LET JESUS EASTER IN US
More Homilies on Biblical Justice

Homily Books by Walter J. Burghardt, S.J.

Tell the Next Generation (1980) (out of print)
Sir, We Would Like to See Jesus (1982) (out of print)
Still Proclaiming Your Wonders (1984)
Preaching: The Art and the Craft (1987)
Lovely in Eyes Not His (1988) (out of print)
To Christ I Look (1989) (out of print)
Dare to Be Christ (1991) (out of print)
When Christ Meets Christ (1993) (out of print)
Speak the Word with Boldness (1994) (out of print)
Love Is a Flame of the Lord (1995)
Let Justice Roll Down Like Waters (1998) (out of print)
Christ in Ten Thousand Places (1999)
To Be Just Is to Love (2001)

LET JESUS EASTER IN US

More Homilies on Biblical Justice

WALTER J. BURGHARDT, S.J.

Paulist Press
New York/Mahwah, N.J.

Acknowledgment
Homily No. 28, "Justice and America's Sixth Child," was originally published in *Just Preaching: Prophetic Voices for Economic Justice,* edited by André Resner, Jr., for Family Promise (St. Louis, MO: Chalice Press, 2003). Used with permission.

Cover design by Sharyn Banks
Book design by Theresa M. Sparacio

Index prepared by Brian Cavanaugh, TOR

Library of Congress Cataloging-in-Publication Data

Burghardt, Walter J.
    Let Jesus Easter in us : more homilies on biblical justice / Walter J. Burghardt.
        p.   cm
    Include bibliographical references and index.
    ISBN 0-8091-4351-8 (alk. paper)
    1. Christianity and justice—Catholic Church—Sermons. 2. Catholic Church—Sermons. 3. Church year sermons. 4. Occasional sermons. 5. Sermons, America. I. Title.
BR115.J8B865 2006
252'.02—dc22

                                                                                    2005026709

Published by Paulist Press
997 Macarthur Boulevard
Mahwah, New Jersey 07430

www.paulistpress.com

Printed and bound in the
United States of America

TABLE OF CONTENTS

PREFACE   ix

FROM ADVENT TO EASTER

1. WAITING: FOR WHOM?   3
   Third Week of Advent, Year 2, Monday

2. GIFTS HUMAN, GIFT DIVINE   6
   Christmas Day

3. A STORY OF TWO CAVES   10
   Monday after Epiphany, Year 2

4. EACH YEAR THIS JOYFUL SEASON   15
   Fourth Week of Lent, Year 2, Monday

5. JUSTICE...EUCHARIST...LENT   19
   Eighth Sunday of the Year (B)

6. RISEN CHRIST, RISEN CHRISTIAN   25
   Easter Sunday (C)

7. THAT THEY MAY ALL BE ONE   29
   Seventh Sunday of Easter (C)

ORDINARY TIME

8. FOR JUSTICE' SAKE   35
   Second Week, Year 1, Monday

9. JUST AS YOUR FATHER IS MERCIFUL   39
   Seventh Sunday of the Year (C)

10. A NEW BIRTH TO A LIVING HOPE   45
    Eighth Week, Year 2, Monday

11. PERSECUTED FOR JUSTICE' SAKE   50
    Tenth Week, Year 2, Monday

12. WHO IS MY NEIGHBOR?   56
     Twenty-seventh Week, Year 2, Monday

13. THIS IS THE FASTING THAT I WISH   61
     Twenty-ninth Sunday of the Year (A)

14. SHE WILL WEAR ME OUT   66
     Twenty-ninth Sunday of the Year (C)

15. GUARD AGAINST ALL GREED   71
     Twenty-ninth Week, Year 1, Monday

16. INVITE THE POOR, THE CRIPPLED, THE LAME,
     THE BLIND   77
     Thirty-first Week, Year 1, Monday

TWO MEMORIALS AND A FESTIVAL

17. LOVE'S "LITTLE WAY"   83
     Memorial of St. Thérèse of Lisieux

18. FROM FIRST COMMUNION TO SERVICE
     UNTO DEATH   88
     Memorial of St. Aloysius Gonzaga

19. THE MIGHTY ONE HAS DONE GREAT THINGS
     FOR ME   93
     Solemnity of the Immaculate Conception

WEDDING HOMILIES

20. WHERE YOUR TREASURE IS, THERE WILL YOUR
     HEART BE   99
     Wedding Homily 1

21. THIS IS A DAY THE LORD HAS MADE   105
     Wedding Homily 2

22. THREE LOVES: GOD, EACH OTHER, THE OTHER   111
     Wedding Homily 3

SPECIAL OCCASIONS

23. FREE AT LAST!   119
    Celebration of Martin Luther King Jr. Day

24. IF YOU HAVE FAITH....   125
    The Radio Mass of Baltimore

25. LET THE LITTLE CHILDREN COME TO ME   129
    Homily for the Baptism of an Infant

26. 'TIS GRACE HATH BROUGHT ME SAFE THUS FAR 133
    Seven Decades a Jesuit

27. DRY BONES, I WILL BREATHE SPIRIT INTO YOU   137
    Mass of the Holy Spirit

28. GOD'S JUSTICE AND AMERICA'S SIXTH CHILD   144
    Children's Defense Fund National Conference 2001

29. TERROR NEXT DOOR   150
    A Homily on Extreme Fear in Our Midst

30. DON'T BE AFRAID TO BE AFRAID   160
    A Pentecost for Priests

31. ALIVE IN CHRIST, ALIVE WITH US   163
    Memorial Mass for Joseph John Burghardt

NOTES   167

INDEX   180

DEDICATED
with delight and gratitude
to
cherished friend and treasured advisor
Katharyn Lois Waldron,
whose encouragement and assistance
greatly facilitated
the publication of this book.
Her courage and love of life
continue to influence my own efforts
to live with hope and joy.

PREFACE

Let Jesus Easter in Us, the fourteenth collection of my homilies published by the Paulist Press, calls for several observations. First, this volume continues and broadens a theme that has increasingly characterized my preaching and publishing for more than a decade. I mean a focus on justice. Ethical justice and legal justice, so necessary for civilized living, must yield pride of place to biblical justice, fidelity to relationships that stem from a covenant with God—relationships to God, to people, and to the earth.

Second, the careful reader cannot fail to notice a certain amount of repetition—the frequent recurrence of the definition of biblical justice, statistics revealing the devastation wrought by injustice, even some favorite phrases and poignant moments. Such repetition could hardly be avoided, since the homilies were addressed to different groups struggling with similar issues.

Third, some readers may wonder why some statistics seem inconsistent—for example, the "fifth" child and the "sixth" child suffering the ills of poverty in the United States. The fact is that within the years covered by these homilies statistics have changed, but each homily tries to reflect the situation at the time each was delivered.

Fourth, devotees of the Jesuit poet Gerard Manley Hopkins (1844–89) will recognize that the title of this volume, *Let Jesus Easter in Us,* is borrowed from the final stanza of his celebrated "The Wreck of the *Deutschland,*" written to memorialize five Franciscan nuns who were exiled from Germany by the Falck Laws and drowned in December 1875. In a 1998 article of *The Living Pulpit* I posed a question stimulated by Hopkins: How does Christ easter in us? My response then was a hope rooted in a reality, in the words of Jesus, "I have life and you will have life." In today's world of growing inequalities, to be alive in Christ is inseparable from the ceaseless call to right relationships. Such inequalities include the gap between the rich and the poor, between the powerful and the powerless, between those only a click away from the Internet and those miles away from the nearest telephone, between those dining with Perrier and those suffering dysentery from unclean water. Closing such divides, actually every act of justice, is another glimpse of a Jesus who easters in us.

Walter J. Burghardt, S.J.
July 10, 2004

FROM ADVENT TO EASTER

1
WAITING: FOR WHOM?
Third Week of Advent, Year 2, Monday

· Numbers 24:2–7, 15–17
· Matthew 11:2–11

For most Christians, Advent is a month of waiting, four weeks on tip-toe of expectation. But, waiting for what, waiting for whom? To answer that question, the Advent liturgy highlights three prominent persons from the Old Testament and the New: the prophet Isaiah, John the Baptist, and the Virgin Mary. Let me begin with that triad from the past, and close by focusing that triad on you and me.

I

First, a look at the past. First character, the prophet Isaiah. Here we cannot escape the famous dialogue between the Lord God and Ahaz, king of Judah. "The LORD spoke to Ahaz: 'Ask for a sign from the LORD, your God; let it be deep as the nether world, or high as the sky!' But Ahaz answered, 'I will not ask! I will not tempt the LORD!' Then [Isaiah] said: 'Listen, O house of David!...The LORD Himself will give you this sign: the virgin shall be with child, and bear a son, and shall name him Immanuel'" (Isa 7:10–14).

The Catholic Church has traditionally followed Matthew, who in his Gospel sees the Isaian prophecy fulfilled in Christ and his virgin mother (Mt 1:18–23).

> The prophet need not have known the full force latent in his own words; and some Catholic scholars have sought a preliminary and partial fulfillment in the conception and birth of the future King Hezekiah, whose mother, at the time Isaiah wrote, would have

3

> been a young, unmarried woman....The Holy Spirit was preparing,
> however, for another Nativity which alone could fulfill the divine-
> ly given terms of Immanuel's mission, and in which the perpetual
> virginity of the Mother of God was to fulfill also the words of this
> prophecy in the integral sense intended by divine Wisdom.[1]

Without quite realizing the profound sense of this prophecy, Isaiah
was in fact on tiptoe of expectation, just short of touching the swaddling clothes of the infant Jesus.

Turn now to John the Baptist (Mt 11:2–6). John lies in prison. It
seems that he is not sure whether this Jesus is "the one who is to come"
(Mal 3:1), the one for whom he has been waiting. Perhaps it was because
the mission of this Jesus had not been one of fiery judgment as John
had expected (cf. Mt 3:2). And so he sends his disciples to Jesus: "Are
you the one who is to come, or should we look for another?" (Mt 11:3).
Jesus' reply is not a simple yes. "Go and tell John what you hear and see:
The blind regain their sight, the lame walk, lepers are cleansed, the deaf
hear, the dead are raised; and the poor have the good news proclaimed
to them" (vv. 4–5). Here is what to expect: not fire and brimstone, only
the healing power of God and the gospel of forgiveness.

Turn now to an Advent Mary. For whom was she waiting? For a
unique child, the "Son of the Most High" (Lk 1:32). But how was she
waiting? For all the angel's "Do not be afraid, Mary" (v. 30), she must
have been puzzled, perhaps concerned. What would such a child be
like? How mother someone who was at once her Son and God's Son,
her baby and Israel's promised one?

But Mary's Advent was hardly a head trip. She walked briskly to
a town in the hill country of Judea, walked perhaps 67 miles. Why? To
help her kinswoman Elizabeth, aged and six months pregnant. But not
simply to help; Mary herself needed to be helped. Someone to talk to,
someone who would understand. She could hardly explain to her
neighbors that this child was conceived of the Holy Spirit, when even
Joseph needed an angel to keep him from "divorcing her quietly" (Mt
1:19). Elizabeth would understand.

II

Move on now to ourselves. What can the experiences of Isaiah,
John, and Mary suggest for your Advent and mine?[2]

Isaiah suggests more than he knew. Here the suggestive word is
Immanuel: "God is with us." In Advent we need not pretend, need not

live in "he who is to come." He has come. He is here. We do well to recapture his coming in loving contemplation: the glad tidings from Gabriel, full hotels in Bethlehem, God in swaddling clothes ("Omnipotence in bonds"), the song of angels, the adoration of astrologers. But paradoxically, such contemplation is possible only because "God is with us"; because, as Ignatius Loyola indicated in his *Spiritual Exercises,* Christ is creatively active, like a laborer, in all that is, from the amoeba to nuclear energy; because Jesus graces us with his body and blood, soul and divinity. For us who believe, every day is Advent, for every day "God is with us." What are *we* waiting for? A deeper, ceaseless awareness of God with us, within us, in all that is.

John the Baptist's experience takes us a giant step forward. Jesus told him why he and his disciples should not "look for another." As with John expecting a fiery reformer, so with us: What sort of Christ are we looking for, waiting for, hoping for, worshiping, even perhaps preaching? Is it the timeless Christ of the Council of Chalcedon, detached from what is going on in the human community, from the social structures that cause human suffering, simply "God-man consubstantial with the Father, consubstantial with us"? Or is the Christ we expect one for whom salvation is rooted on Calvary, is intimately involved with poverty and pain, AIDS and Alzheimer's, violence and war, despair and death?

And our Lady, dear Mary? In trudging to the home of Zechariah and Elizabeth, this pregnant young lady could win Ignatius' approval as a contemplative in action. Our vocation as well. The Advent season, its liturgies and its traditions, invite contemplation as richly as does Lent. But that very contemplation should impel us to action. For we are to find Jesus not only in a manger but in his images, especially in those who hunger and thirst, in the homeless and the naked, in the housebound and the imprisoned. There he is, Jesus told us in that famous passage in Matthew (25:31–46). "Whatever you did for one of these least brothers [or sisters] of mine, you did for me" (v. 40).

A final thought just struck me. Today, at Gonzaga, Jesus might well be saying to most of you, "Whatever you did for one of these young eagles, you did for me."

Our Lady's Chapel
Gonzaga College High School
Washington, D.C.
December 16, 2002

2
GIFTS HUMAN, GIFT DIVINE
Christmas Day

· Isaiah 52:7–10
· Hebrews 1:1–6
· John 1:1–18

For different people, different images sum up what Christmas is about. For some, the image is a tree—tinsel, ornaments, lights. For others, a crib—a feeding trough for animals—a manger cradling a newborn child. For others, a star guiding three astrologers from the East. For others, Christmas is people: angels "sweetly singing o'er the plains"; shepherds watching their flocks by night; Santa climbing down chimneys with toys for good girls and boys. For others, Mass at midnight. For still others, an exchange of gifts, such as you experienced yesterday.

All of these indeed have their place. But this morning it is the exchange of gifts I want to stress—an exchange all too easily forgotten. On the one hand, our human world, in the person of Mary, giving our humanity to the Son of God; on the other hand, God One in Three giving to our world a share in divinity. A word on each gift, with a final personal word to each and all of you.

I

First, our human world, in the person of Mary, giving our humanity to the Son of God. To understand this gift is to admit a reality that surpasses the capacity of the human mind. In his *Spiritual Exercises*, Saint Ignatius Loyola presents a contemplation on the Incarnation that is wonderfully imaginative. He asks the retreatant, he asks us, to imagine the Holy Trinity—Father, Son, and Holy Spirit—gazing down "in Their eternity" upon the whole circuit of the world.

What do They see? Untold millions of men and women diverse in origin and background. What are these people saying and doing? In Ignatius' own words, "swearing and blaspheming, wounding and killing." Then a terribly strong phrase: "going down to hell."[1]

The reaction of the Trinity? A plan for human redemption, to bring God and God's creation together in a fresh life of love. How? God's very own Son would touch our earth in person. Not merely with a word of forgiveness; not as a full-grown man; not in the robes of a king. No. God's Son would be born as we are born, would grow as we grow, would experience life as we experience it, would die as we die but even more cruelly than most of us. Still difficult to believe, this humanness of God's Son would be humanity's gift to God. In response to God's invitation to mother the "Son of the Most High," a young Jewish woman replied simply, "Behold, I am the handmaid of the Lord. May it be done to me according to your word" (Lk 1:32, 38).

II

Turn now to the gift Jesus Christ, God and man, has given to humanity, has given to us. Actually, two remarkable gifts. First, what Ignatius Loyola once again phrases with remarkable brevity and insight in his *Spiritual Exercises*. He asks us to consider

> how God [specifically, Jesus Christ] dwells in creatures: in the elements, giving them existence; in the plants, giving them life; in the animals, giving them sensation; in human beings, giving them intelligence; and finally, how in this way He dwells in myself, giving me existence, life, sensation, and intelligence; and even further, making me His temple, since I am created as a likeness and image of the Divine Majesty....

Then Ignatius asks us to consider

> how God labors and works for me in all the creatures on the face of the earth; acts in the manner of one who is laboring. For example, He is working in the heavens, elements, plants, fruits, cattle, and all the rest—giving them their existence, conserving them, concurring with their vegetative and sensitive activities, and so forth....

Then we should consider

> how all good things and gifts descend from above; for example, my limited power from the Supreme and Infinite Power above;

and so of justice, goodness, piety, mercy, and so forth—just as the
rays come down from the sun, or the rains from their source....[2]

A second gift is incredibly imaginative. I mean the Lord's
Supper, Jesus' gift to us the night before he died, a kind of last will
and testament: his body and blood, soul and divinity as our food and
drink, the promise of eternal life. For, as Jesus told his fellow Jews,
"unless you eat the flesh of the Son of Man and drink his blood, you
do not have life within you. Whoever eats my flesh and drinks my
blood has eternal life, and I will raise him on the last day. For my flesh
is true food, and my blood is true drink. Whoever eats my flesh and
drinks my blood remains in me and I in him" (Jn 6:53–57).

III

Finally, a personal word to each and all of you. Year after year I
have been privileged to share Christmas Eve with the extended
Flanigan family and some very close friends. Unfailingly I have been
impressed and delighted by your exchange of gifts. Why? Because it is
strikingly clear that the gift given by each of you is not merely physical—the tie, the bracelet, the latest in technological games, however
costly. Even more striking than the physical gift is the spirit that ani-
mates it: the friendship, the admiration, the affection, the love. In
other words, you are giving to each other something of yourself.

What transforms a physical gift into the giving of self? That Gift
is splendidly summarized in a single sentence from John's Gospel:
"God so loved the world that he gave his only Son..." (Jn 3:16). God so
loved "the world." Not some impersonal globe. The "world" God
loved was and is every human person from the first Adam to the last
Antichrist. The "world" God loved and loves includes you and me.

Happily, this Gift of God to us in Christ Jesus is precisely what
enables you and me to give ourselves in these Christmas gifts. "In this
way," the First Letter of John declares, "the love of God was revealed
to us: God sent his only Son into the world so that we might have life
through him. In this is love: not that we have loved God, but that he
loved us....Beloved, if God so loved us, we also must love one another"
(1 Jn 4:9–11).

Such, dear friends, is the more profound sense of Christmas giving. (1) God's Gift: God's own Son in our flesh, walking with us, living in us, showing us how to live and how to love. (2) Our gifts: not
only humankind giving humanity to God's Son, but our self-giving to

others, something of ourselves in each physical gift, loving the other like another self, like another Christ, loving the other as Christ loves us. Rich gifts indeed; rich enough to make Christmas not only a holy day but quite a merry day as well.[3]

Baltimore, Maryland
December 25, 2003

3

A STORY OF TWO CAVES
Monday after Epiphany, Year 2

- 1 John 3:22–4:6
- Matthew 4:12–17, 23–25

During the past four months you and I have experienced the lows and the highs of our existence, fear at its deadliest and hope at its liveliest. Concretely, September 11 and December 25. While these experiences are still fresh in our flesh and blood, allow me to tie them together, to make some human sense of them. Three movements to my mulling— or my meandering: (1) a swift flight of my imagination; (2) imagination translated into theology; (3) the relevance of all this for the biblical justice which draws us together this week.

I

First, recent weeks have caused my imagination to fly high. To fly to two caves. One cave is in Western Asia, in Afghanistan, in the White Mountains of Tora Bora. Somewhere here, some suspected, in one of the numerous man-made caves stuffed with arms and weapons, caves the Russians had found impenetrable during their disastrous occupation, a Muslim named Osama bin Laden is hiding. Hiding because there is a $25 million bounty on his head. Hiding because the Bush administration wants him dead from a bullet, a bomb, or an American court of justice.

The other cave is in the Middle East, in a little town called Bethlehem. No weapons here, at best an animal or two; and now a husband and his pregnant wife. For in this cave, according to an early tradition, a baby boy was born.[1] He had been conceived not of man but of the Holy Spirit. He came to birth in a cave "because there was no room for them in the lodge."[2] A despotic King Herod, unaware that

this infant was the Prince of Peace, thinking him a threat to his king-
ship, instituted a search for him and "ordered the massacre of all the
boys in Bethlehem and its vicinity two years old and under" (Mt 2:16).

II

Second, good brothers in Christ[3]: The image of two caves (one
terribly real, the other simply a possible interpretation) struck me as
an interesting way to relate two events that at first glance seem to have
no connection. But they do, indeed they do. They represent two
extremes that are significant for human and Christian living.

On the one hand, there is terror and its consequence, extreme
fear. On September 11, 2001, America as a nation experienced terror
and fear as never before. Not even on December 7, 1941. For all the
horror of that "day of infamy"—18 ships sunk or severely damaged,
about 170 planes destroyed, about 3,700 casualties—Pearl Harbor was
"over there," somewhere west of Honolulu. Like most Americans, this
theological student in rural Maryland was stunned, but felt no personal fear. I did not feel assailed in my flesh and bones. "Remember Pearl
Harbor" became a rallying cry for our involvement in World War II.
But last November, when I stood in the rubble of "ground zero" with
half a hundred Preaching the Just Word retreatants, I not only felt profoundly sad over a unique calvary; I experienced what it means to be
afraid—like untold millions across the country, afraid to fly, afraid to
open an envelope, afraid of the unknown, the unexpected. We have
gathered, uncounted thousands, in shrines and churches, not only to
pray for our dead, not only to honor our heroes, but often with the
perplexity of Job: Why, dear God, why this? And with bin Laden still
alive, perhaps in Pakistan, with innumerable cells of terror scattered
around the globe, with biological and chemical death in our very air,
we walk ever so fearfully in a new kind of world.

Precisely here, I suggest, is where the Christmas cave came to
our rescue. For if, as the First Letter of John declares, "perfect love
drives out fear" (1 Jn 4:18), not only fear of God's final judgment but
fear in the face of man-made terror, then the little town of Bethlehem
is God's answer to bin Laden's capital, Kabul. Not that we can waltz
through life without ever being afraid. After all, St. Paul advised the
Christians of Philippi, "work out your salvation with fear and trem-
bling" (Phil 2:12).[4] Rather that Bethlehem's Child brought with him,
for us, an intimacy with God that subordinates fear to love. If we love
God above all human idols, if we love one another at least as much as

we love ourselves, then the peace of Christ will reign in our hearts, despite an understandable apprehension in an atmosphere of terror. "Peace I leave with you; my peace I give to you. Not as the world gives do I give it to you" (Jn 14:27).

III

Third, what is the relevance of 9/11 and 12/25 for the biblical justice that has brought us together this week? Recall what biblical justice is: fidelity to relationships, to responsibilities, that stem from a covenant. For us, the covenant cut by Christ in his own blood. What relationships, what responsibilities? To God, to people, to earth. To *God*. What Jesus called "the greatest and the first commandment: You shall love the Lord, your God, with all your heart, with all your soul, and with all your mind" (Mt 22:37–38). To *people*. The second commandment, the commandment Jesus said "is like" the first, is like loving God: "You shall love your neighbor as yourself" (v. 39). Your neighbor. Not only the man, woman, and child next door. My neighbor is the Jew of Jesus' parable: the Jew who "fell victim to robbers as he went down from Jerusalem to Jericho" (Lk 10:30), the Jew helped not by his priest, not by his Levite, but by a Samaritan, a hated enemy. My neighbor is each person in pain, in trouble, in need. To *earth*. God's material creation, all that is not human or divine. Touch all of this with reverence, with awe, as a gift of God, not as despot but as steward.

How does this relate to 9/11? Intimately, painfully, with difficulty. Focus on the second commandment. My neighbors are the terrorists who crashed the Twin Towers and the Pentagon, massacred several thousand men and women. My neighbor is bin Laden, who orchestrated the tragedy and laughed with joy when shown he had succeeded beyond his fondest dreams. My neighbors are those Muslims who see us as infidels, to be destroyed by Allah's wishes. I find it frightening that in self-defense, for a greater good, we must kill what we love. I can only pray that we do so reluctantly, as a last resort, with regret in our hearts, not revenge. I pray that, if and when we uncover bin Laden, we will not honor a presidential "dead or alive." To a Christian, a just Christian, each life is sacred; even bin Laden is fashioned like God, however flawed the image.

Turn to the thousands of tons of food and medicines we dropped on the impoverished in Afghanistan while we were dropping bombs on the Taliban. We showed that we cared, that we loved. But why did it take a war to feed the hungry, to heal the ailing? Listen to some disturbing facts.

> Back in August, the United Nations published a paper on "The Deepening Crisis in Afghanistan" which detailed plans to respond to drought, conflict and displacement. The report went largely unnoticed then, despite its prediction that 5.5 to 6 million Afghans out of a total population of 25 million were at risk of hunger and starvation....It is a tragic irony that since 11 September, the focus on Afghanistan has been such as to bring pledges from the international community of more than was asked for....[5]

Is there not reason here for a critical self-examination?

Turn, finally, to Pope John Paul II. In several December 2001 speeches he revealed his growing anxiety over the world situation since September 11. In separate messages to each of nine new ambassadors to the Holy See, "he expressed alarm over the tenuous state of peace in the world. All the letters were marked with a sense of urgency, highlighting the primary role of diplomacy and dialogue and the urgent need to set about solving social and economic problems that helped breed terrorism and conflict."[6]

How does this relate to 12/25, to the Christmas cave? Age allows me to cite the title of my most recent collection of homilies: *To Be Just Is To Love.*[7] You see, the philosopher can tell you what his mistress, naked reason, demands: Give to each what is due to each, what each can claim as a human right. The jurist can tell you what his blindfolded Lady Justice demands: impartiality, no favoritism, simply the law on the books. Neither—neither philosopher nor jurist—can command that we love. Only God can demand love. Only the Jesus of Bethlehem's cave and Calvary's cross can demand that we love as he loved. Such is the justice that rises above the ethical and the legal, the justice that is divine, the justice of God.

This above all is the justice you and I must preach; for this above all is the justice our people must live. Only then can we be servants of justice in line with Isaiah's servant applied by the Church to Christ, the Servant par excellence who "shall bring forth justice to the nations" (Isa 42:1). Here, in Bethlehem's cave, is Justice incarnate. Justice in the flesh he borrowed from you and me. Marvel at the wonder of it all: This Child of Bethlehem, he *is* Justice—for us, for our people, for the terrorist. Justice alive in your very gathering for worship, Justice speaking in the word proclaimed, Justice joined to your whole self and mine in the body broken and the blood poured out.

Pointedly, the Suffering Servant, "pierced for our offenses, by [whose] stripes we were healed" (53:5).

But before we leave the cave for the cross, let us rejoice and be glad—joy and gladness that, with "a little child to guide" us (Isa 11:6), we can preach to Christian and Muslim alike, "To be just is to love." The love that drives out fear.

St. Joseph's-in-the-Hills
Retreat House
Malvern, Pennsylvania
January 7, 2002

4
EACH YEAR THIS JOYFUL SEASON
Fourth Week of Lent, Year 2, Monday

• Isaiah 65:17–21
• John 4:43–54

My homily this evening stems from the first Preface for Lent. There the Catholic people declare to God our Father through the celebrant, "Each year you give us this joyful season." Joyful season? With fish and fasting, penance and purgation, sacrifice and self-denial, Jesus in the desert and Jesus on a cross? Is Lent for laughing or for weeping, for joy or sadness? I shall suggest that here we face not an "either-or" but a traditionally Catholic "both-and." Lent is for laughing *and* for weeping. I begin with Jesus, move on to Lent, close with you and me.

I

I begin with Jesus. Here I recall an old favorite of mine, a piece of art. In the famous abbey of Lérins, on an island off the southeast coast of France, there is an unusual sculpture. It may go back to the twelfth century, and it has for its title *Christ souriant,* "the smiling Christ." Jesus is imprisoned on a cross; his head is leaning somewhat to the right; his eyes are closed—in death, I think; but on his lips there is a soft, serene smile.[1]

I do not know whether Jesus died with a smile on his lips. But that is not quite the point. The very idea, this somewhat wild idea, tells us something important about Jesus. We know from the Gospels that he wept—wept over Jerusalem and over Lazarus, over his city and his friend. Yet the Gospels never tell us that Jesus laughed or smiled. But I refuse to believe that this man who was like us in everything save sin failed to smile when he cuddled a child comfortably in his arms, or when the headwaiter at Cana wondered where the good wine had

15

come from, or when he spied little Zaccheus up a tree, or at times when Peter put his foot in his mouth. This man who moved through life very much as we do attracted not only fishermen and centurions but little children, simple folk, women like Mary of Magdala. He could hardly have done so if his face never creased into a smile or broke out into merry laughter.

But on the cross? Pain may well have prevented a look of joy. Still, when he spoke those final words, "It is finished" (Jn 19:30), deep inside there must have been a feeling quite different from the agony in his earlier words, "There is a baptism with which I must be baptized, and how great is my anguish until it is accomplished [finished]!" (Lk 12:50).[2] Finished—why not "a soft, serene smile"?

II

Move on to Lent. Is there any place for the smiling Christ these 40 days? I believe there is. You see, neither in Lent's liturgy nor in Lent's living dare we pretend, dare we make believe that Christ is not yet risen, that we have to wait for Easter to enjoy resurrection. Even in Lent you and I are *risen* Christians. And the twin fact that Jesus is risen and that we have risen with him into a new life must color the way we celebrate Lent, the way we fast on Ash Wednesday, the way we eat a "simple soup" on Friday evenings. Oh yes, during these weeks we re-present the stages of our Lord's journey to Jerusalem, his way to the cross, but we do it as *risen* Christians. And that means we do right to reproduce in our own Lent, in our own suffering, on our own cross, the smiling Christ of Lérins. The cross is victory, not defeat, and we do not have to wait for that victory, wait for Easter to dawn.

But we cannot pretend the other way either. Simply because we have risen with Christ in baptism, we cannot make believe that Lent does not really exist. Risen we are, but not yet *fully* risen. "We ourselves," St. Paul agonizes, "who have the first fruits of the Spirit, we also groan within ourselves as we wait for...the redemption of our bodies" (Rom 8:23). And so we must ceaselessly reproduce the journey of Jesus to Jerusalem, not only symbolically, not only liturgically, but in our flesh and bones and in the wrenching of our spirit. That is why our laughter is not yet full-throated; why it is often through tears that we smile; why we still have to pray "Father,...take this cup away from me" (Lk 22:42). We have not been transformed completely into the risen Christ; that transformation will take place only if we trudge to Jerusalem with Jesus. The smiling Christ rests on a cross.

Is Lent for laughing or for crying? I say, for both. But I am stressing the laughter of Lent because for so many Christians it is far removed from their spirituality. It is almost as rare to find a smiling Christian on Good Friday as it is to find a smiling Christ in crucifixion art. In my memory, all too many of us who took Lent seriously, from Ash Wednesday's "Dust thou art" to Holy Saturday's empty tomb and tabernacle, only confirmed Nietzsche's cutting critique about Christians: We "do not look redeemed."

III

Finally, you and I: What now till Easter? I do not reject Jesus' injunction "Repent" (Mk 1:15). All of us stand in need of constant conversion, ceaseless turning to Christ. But since you are already on the road to Jerusalem with Jesus, I suggest a fresh approach to Lent, a twin approach a splendid spiritual writer has called "an asceticism of humor" and "a diaconate of humor."[3]

For ourselves personally, individually, an asceticism of humor—a fresh form of self-denial. I am suggesting that we give up something sweeter than candy, more difficult than the cream in our Starbucks, perhaps more destructive than sin. I mean an absorption in myself—where I take myself too seriously, where the days and nights rotate around *me*, my heartache and my hiatal hernia, my successes and failures, my problems and frustrations. For an asceticism of humor, I must distance myself from myself, see myself in perspective, as I really am. And what is that?

Each of us is a creature wonderfully yet fearfully made, a bundle of paradoxes and contradictions. We believe and doubt, hope and despair, love and hate. We are exciting and boring, enchanted and disillusioned, manic and depressive. We are "cool" on the outside and we hurt within. We feel bad about feeling good, are afraid of our joy, feel guilty if we don't feel guilty. We are trusting and suspicious, selfless and selfish, wide-open and locked in. We are honest and we still play games. Aristotle said we are rational animals; I say we are angels with an incredible capacity for beer.

If it is the incongruous that makes for humor, what does not fit, you and I can indeed smile at ourselves. A generation ago Harvey Cox wrote a book called *The Feast of Fools: A Theological Essay on Festivity and Fantasy*[4] with an engaging chapter on "Christ the Harlequin." Let Christ the harlequin, the clown Christ, into our spiritual life. We are not laughing sacrilegiously at him; he is poking gentle fun at us—through tears.

Ignatius Loyola has a rule for Jesuits: Our "whole countenance should reflect cheerfulness rather than sadness...."[5] Even in Lent. And our smile will turn to lusty laughter if we only realize how lovable we are—not because of anything we have made of ourselves, but because God loves us, died for us, lives in us...now.

But an asceticism of humor dare not remain a private joke. Humor, someone has said, good humor is basically looking at the world, at others, with eyes of love. An asceticism of humor must move out into a diaconate of humor. We "deacon," we minister, the smiling Christ to others. Not a forced smile, not bellowing always with laughter. Simply, with our new-found Christian delight in ourselves, we go out to our brothers and sisters as we are, where they are.

Where they are....Not far from you is someone who is afraid and needs your courage; or lonely and needs your presence; or hurt and needs your healing. Many are weak in so many ways and need for support your own shared weakness. One of the most helpful words I ever spoke was to confess to a troubled lady that I too had doubts about faith. "You?" she cried. "Oh, thank God!"

Christianity needs men and women who repent of their smallness, fast from their selfishness, abstain from isolation. In any case, if the crucified Christ can look redeeming, the crucified Christian can at least look redeemed. For your Lenten penance, therefore, please...look...redeemed.

Our Lady's Chapel
Gonzaga College High School
Washington, D.C.
March 11, 2002

5

JUSTICE...EUCHARIST...LENT
Eighth Sunday of the Year (B)

· Hosea 2:16b, 17b, 21–22
· 2 Corinthians 3:1b–6
· Mark 2:18–22

One of the freedoms we Catholic preachers enjoy is this: We are not compelled in each and every Eucharistic liturgy to preach from one or all of the two or three biblical readings. We are indeed urged to do so, but there are exceptions. I may focus on any of the wondrous prayers in the Eucharistic liturgies—for example, the opening prayer, the Responsorial Psalm, or the Offertory prayers. Or I may focus on an urgent issue of the present moment—for example, the sexual abuse of children or war against Iraq.

This morning I shall take advantage of this freedom. I shall speak of the Eucharist we are celebrating, and I shall touch this Eucharist to the justice we have been discussing this weekend. And this I shall do for a highly practical reason: in order to shed deeper meaning on the Lenten season that begins this Wednesday. So then, three pivotal points: justice, Eucharist, Lent.

I

First, justice. This weekend we have experienced together a gradual growth in our grasp of that elusive word. Widely known is the justice promised by President Clinton after the bombing of a Federal building in Oklahoma City: "We shall bring the criminals to justice." Justice was simply punishment.

Broader is the legal justice from which that remark emerged: giving to each person what he or she deserves because it has been written

19

into law. No sentiment, no favoritism; ideally, only guilt or innocence established by evidence. Presumed innocent until proven guilty.

Move one step higher: ethical justice, a justice that stems from human reasoning. I mean giving to others what each has a strict right to demand, not because she or he is powerful or wealthy or brilliant, attractive to look at, delightful to see. Rather because each is, very simply, a human person. What basic rights? I mean, for example, the right to a decent living, a family wage, affordable housing, safe environment, universal healthcare, a basic education; the right to be treated with respect.

Important, indeed, legal and ethical justice, indispensable if life on earth is not to degenerate into wilderness, where the prize goes to the swift, the shrewd, and the strong and the devil take the hindmost.

Indispensable for human living, inadequate for Christian living. The justice that characterizes the Christian is biblical justice, the justice that runs like a thread through Old Testament and New, through the Hebrew prophets and *ho dikaios,* "the Just One," Jesus. And what is biblical justice? Fidelity. To what? To relationships. What relationships? To God, to people, to the earth. Love God above all earthly idols. Love every man, woman, and child, friend or enemy, as a child of God. Touch "things," God's material creation—from a blade of grass to nuclear energy—with reverence, as gifts of God. Such justice is a share in God's own justice. For God is ever faithful to God's promises, however unfaithful we humans may be.

A crucial difference between biblical justice and ethical or legal justice: Neither philosophy nor law can command love. God does.

II

Second, Eucharist. How does the Eucharist relate to justice? Intimately. For the Eucharist is the most powerful force for all that the Church is and does. Listen to the Second Vatican Council:

> The liturgy is the summit to which the church's activity is directed; at the same time it is the source from which all her power proceeds....The renewal in the eucharist of the covenant between the Lord and humans draws the faithful into the compelling love of Christ and sets them afire. From the liturgy, therefore, and especially from the eucharist, as from a fountain, grace is channeled into us, and that sanctification of men and women in Christ and the glorification of God to which all other activities of the church stretch and strain toward their goal, are most effectively achieved.[1]

Why is the liturgy, especially the Eucharist, so important in the area of justice? Recall, to begin with, that the liturgy, specifically the Eucharist, is the very presence of Jesus, the Servant of Justice, in the people assembled, in the Word proclaimed, in the body and blood shared. Recall that biblical justice is a matter of relationships. And the three relationships? To God, to people, to the earth.

The Eucharist reveals and celebrates our relationship to *God*. Here I confess my daily displeasure as I reach the Eucharistic prayer and I am instructed to pray, "We do well" to give God thanks and praise. "We do well": a dreadful translation or substitution for the old Latin "Vere dignum et iustum est." To praise God and thank God always and every-where "is utterly fitting and a matter of justice." If I do not praise and thank God regularly, constantly, I am unfaithful to my covenant with God cut in the blood of Christ. I am guilty of biblical injustice.

Why are praise and thanks a matter of justice? Because it is God to whom we owe our being, our existence, our life at every moment. Because it is God to whom we owe our salvation in Christ. Because it is "God's love [for us]" that "has been poured out in our hearts through the Holy Spirit that has been given to us" (Rom 5:5). Because it is God who is our last end, our hope, our destiny.

The Eucharist reveals and celebrates our relationship with *one another*. Some years ago liturgist Mark Searle ventured a fresh perspec-tive on the Eucharist: "We stand to one another not as the rich to the poor, the wise to the ignorant, the strong to the needy, the clever to the simple. We stand rather as the poor to the poor, the weak to the weak, the loved to the loved."[2] Back in the 1980s, Robert Hovda expressed in striking syllables the equalizing, leveling power of the Eucharist:

> Where else [other than at Eucharist] in our society are all of us—
> not just a gnostic elite—called to be social critics, called to extri-
> cate ourselves from the powers and principalities that claim to
> rule our daily lives in order to submit ourselves to the sole domin-
> ion of the God before whom all of us are equal? Where else in our
> society are we all addressed and sprinkled and bowed to and
> incensed and touched and kissed and treated like *somebody*–all in
> the very same way? Where else do economic czars and beggars
> get the same treatment? Where else are food and drink blessed in
> a common prayer of thanksgiving, broken and poured out, so that
> everybody, *everybody*, receives and shares alike?[3]

Wondrously true, but even there we cannot help experiencing a torment and a tension.[4] For the liturgical assembly does not adequate-ly reflect the justice of the kingdom; it reflects more obviously the divisions of social groupings. For all our Eucharistic equality, the tensions abide: rich and poor and the in-betweens, black and white and yellow and red and brown, men and women, the famous and the forgotten, CEOs and cleaning folk and the unemployed, Anglos and Hispanics, and all the rest. How can the liturgy affect such divisions? How build up the single body of Christ that Godfrey Diekmann rightly insisted was the soul of the pre–Vatican II pastoral-liturgical movement, the one image he believed can inspire us to grasp and live what it means to share the life of God?

The Eucharist reveals and celebrates our relationship to the *earth,* to material creation. God's "things" can be used to build up relationships or destroy them—from a jug of wine to nuclear energy, from bread shared generously to luxuries clutched feverishly. The breaking of one Bread, our sharing in the one Christ, cries out against the way we turn God's creation committed to our care into a captive of our cupidity—yes, into weapons of power and destruction.

I have focused on the Eucharist. But the pertinent symbols in liturgy are not limited to bread and wine. There is the water, simultaneously symbolic of death and of birth. There is the oil for healing, the oil for consecration, the oil for faith building. There is the wood of the cross, supreme paradox of life through death, symbol of reconciliation with God and neighbor. There is the incense rising to heaven for forgiveness, for veneration, for exorcism. There is the ring, symbol of love and fidelity. There is darkness and there is light.

There are other ways of approaching the relationship between liturgy and justice. I have submitted an approach which has the advantage of linking liturgy specifically with *biblical* justice, and therefore with *all* of our relationships to God, to every human person, and to material creation.

III

Third, Lent. Many decades ago, during an adolescence prolonged into my early years as a Jesuit, Lent was largely approached with the question, "What are you giving up for Lent?" The emphasis was on giving up, sacrifice. If sins were in question, giving up such forbidden activities made sense. But most of us gave up things on a superficial level—sugar in one's coffee, delectable chocolate, movies for forty days. Even the rules on fast and abstinence rarely caused more than inconvenience. Hardly an effective method for living realistically what we call "the paschal mystery," union with the dying/rising Christ.

Fortunately, recent years have provided fresh insights into Lent: self-giving rather than giving up. We can begin with powerful words from Yahweh through Isaiah:

> This, rather, is the fasting that I wish:
>   releasing those bound unjustly,
>   untying the thongs of the yoke;
> Setting free the oppressed,
>   breaking every yoke;
> Sharing your bread with the hungry,
>   sheltering the oppressed and the homeless;
> Clothing the naked when you see them,
>   not turning your back on your own.
> Then your light shall break forth like the dawn,
>   and your wound shall quickly be healed....
> Then you shall call, and the Lord will answer;
>   you shall cry for help, and he will say: Here I am!
>   (Isa 58:6–9)

My point is, we are servants of justice. But only if we do not sever social action from the most powerful source of grace at our command. Only if we and our people recognize that our self-giving to God's justice draws its power from a sacred hour, from the Servant who proclaims to the world through us, "This is my body given for you" (Lk 22:19). Only if, as suffering servants, we are prepared to walk the way of the cross that is inseparable from proclaiming God's justice, prepared to follow the Servant who "was despised and rejected by others, a man of sorrows, one from whom others hide their faces" (Isa 53:3).

A suggestion. During this Lenten season read through Mark's Gospel. Without speaking specifically of justice, Jesus is constantly dealing with the reality, struggling to make all relationships right. For the leper is not only cured; a human person ostracized from society, severed from the synagogue, and banished to the edge of his city is restored to his family and his community (Mk 1:40–45). A paralytic is not simply loosed of his paralysis; he is restored to God's friendship: "Your sins are forgiven" (2:5). Jesus makes a withered hand whole on the Sabbath, to stress a right relationship to God: "The Sabbath was made for men and women, not women and men for the Sabbath" (2:27). A wild man is not only freed from an unclean spirit; Jesus sits with him, talks to him, listens to him, and when he wants to stay with Jesus, Jesus sends him home to his family (5:1–20).

When his disciples argue, centuries before Mohammed Ali, "Who's the greatest?," Jesus shows that their role in his work is one of service. He takes into his arms a little child, an example then of a social nobody—no status, no social significance—and presents the child as a symbol of the *anawim*, the poor in spirit, the lowly in the community: "Whoever receives one child such as this in my name, receives me" (9:37).

Take the widow and her two small coins (12:41–44). For years I have recognized that, in dropping into the temple treasury all she had to live on, "By the totality of her self-giving," she was foreshadowing "the complete self-giving of Jesus on the cross."[5] Instructed by insightful scholars, I now see Jesus lamenting "the tragedy of the day."[6] This widow had been encouraged by religious leaders to give as she did. Jesus condemned the value system that motivated her actions—a poor widow persuaded by the hierarchy of her religion to plunk into the treasury her last penny. It was Jesus' quiet but passionate rebuke to a structure of sin. He was condemning a social injustice.

During Lent, and thereafter, come together in smaller groups to discuss three questions. (1) What are some of the injustices in your diocese? (2) What resources do you have to combat such injustices—spiritual, financial, personal, professional? (3) Since you cannot do everything, which critical injustice cries out for your immediate attention?

I close with a delightful summation by biblical scholar John R. Donahue. "There are two women of justice: one with a scale and her eyes blinded, and the other, who proclaims, 'He has shown might with his arm, dispersed the arrogant of mind and heart. He has thrown down rulers from their thrones, but lifted up the lowly. The hungry he has filled with good things, the rich he has sent away empty' (Luke 1:51–53)."[7]

San Pedro Catholic Retreat & Conference Center
Winter Park, Florida
March 2, 2003

6
RISEN CHRIST, RISEN CHRISTIAN
Easter Sunday (C)

- Acts 10:34a, 37–43
- Colossians 3:1–4
- John 20:1–9

Most of us who have gathered here for Easter came together on Christmas Eve. At Christmas our focus was on a crib, a feeding trough for animals; at Easter our focus is on an empty tomb. At Christmas a choir of angels were "singing o'er the plains"; at Easter two angels ask the women at the tomb, "Why do you seek the living one among the dead? He is not here; he has been raised up" (Lk 24:5–6). Christmas generates a warm feeling because it tells of an infant being born for us; Easter deepens that feeling by stressing that the child not only died but rose for us.

If Christmas is the overture of salvation, Easter is its crescendo, its climax.

I

First, Jesus Christ actually rose from the dead, from death to life. Many indeed are those who deny it or hesitate to affirm it. Recall Jesus' closest friends. Two of his disciples making their way to Emmaus on the first Easter confessed their disappointment over their Master's death: "We were hoping that he was the one who would set Israel free" (Lk 24:21). The apostle Thomas stubbornly refused to believe in a resurrected Jesus: "Unless I see the mark of the nails in his hands and put my fingers into the nailmarks and put my hand into his side, I will not believe" (Jn 20:25). Down through the centuries untold numbers have written off a risen Jesus as a product of a fertile imagination or as a substitute for an immature faith.

25

But a homily, especially an Easter homily, is not the place to refute unbelief. On this blessed day you and I thank God for the incredible grace to declare in the Sunday Creed, "On the third day he rose again in accordance with the Scriptures; he ascended into heaven and is seated at the right hand of the Father. He will come again in glory to judge the living and the dead." Jesus Christ is alive today, alive in his humanity and in his divinity—the very same person who was born in Bethlehem, walked the paths of Palestine, anguished on Calvary's cross. All this is expressed vividly in St. Paul's blunt declaration to the Christians of Corinth: "If the dead are not raised, neither has Christ been raised, and if Christ has not been raised, your faith is vain; you are still in your sins" (1 Cor 15:16–17). Paul's declaration leads naturally to a second issue: For whom did Jesus rise?

II

For all their differences, one essential similarity links Christmas and Easter—two momentous monosyllables: *for us*. Not for a misty mass called humanity. Jesus rose for every human being, for the whole family of God, from the first Adam to the last Antichrist. He rose not simply for the good and the "nice." He rose not only for the Virgin Mary who mothered him but for the Judas who betrayed him and for the Peter who denied him thrice. Importantly for our presence here today, Jesus rose to life for each of us, regardless of age: from great-grandparents Pierce and Mary Ann to toddler Katie, all of us in-between, and those yet to come.

Despite their human attractiveness, the essence of Easter lies not in the return of spring, not in the radiant colors of new blossoms, not in egg-rolling on the White House lawn. Easter in its essence is Jesus: Jesus risen, Jesus gloriously alive, Jesus risen and alive for us. What this "for us" means in the concrete is that we Christians are risen with Christ. Hence, my third point.

III

What does it mean to say we are risen Christians? Again, as so often, St. Paul provides an answer. In his letter to the Christians of Rome, he asks a question all of us should ask ourselves time and again, especially at Easter: "Are you unaware that we who were baptized into Christ Jesus were baptized into his death [were plunged into his death]? We were indeed buried with him through baptism into death, so that, just as Christ was raised from the dead by the glory of the Father, we too might live in newness of life" (Rom 6:3-4).

The phrase "baptized into Christ Jesus" is fascinating, but its rich meaning is not often understood. You see, the verb "to baptize" in its origin means "to plunge." So, what Paul is saying is that in our baptism we are plunged into Christ Jesus. The significance of this becomes clearer when we realize that in the early Church the child or adult being baptized was plunged totally into a body of water.

Unfortunately, in most Roman Catholic churches the baptismal font is rather small—only large enough for the head to be held over the water. The priest then sprinkles a small amount of water over the forehead of the one being baptized. No immersion here, no sense of dying to sin and to self, no rising together with Christ Jesus to a new life, life in the community of the baptized.

What is this "new life" that we celebrate on Easter? Not simply Mass every Sunday, not just the ten commandments. Good indeed, but not good enough. I make bold to commend to you a significant charge given by the Hebrew prophet Micah to his fellow Jews: "This is what Yahweh requires of you, only this: to act justly, to love tenderly, and to walk humbly with your God" (Mic 6:8).

"Act justly." The "justice" here is not man-made, the product of human intelligence: giving to every man, woman, and child what they can claim as a strict right. God's justice is fidelity to relationships, to responsibilities, that stem from our covenant with God. What relationships, what responsibilities? To God, to people, and to the earth. Love God above all else, above every human idol. Love every human person, friend or enemy, as a child of God, another self. Touch "things," God's material creation, all that is neither God nor a human person, earth and sea and sky, with reverence, as a gift of God, not to be clutched selfishly but shared generously.

In particular, the risen Christian should live the charge Jesus said would determine if we are to rise together with him for ever: "I was hungry and you gave me food, I was thirsty and you gave me drink, a stranger and you welcomed me, naked and you clothed me, ill and you cared for me, in prison and you visited me....Whatever you did for one of these least brothers [or sisters] of mine, you did for me" (Mt 25:35-45).

Such fidelity to relationships is the new life of risen Christians— your life and mine. A taxing task, for it touches our responsibilities to all that is: to God, to people, to earth. And still a thrilling task, for the Christ Jesus who rose from death to life on the first Easter, the same

Christ Jesus who raised us to new life with him in our baptism, wants with all his heart to share that life and its responsibilities. In fact, unless he shares that life, our new life would not exist; we cannot live it alone. And so, my prayer for all of us this sacred day is the exciting exhortation of Jesuit poet Gerard Manley Hopkins, "Let [Jesus] easter in us!"[1]

Pasadena, Maryland[2]
April 11, 2004

7
THAT THEY MAY ALL BE ONE
Seventh Sunday of Easter (C)

- Acts 7: 55–60
- Revelation 22:12–14, 16–17, 20
- John 17: 20–26

Good brothers and sisters in Christ: Today you and I come face-to-face with a striking contrast; you might almost call it a contradiction. On the one hand, the Gospel reading leaves us feeling good about ourselves, suffuses us with a pleasant glow. On the other hand, what we shall experience on the Capitol Mall this evening[1] may well raise questions, doubts, if not about ourselves, surely about the country we are proud to call our own, this "land of the free and home of the brave." So then, three issues: (1) the glow from the Gospel; (2) the downside from a contemporary experience; (3) some serious reflection on the Gospel and the experience.

I

Begin with the Gospel that makes us feel so good. What you have just heard is part of Jesus' farewell address, "one of the most majestic moments in the Fourth Gospel, the climax of the Last Discourse where Jesus turns to his Father in prayer."[2] He turns from his disciples to address his Father. What does he ask? Nothing for himself—not, as in Gethsemane, to have the chalice of suffering pass him by. No. Jesus' prayer is for his disciples. Not only the disciples around him then, the favored Twelve. Even more so for Christians of the generations to come. His prayer is not dated; it is a living message. He was praying for you and me.

But what was Jesus asking for his disciples, those who believe in him, then and now? He wanted them, he wanted us, to be one. But

29

what did Jesus mean by that powerful but vague monosyllable "one"?[3] How exactly are all of us who believe in Jesus expected to be one? It is not easy to say from what the evangelist John has given us, and so biblical scholars have come up with a number of different opinions. Since you are not gathered here for an academic lecture, let me simply summarize what I think it safe to say.

First, whatever the oneness is, it is not something we humans, you and I, can produce by ourselves. The fact that Jesus prays to the Father for this unity, the fact that our oneness is to resemble the oneness that exists between God the Father and God the Son, tells us that such oneness comes from God, is a gift of God. Not that you and I are purely passive; simply that our activity is not the primary source of our oneness.

But still, what is this oneness? Surely it involves all that Jesus has said about love, summed up in one immortal commandment, "Love one another as I love you" (Jn 15:12). Can there possibly be any greater, more intimate oneness on earth than the oneness that would be here if all Christians were to love all others with the type of love Jesus lived from the crib in Bethlehem to the cross on Calvary?

Further, this oneness, this love, is not just inside us, not just spiritual; it has to be visible, expressed in deeds, in action. Otherwise it could not do what Jesus wants it to do: challenge the world to believe in Jesus: "that the world may believe that you [the Father] sent me, and that you loved them even as you loved me" (Jn 17:21, 23).

And if you remember "I am the vine, you are the branches" (Jn 15:5), if you recall Jesus' prediction "one flock, one shepherd" (Jn 10:16), such love presupposes a Christian community, not simply untold individuals each doing his or her own thing.

What did Jesus ask for? A community of love, where our love for others mirrors the love of Jesus, where the deep love within us is shown in deeds, by the way we live for one another. Such is the oneness Jesus wanted, commanded, in his last will and testament.

II

Move now from the first century to the twenty-first, from the love Jesus commanded to a contemporary experience that must challenge our calling to love as Jesus loves. This experience is the heart of the memorial concert you and I, perhaps a quarter million spectators, and untold numbers of TV watchers will share this evening. I mean the experience of our homeless veterans.

Some basic facts. Who are these homeless veterans? Mostly male (2% are women), the vast majority are single; most come from poor communities; 45% suffer from mental illness; half have substance-abuse problems. Where have they served? World War II, the Korean War, the Cold War, Vietnam, Grenada, Panama, Lebanon, the first Gulf War; 47% served during the Vietnam era. More than 67% served at least three years; 33% were stationed in a war zone.

How many homeless veterans are there? No national records are kept. The U.S. Department of Veterans Affairs (VA) estimates? On any given night, more than 275,000. Over the course of a year, more than half a million—one of every four homeless males.

Why are these veterans homeless? Not only because affordable housing, a livable income, and healthcare are often unavailable. "A large number of displaced and at-risk veterans live with lingering effects of post-traumatic stress disorder and substance abuse, compounded by a lack of family and social support networks."[4] And most housing money in federal programs for the homeless goes to families or homeless women with dependent children.

The Department of Veterans Affairs? It is indeed the nation's largest provider of services; but with an estimated half million veterans homeless at some time during a year, the VA reaches less than 10% of those in need—leaving 460,000 still without services.

III

My third question: What have all these statistics to do with today's Gospel—ultimately with you and me? It's true, in the passage proclaimed to you, Jesus is speaking of the oneness he wants to see among his disciples, among all those who believe. Still, our oneness in love is expected to draw others to the same belief, to the same kind of love. And it is precisely this love that we are to lavish on every sister and brother, whatever their belief or unbelief, but especially on the less fortunate, on the downtrodden, on the ailing and the afflicted, on those who experience more of Christ's crucifixion than of his resurrection. Why these especially? Simply because they stand in greater need. That is why Jesus could present so concrete a criterion for entrance into his kingdom at the Last Judgment: "I was hungry and you gave me food, I was thirsty and you gave me drink, a stranger and you welcomed me, naked and you clothed me, ill and you cared for me, in prison and you visited me....[For] I say to you, whatever you did for one of these least brothers [and sisters] of mine, you did for me....[And] what you did not do for one of these least ones, you did not do for me" (Mt 25:35–45).[5]

"Ill and you cared for me." Yes, in caring for the homeless veteran, we care for Jesus. But what does such caring involve where, for example, the homeless veteran has for years been stressed mercilessly by his experience in Vietnam? Solutions are hardly the function of a homily. But this much I dare to utter with confidence: Our first task is to get the facts. What's going on here? And why?[6] This evening Jerry Colbert is making a magnificent beginning, opening the eyes of millions to the tragic situation of a half million Americans who have put their lives on the line for us and are all but forgotten by their country. After tonight, millions of us will have no excuse for forgetting.

As for myself, I know that from this day forward I shall never again pass by a group of the homeless without remembering that, in all probability, one of them was once willing to die for me.

What next? Keep abreast of the problems, the needs, and the resources of homeless veterans, and let Jesus suggest where you might take action. After all, he did already pray for you when he said to his Father, "I pray not only for [the Twelve], but also for those who will believe in me through their word, so that they may all be one, as you, Father, are in me and I in you, that they also may be in us, that the world may believe that you sent me" (Jn 17:20–21).

Have you ever heard a more attractive invitation?

Washington Court Hotel
Washington, D.C.
May 27, 2001

ORDINARY TIME

8
FOR JUSTICE' SAKE
Second Week, Year 1, Monday

> • Micah 6:8
> • Matthew 5:1–12

Biblical justice—your theme and mine for five days. Not simply a neat idea, a concept. Like its sisters ethical and legal, it is born of everyday life, the holy and the horrific. It is born of a covenant sealed and broken. It is born of Sinai and the desert, of exile and return, of David the shepherd and David the adulterer, of Solomon's wisdom and Solomon's 800 concubines. It is born of a crib and a cross, of Jesus "the Just One" and Judas the betrayer.

But importantly, biblical justice is not stagnant, is not enclosed in one age, one people, one culture. It develops, it grows, it changes as it touches new ages, new peoples, new problems. In that context, I suggest that this evening we touch justice—biblical and ethical—to one contemporary problem. I mean the scandal of poverty in the richest country on earth: (1) facts, (2) justice, (3) a personal word to each and all of you.

I

First, some basic facts. In this land of the free, the younger you are, the more vulnerable you are. In the richest country on earth, one out of every five children is growing up poor, hungry, ill-educated. Among industrialized countries the United States ranks 14th in the proportion of children in poverty, 16th in efforts to lift children out of poverty, 18th in the gap between rich and poor children, last in protecting our children from gun violence.[1] According to the Centers for Disease Control and Prevention, U.S. children under age 15 are 12 times more likely to die from gunfire, 16 times more likely to be murdered with a gun, 11 times more likely to commit suicide with a gun, and 9 times more likely to die in a firearm accident than children in 25 other industrialized countries combined.[2] In my own backyard, the capital of the United States, in one five-year period, 245 children died of gunshot wounds. Between 1975 and 1998, nearly 84,000 American children were killed by guns—more than all our battle fatalities in Vietnam.

In fact, all our children are at risk—not only from the proliferation of guns but from the pollution of our air, water, and earth; from toxic substances and Internet smut; from domestic violence and the breakdown of family life.[3] Endangered too by a strange absence of adequate healthcare. Twenty-three industrialized countries have safety-net policies for children: (1) universal health insurance/healthcare, (2) paid maternal/paternal leave at childbirth, (3) family allowance/child dependency grants. The United States has none of these. Eleven million of our children are uninsured; 11 million images of God.[4]

I have not studied Beaumont poverty in detail, and you have no need of a justice homily fashioned of ignorance. Still, the census of 2002 reveals some disturbing data. In 2002, 14 percent of people in Beaumont-Port Arthur lived in poverty. Sixteen percent of related children under 18 lived below the poverty level, compared with 11 percent of people 65 years and over. Ten percent of all families and 37 percent of families with a female householder and no husband present had incomes below the poverty level. Seventeen percent of the households in Beaumont-Port Arthur MSA (metropolitan statistical area) received means-tested public assistance or noncash benefits.[5]

II

My second point: To what purpose such statistics? I list them with such cold, unadorned brevity because behind the word "percentage" lie flesh and blood—millions of creatures as human as you and I, shaped by God with minds to know and hearts to love, with fingers to feel and emotions to burst forth in joy unbounded. Children of one divine Father, sisters and brothers of the one Christ who lived and breathed and died for them.

And these sisters and brothers of "the Just One" are suffering from one ailment that embraces all their addictions. One word sums it up: injustice. Injustice on two levels. One level we call ethical or philosophical, because it has to do with rights our minds tell us the impoverished can claim simply as members of the human family. I mean the right to a decent human existence, some substantial share in the incredible richness God intended not for a favored few but for all of us without exception. I mean food that would satisfy their stomachs, the incalculable waste your Beaumont and my Washington indulge that could feed all our hungry each day. I mean the jobs that would feed their families but from no fault of theirs are out of their anguished reach. I mean the education that would lift their children from the asphalt jungle, prepare them to take their rightful place in today's society, tributes to their professions. I mean the right to be treated with respect.

All this, and so much more, is human justice, the product of the minds God gave us. But our God did not leave us to our own unaided thinking. God spoke to us, coauthored a unique book with a wondrous theme that runs from the first man and woman to the Last Judgment. The theme is justice, God's justice. And what is God's justice? Fidelity to relationships, to responsibilities, that stem from a covenant. What relationships, what responsibilities? Three: to God, to our sisters and brothers, to our earth. Love God above all human idols; love every man, woman, and child, enemy as well as friend, like another self. Touch all of God's material creation with reverence, as a gift of God.

Love—the most wondrous four-letter word on earth as in heaven. A word that raises human justice to a new level. Ethical justice can lay many commands on us; it cannot command love. Only God can say, "This is my commandment: Love one another." Not only that but "Love one another as I have loved you" (Jn 13:34). Here, more powerfully than anywhere else, lies our motivation for justice. Love the poor, the hungry, the downtrodden; love the homeless and the naked; love the ill and the imprisoned. Yes, love your enemies. A hard command, a harsh command, for we are commanded to love not only the poor and the unfortunate, but bin Laden and Hussein.

No, good brothers in Christ, the statistics on poverty are not abstractions. But neither do they tell the whole story. Much of the story, the story close to your home, you have just written yourselves. And those injustices will confront you each time you reach this room. And even they are part of a much larger picture.

III

Finally, a personal word to each and all of you. For all the woes I have recited, I am delighted to add a positive note. I mean the admirable parish social ministry (PSM) within your diocese. A fresh beginning, I am told.[6] You now have a fully-staffed PSM office and, in the words of your director, are "fixing to charge out of the gate." Last year among much else, PSM funded six local organizations that provide the community with a literacy program, food and prescriptions for the poor, aid to the mentally ill and the physically challenged. On January 28, Beaumont Catholic Charities will join other Catholic Charities agencies across Texas in a massive gathering at the Capitol in Austin to plead the cause of the poor and vulnerable.

Yes, such committees, such commitments, delight me. Let me simply add to such organized activity a dream of mine. An incurable optimist, I dream of a massive movement among families. I mean a movement where every Catholic family with more than a mere sufficiency of God's gracious gifts would "adopt" one of the imperiled children in your area. Not legal adoption. Rather, a family friendship, within which the special needs of one child would be addressed: food that builds energy, funds for a basic education, books to read, braces for uneven teeth, a pair of skates, a summer-camp vacation, perhaps even a job for the youngster's father. The needs are legion. With persistence, imagination, time, and some sacrifice, your people can transform a parish, parishes transform a diocese. And if the dream were to carry over to diocese after diocese, the country we love might well become known, be envied, not for its wealth but for its justice—the justice of God, the justice that is penetrated by love.

Far out, off the wall, a mission impossible? Perhaps. But remember, the most improbable transformation in history began with a single child, a helpless child, in a tiny corner of our world, with no one to care save a virgin mother and a foster father. If we Christians could only see, in each little one in need, an image of Bethlehem's child, we could remake our troubled world. Together with your people, don't be afraid to take the first step, to reach out to another little Christ. Let none of us be afraid—for one remarkable reason: It is Christ who reaches out through you, the same Christ who told you, "Blessed, fortunate, happy are you who hunger and thirst for justice."

Holy Family Retreat Center
Beaumont, Texas
January 20, 2003

9

JUST AS YOUR FATHER IS MERCIFUL
Seventh Sunday of the Year (C)

- 1 Samuel 26:2, 7–9, 12–13, 22–23
- 1 Corinthians 15:45–49
- Luke 6:27–38

Today's readings from Paul and Jesus have evoked from me three reactions: (1) a true story, (2) a Gospel behind the story, and (3) a personal word for permanent deacons and your permanent wives.[1]

I

A true story.[2] The scene: Central Park in New York City on a hot summer night in 1986. The context: a rash of bicycle thefts by teenagers armed with guns and knives. This night Detective Steven McDonald and his partner chase and stop two youngsters, 14 and 15. McDonald bends down to check out a gun he thinks he sees in the younger boy's sock. He looks back, sees the other youth, Shavod Jones, pointing a pistol at his head. Jones squeezes the trigger, fires three shots, hits McDonald above his right eye, in his neck, and in his arm. "I was lying on the ground. I was in pain and frightened. I heard later that my partner was holding me in his arms, crying. I was dying." McDonald survived the shooting. But the bullet in his neck had severed his spine. It left him unable to use his hands or his feet, unable to breathe on his own. At the time, his wife, Patti, was pregnant with their son, Conor.

Last month Steven McDonald spoke to the children of St. Anthony of Padua Church in Paterson, New Jersey. He was strapped into his motorized wheelchair. Two small tubes carried the wheelchair's driving and steering controls into his mouth. His voice

39

wheezed between sentences as a respirator gasped to pump oxygen into his lungs. Periodically his head jerked back and forth.

What did Officer McDonald tell the children? In soft tones, almost like a whisper, "I forgave him. If I was angry or bitter toward the person who did this horrible thing to me, I needed to free myself from these terrible emotions so I could be free to love. It's possible to forgive. It's a beautiful expression of love to others and of nonviolence."

The shooter? McDonald's decision to forgive touched Jones' troubled heart. From prison he called McDonald and his wife, crying as he apologized for the pain he had caused. Shortly after his release from prison in 1995, Jones was killed in a motorcycle accident. Praised for his act of forgiveness, Officer McDonald said, "Mine is a minor example of forgiveness. The biggest example of forgiveness is Jesus on the cross. He died for our sins."

II

"I forgave him." What lies behind those three words? Today's Gospel, as tough a Gospel as you will ever hear. "To you who hear I say, 'Love your enemies, do good to those who hate you, bless those who curse you, pray for those who mistreat you'" (Lk 6:27–28). Those four commands constitute the core of Jesus' Sermon on the Plain; therefore they are crucial for Christian living. For the command to love your enemy is rooted in the very nature of God. It is etched indelibly in Psalm 103, the song you sang in today's Responsorial Psalm:

> Bless the Lord, my soul;
>   all my being, bless His holy name!
> Bless the Lord, my soul;
>   do not forget all the gifts of God.
> He pardons all your sins,
>   heals all your ills,
>   delivers your life from destruction,
>   surrounds you with love and compassion.
> Merciful and gracious is the Lord,
>   slow to anger, abounding in kindness,
>   has not dealt with us as our sins merit,
>   nor requited us as our deeds deserve.
> As far as the east is from the west,
>   so far have our sins been removed from us.
> As a father has compassion on his children,
>   so the Lord has compassion on the faithful.
>   (Ps 103:1–4, 8, 10, 12–13)

And what Jesus proclaimed Jesus lived. We all treasure the so-called first words from the cross, "Father, forgive them, they know not what they do" (Lk 23:34a). Would you be surprised to know that those words do not appear in some Catholic translations of Luke? Why? Because they do not appear in very early manuscripts of Luke, important manuscripts, manuscripts from different geographical areas; they are absent from some ancient translations.

Are you shocked? Don't be. You see, deep down it doesn't really matter whether Jesus *spoke* those words from the cross. Why not? Because apart from forgiveness Bethlehem and Calvary make no sense. The crib and the cross are themselves mute cries for forgiveness. In Bethlehem God's forgiveness took flesh. Everything Jesus did from Bethlehem to Calvary welled up from the bowels of his compassion. His ministry was summed up when he taught us how to pray: "Forgive us as we forgive" (Mt 6:12). And Calvary? Calvary is the climax of his earthly compassion. It began a massive, marvelous work of reconciliation, undoing the damage that was done in Eden. Once again I can be one with my God, can tabernacle Trinity in my inmost being. I am forgiven. Forgiven, I can mimic God's own forgiveness by forgiving others.

Fine words. And yet, as a splendid Scripture scholar recently remarked, "Virtually no Christian group has adopted Jesus' teaching on love of enemy as a critical test of orthodoxy."[3] This despite the fact that Jesus declared, "This is my commandment: Love one another as I love you" (Jn 15:12). Love is not simply or primarily heavy breathing, a sexual attraction, chemistry between bodies. I love when I seek what is good for another, when I respond to another's need. I know I love when Jesus says to me, "I was hungry and you gave me food, I was thirsty and you gave me drink, I was a stranger and you welcomed me, naked and you clothed me, ill and you cared for me, in prison and you visited me" (Mt 25:35–36). Not only those I like and who like me. The foul-mouthed beggar, the undocumented immigrant, the strange-looking stranger, the black and the yellow, yes the terrorist and the child abuser. Powerful are the words of Jesus, "If you love those who love you, what credit is that to you? Even sinners love those who love them" (Lk 6:32).

Why such love, even for enemies? Because each human person is fashioned in God's image. And every man, every woman remains a reflection of God, however defective. Somewhat as a work of art, Michelangelo's *Last Judgment*, howsoever mutilated by the ages, never ceases to be his creation, never ceases to be his, so too we: shaped in God's image, reshaped in the image of Christ, none of us can ever lose that basic relationship, that link to the Lord through creation and the cross. In forgiving the sinner, in turning the other cheek, we are not saying yes to evil, passively enduring violence, rejecting all punishment. Quite the contrary. In forgiving as God forgives, in reflecting God's own love, in treating criminals as images of God, we are helping to free enemies of their enmity, of their hatred, of their violent destructiveness.

Does it always work? Obviously not. The more serious problem? As Chesterton said of Christianity, it's not really been tried. Not often enough.

III

This leads finally to a more personal word to you—to you as deacons in the Church of Christ. A significant facet of your ministry, as I conceive it, is preaching. Not just in general. Preaching the just word. The word you preach above all else is the one indispensable word, God's written Word, Scripture. An endless theme in Scripture: justice. Not simply human justice: giving every man, woman, and child what they deserve, what they have a strict right to demand, because it can be proven from philosophy or has been written into law. With that, and above that, God's justice: fidelity to relationships that stem from our covenant with God cut in the blood of Christ. What relationships? Three. Love God above all else, above all human idols. Love every human person as an image of God. Touch God's material creation, earth and sea and sky, all that is not God or the human person, with reverence.

Our focus today is clearly relationship number two: others. Specifically, those the Gospel calls "enemies." How touch what I have said about principles to actual living in today's world? How make concrete what is clear enough on principle? How preach it to a skeptical or hostile congregation?

To preach forgiveness effectively, I must live it. Where I myself have been hurt. Not necessarily paralyzed in body like Officer McDonald. Still, actually suffered injustice and no apologies offered, no reparation made, paralyzed in spirit. I must love those who have sinned against me as Jesus loved and loves me; as Jesus loves them. I must sincerely desire what is good for them, what will make them better persons. I must learn to forgive those who have sinned against me as Jesus has forgiven me, continues to forgive me. Not a sentimental feeling; rather a firm act of my mind and will.

But even if you the preacher live forgiveness, preaching it remains a problem. People, good Christian people, will turn you off.

Forgive the child molester? Forgive the serial killer? Forgive the Oklahoma City bombers? You're out of your cotton-pickin' mind. You're a bleeding heart. The father of the prodigal son, the Good Samaritan—touching indeed, great stories, but hardly realistic. One writer put it powerfully in *Time* magazine:

> ...the problem with forgiveness has been that of all acknowledged good acts, it is the one we are most suspicious of. "To err is human, to forgive, supine," punned J. S. Perelman. In a country where the death penalty has been a proven vote getter in recent years, forgiveness is often seen as effete and irresponsible. Sometimes it even seems to condone the offense, as noted centuries ago by Jewish sages who declared, "He that is merciful to the cruel will eventually be cruel to the innocent."[4]

Preaching forgiveness calls not only for courage but for patience. It calls for a serious, long-term education in a basic Christian virtue that has gone out of style even among Christians. You must assure your people that you are not condoning crime, not excusing evil, not protesting against punishment. Admit that it's not reasonable, isn't logical, doesn't make down-to-earth sense. You are preaching what St. Paul calls "a still more excellent way" (1 Cor 12:31). A more excellent way because it is Christ's way. More excellent because it moves from Jesus to myself, a sinner time and again forgiven by God. More excellent because it sees in the sinner what Jesus saw: an image of God, a child of God, my brother, my sister. More excellent because it looks beyond retribution to restoration—restoration to God's friendship, restoration to the human community, to the Christian community. More excellent because it is based not on vengeance but on love.

I am not suggesting that in your homilies you will demand instant forgiveness no matter what: that a Polish American forgive the Nazis who gassed his father and mother; that Chileans forgive the Pinochet who forced thousands of their dear ones to "disappear"; that a mother forgive the rapist who ravished and murdered her daughter; that mothers forgive the thugs who killed the four American missionary women in El Salvador; that two families will forgive the teenage student who recently killed their sons at Washington's Gallaudet University for the deaf. To forgive under such circumstances is a grace we cannot merit.

What, then, shall preachers ask, suggest, demand? That those who hear us and are hurting will pray God to lessen not only their hurt but their anger, their bitterness; pray God to change the hearts of their enemies; pray God to place in their own hearts some semblance of the forgiveness that burst from the lips of Christ on Calvary; that God will make of them what St. Paul said of himself when he wrote to the Christians of Corinth: "Whoever is in Christ is a new creation; the old things have passed away; behold, new things have come. And all this is from God, who has reconciled us to Himself through Christ and has given us the ministry of reconciliation, namely, God was reconciling the world to Himself through Christ. Not counting their trespasses against them and entrusting to us the message of reconciliation. So we are ambassadors for Christ, as if God were appealing through us" (2 Cor 5:17–20).

Appealing *to* you, appealing *through* you: "Be merciful, just as your Father is merciful" (Lk 6:36).

Diocese of Little Rock
Little Rock, Arkansas
February 18, 2001

10
A NEW BIRTH TO A LIVING HOPE
Eighth Week, Year 2, Monday

- 1 Peter 1:3-9
- Mark 10:17-29

Today, as usual, I face a fascinating task: how to link three realities—Scripture, this congregation, and the world you inhabit. Concretely, three movements. I shall (1) touch rather briefly on the obvious meaning of "a new birth to a living hope" (1 Pet 1:3); (2) expand that newness to the biblical justice that is your primary concern this week; and (3) suggest how all this might speak to a Memorial Day that for the first time includes September 11.

I

The passage proclaimed to you from the First Letter of Peter is surely one of the most thrilling in the New Testament—in content, in language, in rhetoric. From its beginning, "God the Father of our Lord Jesus Christ, who in His great mercy gave us a new birth to a living hope through the resurrection of Jesus Christ from the dead," to its closing, "you rejoice with an indescribable and glorious joy as you attain the goal of your faith, the salvation of your souls" (v. 9), you have heard in rapturous syllables the new thing that is the Christian story, your story and mine—our firm faith, our basic belief.

Why do I say this? Because here, in the Christian's rebirth, is Jesus' insistence that we must be born again, "born from above," "born of water and Spirit" (Jn 3:3, 5). Here is Jesus' pithy and pregnant "I live and you will live" (Jn 14:19). It is Jesus' prayer to the Father for us that we "may all be one, as you, Father, are in me and I in you, that they may also be in us" (Jn 17:21). This is St. Paul's "whoever is in Christ is a new creation; the old things have passed away; behold, new things have

45

come" (2 Cor 5:17). The "living hope"? This is Paul's "hope [that] does not disappoint, because God's love has been poured out in our hearts through the holy Spirit that has been given to us" (Rom 5:5). Because of the Spirit at home within us, we rejoice in the assurance of 1 Peter, "Although you have not seen [Christ], you love him; even though you do not see him now, you believe in him" (1 Pet 1:8).

Such, good brothers in Christ, such is our newness, such in brief is our faith.

II

Second, let me expand a bit beyond the obvious meaning of 1 Peter. You see, part of being "a new creation," part of being "a chosen race, a royal priesthood, a holy nation, a people of [God's] own" (1 Pet 2:9) is that we may not be satisfied with our obligations on simply a human level. Yes, as 1 Peter urges us, we are "subject to every human institution for the Lord's sake, whether it be to the king as supreme or to governors as sent by Him for the punishment of evildoers and the approval of those who do good" (1 Pet 2:13–14). But if the New Testament, our gospel, tells us anything, it tells us to rise above what is expected of this world's citizens. It is the Christ's "You have heard...but I say to you."

Precisely here justice enters in. But how? Fifteen years ago a Jesuit social scientist, Philip Land, opened an encyclopedia article on justice with a quotation from the Hebrew prophet Amos: "Let justice roll down like waters" (Amos 5:24).[1] Land continued:

> Prior to Vatican II no Catholic treatise on justice would have begun with scripture. It would have taken its start from the [ethical] definition of justice—*Suum cuique tradere*–to render to each one [what is] one's due and proceeded then to analyze in the light of reason the various relations this involves. With Vatican II but especially with the 1971 Synod, Justice in the World, justice becomes a call to the Christian from the God of the two Testaments.[2]

The primary justice is now biblical. And what is biblical justice? Fidelity to relationships that stem from a covenant—for a Christian, the covenant with God cut in the blood of Christ. What relationships? Three. There is the greatest commandment of them all: "You shall love the Lord, your God, with all your heart, with all your soul, and with all your mind" (Mt 22:37; see Deut 6:5). There is the second commandment, which Jesus said "is like" the first: "You shall love your neighbor as yourself" (Mt 22:39; see Lev 19:18). There is the injunction to care for the earth, for God's material creation, to treat the "things" of God with reverence and respect. "Like ancient kings, men and women are to be mediators of prosperity and well-being. Reverential care for God's creation rather than exploitation is the mandate given humanity in [Gen 1:27–28]."[3]

The first two injunctions—love God, love neighbor—clearly fall under the *faith* that does justice, the faith over which 1 Peter lyricizes. But what of our care for creation? If you are not convinced by biblical scholars, listen to John Paul II's message for the World Day of Peace, January 1, 1990: Christians must "realize that their responsibility within creation and their duty toward nature and the Creator are an essential part of their faith."[4] The faith that does justice is not a matter of philosophy or law. Not that ethical and legal justice are insignificant; without them, life on earth becomes a jungle, the survival of the fittest, the playing field of the shrewd and the powerful. It is rather that reason and law are insufficient for the Christian. To give others what they deserve, what they can claim as a right, to realize from reason alone that we are not earth's despots, this is good but not enough. Where God and people and creation are concerned, we have been given "a new birth." We are to love as Jesus loved—love enemy as well as friend, because each man, each woman, each child is an image of God marred but never destroyed; each is a reflection of Christ. And as for the earth, I suggest that Elizabeth Johnson's insight on *communio sanctorum* ("communion in the holy") must become our own:

> ...the universe itself is the primordial sacrament through which we participate in and communicate with divine mystery. Since the same divine Spirit who lights the fire of the saint also fuels the vitality of all creation, then "communion in the holy" includes holy people and a holy world in interrelationship. By this line of thinking, a door opens from within the symbol of the communion of saints itself to include all beings, sacred bread and wine certainly, but also the primordial sacrament, the earth itself....[5]

III

From faith and hope to justice—ordinarily enough for a homily. But this is Memorial Day, and for the first time in our lives Memorial Day can hardly be separated from September the eleventh. Year after year we have memorialized, commemorated the men and women who have given their lives for their country, for us—from the Civil War through the

Spanish-American War, World Wars I and II, to the Korean War and the Vietnam War. And it is fitting that we do so; for in large measure those who died bore witness (even if unknowingly) to the declaration of Jesus, "No one has greater love than this, to lay down one's life for those whom one loves" (Jn 15:13). Add to them now the hundreds of police and fire fighters who perished for us on 9/11. But today, in the midst of solemn warnings about terrorism yet to come, I am particularly concerned over injustice. I am not excusing 9/11, but I wonder at times if that day of infamy might have been averted if the powerful among believers had shown biblical compassion to the needy beyond our borders—perhaps even to Afghanistan. One sad statistic:

> Although it is the richest country in the world, the United States is the least generous in foreign aid. It allocates only 0.1 percent of its gross national product—much of it for military purposes. Of this 0.1 percent, only one-eighth goes for health. In March, the Bush administration announced a plan to add $10 billion to overseas aid over the next few years, and the president himself said in Monterrey that the wealthy countries need to do more to help the poorest. But as noted in a report jointly issued around the same time by the Center for Global Development and the Center on Budget and Policy Priorities, the proposed increase would lift the amount of foreign aid to only 0.13 percent, so "the United States would continue to contribute a far smaller portion of its economy to aid than nearly every other donor country."[6]

And I must ask, does it make for justice to divide God's one world into "us" and "them," to characterize three countries as an "axis of evil"? And since justice, like charity, might well begin at home, should it not shame us that in the United States the younger you are, the poorer you are, that every sixth child grows up below the poverty line, with all the risks to bloated bellies and famished minds? Should it not distress us that one in seven children has no health insurance, that one in eight is born to a teenage mother, that one in 24 lives with neither parent, that one in 139 will die before his or her first birthday, that one in 1,056 will be killed by guns before age twenty?[7]

Why so much on faith/justice to my knowledgeable Jesuit brothers?[8] Because the faith that does justice has been officially declared the mission of the contemporary Society.[9] Because our revered Father General Pedro Arrupe let it be known that this mission was the most difficult he had to sell to Jesuits. Because even the 32nd Congregation (1974–75) was not in a position to identify and stress *biblical* justice. Because most Catholic priests are still preaching only ethical justice, giving everyone what each can claim as a right. Because our Catholic people will never rise above mere human justice unless we preach God's justice with clarity and conviction.

Despite new fears of terrorisms to come, I still hope—and pray—that the leaders who make world-shaking decisions on our behalf will find fidelity to relationships preferable to self-interest. The Christ who was crucified for all of us would find this very much to his liking.

Jesuit Retreat House
Oshkosh, Wisconsin
May 27, 2002

11
PERSECUTED FOR JUSTICE' SAKE
Tenth Week, Year 2, Monday

> • 1 Kings 17:1–6
> • Matthew 5:1–12

I find it fascinating that over the centuries justice has consistently been accompanied by persecution.[1] In swift succession, let me explore this link (1) briefly from antiquity, then (2) in the story of the Society of Jesus, finally (3) as it might touch you and me.

I

From the Hebrew Testament, a pertinent prophet is Jeremiah. Jeremiah reproached Judah for its foreign alliances and its idolatry, attacked the superficiality of the Temple cult. The priests and other prophets threatened him with death; the princes had him beaten and thrown into a dungeon; other princes buried him in a cistern, where he sank into the mud. Forced into Egyptian exile, he was murdered by his own countrymen. Indeed persecution for justice' sake.

Move to the New Testament and John the Baptist. Why imprisoned by King Herod? Says evangelist Matthew: because he had reproached Herod for his unlawful marriage. Why beheaded? Says Matthew: because unlawful wife Herodias had asked Herod for John's head (Mt 14:3–12). Not so, implies ancient historian Josephus: John was imprisoned and executed because Herod was afraid that the Baptist's influence over the people might enable him to lead a rebellion.[2] In either case, persecution for justice' sake.

Forget not Jesus himself, *ho dikaios*, the supremely "Just One" of the new covenant (Acts 7:52; Mt 27:19; Lk 23:47; 1 Jn 2:1; 3:7). Uniquely persecuted for justice' sake. For Jesus was marked for death from his birth by a Herod who feared for his kingdom, who in his fury at being deceived by the magi "ordered the massacre of all the boys in Bethlehem and its vicinity two years old and under" (Mt 2:16). Uniquely persecuted for justice' sake when his own fellow Nazarenes tried to kill him for claiming to be a prophet like Elijah and Elisha (cf. Lk 4:24–30). Uniquely persecuted for justice' sake because this was the uniquely Just One unjustly condemned to a criminal's cross. Pilate's wife spoke more accurately than she knew when she warned him, "Have nothing to do with that just man" (Mt 27:19). As was the centurion who witnessed his dying and exclaimed, "This man was just [innocent] beyond doubt" (Lk 23:47).[3]

II

Turn now from Jesus to our own Society of Jesus, to Jesuits who were persecuted for justice' sake.[4] Not all by any means; merely a handful, a random selection, to illustrate the link between justice and persecution, the link that might suggest why Jesus called such individuals "blessed," "fortunate," perhaps even "happy."

We could begin with Ignatius Loyola. In 1527, a decade before his ordination, while preaching the gospel in Alcalá, he was arrested by the Inquisition and imprisoned, was released after 42 days and forbidden to teach in public. Three months later he was preaching in Salamanca, but within two weeks Dominicans in the city suspected him of heresy and had him imprisoned. Found to be without fault, he was released after 22 days, told he could teach children but could not discourse on more complicated theological matters.

As persecutions go, Ignatius was not nearly as blest as his sons down the ages. From a striking list I choose only two. First, cross over from Spain's Loyola to not so Merrie Elizabethan England. Mull a moment over Edmund Campion, the most famous of the English martyrs. Entering hostile England secretly, he writes a manifesto of his mission; we know it as "Campion's Brag." Intended to be used if he is captured, it declares he has come to England on a religious mission, not for political purposes. He publishes his little book *Ten Reasons,* ten arguments for the truth of Catholicism; many of the 400 copies are left on the benches of Oxford's Church of St. Mary. Eighteen months of secret ministry and he is betrayed by a professional priest-hunter. Since he refuses to apostatize to the Established Church, he is tortured on the rack. With seven others he is charged with forming a conspiracy against the life of Queen Elizabeth, exhorting foreigners to invade the country, entering England to stir up rebellion in support of an invading force. All eight are found guilty of high treason, condemned to be hanged, drawn, and quartered. Asked to confess his treason on the scaffold, Campion replies: "If you esteem my religion treason, then I am guilty; as for other treason, I never committed any. God is my judge." He forgives those who condemned him; the cart is driven from under him, and he is left hanging. The executioner cuts out his heart and his intestines. It is December 1, 1581. Blessed indeed are you, St. Edmund Campion, persecuted for justice' sake.

Fly back to New York and Canada: eight North American martyrs, six of them Jesuits, two lay associates. Isaac Jogues and Jean de Brébeuf we know well, but muse a moment over Noel Chabanel. A brilliant professor of rhetoric in France, very sensitive, he is transported to a wilderness. He detests the Huron way of life: the smoke and the vermin, the filth in the food and the utter absence of privacy, the howling dogs and screeching children. Five years and he still cannot learn the Huron language. Tempted to return to an appreciative France, he takes a vow, binds himself to remain in the Huron mission to the day of his death. He wants to be "a martyr in obscurity." And so he is, his very fate shrouded in mystery until an apostate Huron admits he murdered Chabanel, threw his body into a river. Why? Because he hated the Christian faith. Blessed indeed are you, St. Noel Chabanel, persecuted for justice' sake.

III

Finally, what might all this say to you and me, to Jesuits of any province? My response begins with a declaration of the 32nd General Congregation of the Society of Jesus:

> The mission of the Society of Jesus today is the service of faith, of which the promotion of justice is an absolute requirement. For reconciliation with God demands the reconciliation of people with one another.
>
> In one form or another, this has always been the mission of the Society; but it gains new meaning and urgency in the light of the needs and aspirations of the men and women of our time....[5]

And a little later on: "Each one of us must contribute to the total mission according to his talents and functions which, in collaboration with the efforts of others, give life to the whole body...."[6]

Second, the inseparable unity of the service of faith and the promotion of justice is a concept which Father General Pedro Arrupe admitted in Manila is "the concept which has been most difficult to put across."[7] He knew that on this issue some of our most loyal friends and benefactors thought us traitors to the Ignatian ideal. He knew that more than a few Jesuits echoed the remark I overheard in a Jesuit recreation room about the desperate plight of Latin America's poor: "not unjust, simply unfortunate." He knew there were idealistic Jesuits who carried the struggle to extremes, to a violence hardly in conformity with the cross of Christ. Yet he never wavered in his core conviction, the memorable message John Paul II proclaimed in Puebla: "The Church has learned that an indispensable part of its evangelizing mission is made up of works on behalf of justice and human promotion...."[8]

Third, the faith/justice in question is best understood in our time as the biblical justice that is the centerpiece of this week's retreat/workshop: fidelity to relationships that stem from our covenant with God cut in the blood of Christ. Relationships to God, to people, to the earth. Love God above all human idols. Love every human being, friend or enemy, as Christ loved and loves us. Touch "things," God's material creation, all that is not God or the human person, with reverence, with respect, as a gift of God, a "trace" of divinity.

Fourth, the beatitude which stimulated this homily: "Blessed are they who are persecuted for the sake of justice." My point is, living and preaching the faith that does justice is not something that falls under what Dietrich Bonhoeffer called "cheap grace," something paid in advance by Christ, therefore can be had for nothing. No, biblical justice is a "costly grace." Costly because, to borrow Bonhoeffer's words, "it costs a man his life,"[9] as it cost the life of God's only Son.

At times preaching and living justice is costly enough to lose one's life. Recall Jeremiah, John the Baptist, and Jesus; recall Campion and Chabanel. Recall, in our own time, Archbishop Romero shot to death at the altar, the six Jesuits massacred at the University of Central America. But for the most part, preaching and living justice does not make a bloody entrance, is literally unbloody, does not kill. It takes its toll in your living; its cost is in courage. As Arrupe experienced, you will alienate some of your own people, especially if you are questioning their justice. Whether you raise an issue with a gospel answer or simply raise an issue for consideration, some will turn you off or even turn on you.

Proclaiming justice calls not only for knowledge but for discretion, awareness of conflicting claims and doing justice to their merits. Justice is not always an either/or. I learned that after a homily in Montana, where I had praise galore for the environmentalists, only learned too late the legitimate claims of loggers. Preaching justice just-ly murders my sleep, forces acid from intestines to esophagus, tenses every tendon and muscle in my body, even builds a walkway between my computer and the bathroom.

Despite the difficulties, you and I may not disregard the call of Christ and the Society. There are indeed different levels of response—from the parish priest, from the professor of poetry, from the spiritu-al father, from the treasurer in a community. But each of us, I suggest, can and should co-operate in three ways with the faith that does justice.

1) *Listen.* Listen to Jesus: "*I* was hungry and you gave me food" (Mt 25:35). Listen to the Church—the whole Church, clerical and lay, as it speaks to you from its vast experience of injustice. Listen to one another, even or especially when you disagree. Listen to Jewish lead-ers as they rehearse the litany of age-old Christian crimes against God's chosen people. Listen to other cultures: American Indian, African American, Hispanic, Vietnamese, as they tell of American injustice. Listen to professionals as they tell you that the death penal-ty "actually hinders the fight against crime."[10] Listen to land mines as every 22 minutes they maim or kill a man, woman, or child some-where in our world. Listen to the cries of America's children, every sixth child growing up in poverty. Listen, listen, listen.

2) *Live.* Live justice. I don't mean a menu of "locusts and wild honey" with John the Baptist (Mt 3:4). I mean loving God above all else. I mean loving every man and woman and child as Jesus has loved and loves you. I mean touching every thing that is not God or human per-son with reverence. And share. We profess to own nothing. But as I look into my closet, there is so much I no longer need; no superior will object to my giving to the needy what I simply do not need. And, perhaps above all, share yourself, your ideas, your compassion, your love.

3) *Proclaim.* Whatever your assignment by the Society, tell your little world how to be faithful to relationships that stem from their covenant with God. From the pulpit or in conversation, by e-mail or phone, using the modern miracles of communication, proclaim to all within your reach how good our God is, how precious they are to God and to you, how to forgive and be reconciled, how to use God's good earth not as despots but as stewards.

Good brothers: From over a decade of experience, I can assure you of one thing about biblical justice. Rarely will you experience such satisfaction, such delight, such peace, such intimacy with God, as when with God's grace you bring a smile to a hungry child's lips and eyes, or when through our Lady's intercession you watch two bitter enemies shake hands in reconciliation, or when with St. Paul you sense some part of creation no longer "made subject to futility" but "set free from slavery to corruption" and beginning to "share in the glorious freedom of the children of God" (Rom 8:20–21).

Jesuit Retreat House
Parma, Ohio
June 10, 2002

12
WHO IS MY NEIGHBOR?
Twenty-seventh Week, Year 2, Monday

- Galatians 1:6–12
- Luke 10:25–37

"Who is my neighbor?" To confront this question, allow me to fly you to Australia, then on to Palestine, and end up in Scranton, Pennsylvania.

I

First, imagine you are in Australia near midnight on Friday, September 23, in the city of Sydney, in the largest Olympic stadium ever built. Before 110,000 people singing "Waltzing Matilda," a brown woman stands proudly. Granddaughter of an Aboriginal woman taken by authorities as a child and given to a white family, she waits patiently for a torch that was lit in Greece and has passed through 11,200 hands. Taking the torch, she climbs a set of stairs and steps into a pool beside a waterfall cascading from the top of the stadium's second tier. She bends and lights a circle of flame, the inner rim of a nine-ton platter of steel, the Olympic cauldron, which rises above her like a spaceship to the 14-story stadium's top.[1]

Several days later, the same Aboriginal, Cathy Freeman, ran the 400-meter race. On the morning of the race, a front-page article in the *Sydney Morning Herald* read, "There has been no single occasion when more has been expected of an Australian sportsperson....Rightly or wrongly, Cathy carries with her not just the nation's sporting hopes but its political aspirations."[2] She won "in 49.11 seconds as the huge stadium shook from the roar of more than 112,000 people....[A]nd then she circled the stadium with Australian and Aboriginal flags knotted together."[3]

56

It is this scene that flooded my mind and my emotions as I worked over today's all-important Gospel question, "Who is my neighbor?" But that means leaving Sydney for a while, moving on to the Holy Land, where the featured characters are not an athlete and a torch but a lawyer and the Son of God.

II

In Palestine, begin with the lawyer's question, "Who is my neighbor?" It's a terribly important question, not only for the lawyer but for everyone who is concerned with his earlier question, "Teacher, what am I to do to inherit eternal life?" A Jew would have been aware of the sentence in the Book of Daniel, "Many of those who sleep in the dust of the earth shall awake, some to life eternal, some to shame and eternal disgrace" (Dan 12:2). The lawyer knows what is written in the Mosaic law: Love God with all your heart and soul, all your mind and strength; love your neighbor as yourself. Hence his question.

Here the lawyer's problem is very real: Who qualifies as his neighbor? Surely his fellow Israelites; but just as surely the resident alien; for he must have been aware of the legislation in Exodus, "You shall not oppress a resident alien; you know the heart of an alien [you know how an alien feels], for you were aliens in the land of Egypt" (Exod 23:9). Not only not oppress; listen to Deuteronomy, "You shall love the resident alien, for you were aliens in the land of Egypt" (Deut 10:19).

Why, then, the question, "Who is my neighbor?" Who might *not* be considered a neighbor? Hebrew slaves, I suspect. Could the lawyer possibly have been thinking of the Samaritans, schismatics in the eyes of the Jews? Remember how the evangelist John remarked in the story of the Samaritan woman at the well, "Jews have nothing to do with Samaritans [or: use nothing in common with Samaritans—e.g., vessels for food and drink]"? Perhaps. At any rate, the lawyer's question is real, deserves a reply.

What precisely is Jesus' answer? He does not answer the question directly. The lawyer wanted a *definition* of neighbor. There the neighbor would be the *object* of benevolent action. Whom must I treat as a neighbor, as a friend? What are the limits of my responsibility? Whom can I exclude? Foreigners? Heretics? Personal enemies? The occupying Romans? Jesus turns the question on its head. The neighbor in his parable is not the person who *receives* benevolence; it is the person who *shows* benevolence, *shows* kindness, *shows* neighborliness.

True, Jesus' parable answers the lawyer's question implicitly: Your neighbor is anyone in need who somehow touches your life. But the question Jesus asks at the end of the story, "Which of these three [priest, Levite, Samaritan] seems to you to have been neighbor to the man who fell into the hands of the robbers?" and the grudging response of the lawyer, "The one who showed him kindness," compassion (Lk 10:36–37), cast the question into a larger perspective. "It is no longer whether the victim of the highway robbery could be considered legally a 'neighbor' to either the priest, the Levite, or the Samaritan, but rather which one of them acted as a 'neighbor' to the unfortunate victim."[4] The principle underlying Jesus' question? "[While] mere neighborhood does not create love, love does create neighborliness."[5]

Here, for Luke, is a concrete example of the love that leads to eternal life. The story of the Good Samaritan is a striking example of the human love Jesus commanded in the Sermon on the Plain: "I say to you: Love your enemies, do good to those who hate you, bless those who curse you, pray for those who abuse you" (Lk 6:27). "It also contributes to the larger picture of Lucan 'universalism,' which includes a Samaritan and makes him a paradigm for Christian conduct; it suggests that even a Samaritan has found the way to eternal life."[6]

III

Back in Scranton.[7] To yourselves and the people you serve. You see, the story of Cathy Freeman, the parable of the Good Samaritan, and the experiences of priests and deacons of Scranton are not unconnected, isolated realities. They are significant moments in the long history of injustice—specifically discrimination.

How the Jews split from the inhabitants of Samaria is shrouded in mystery. But the dissension, the dislike, the discrimination is clear. Clear from the question put to Jesus by the woman at Jacob's well: "You are a Jew—how can you ask me, a Samaritan, for a drink?" (Jn 4:9). Clear from the Samaritan villagers who would not welcome Jesus because "his face was set toward Jerusalem" (Lk 9:53); that is to say, his intention was to proceed to Jerusalem. Clear from the reaction of James and John: "Lord, do you want us to call down fire from heaven to consume these people?" (v. 54). The Samaritans restricted their Scriptures to the Pentateuch, built a temple on Mount Gerizim, had developed their own form of the Pentateuch, their own liturgy, their own liturgical literature in both Hebrew and Aramaic. The historian

Josephus relates the problems Galilean pilgrims had "at the time of a festival to pass through Samaritan territory on their way to the Holy City."[8] No, Jerusalem's Jews in general would not have found the parable of the Good Samaritan to their liking.

And what of Australia? Cathy Freeman's victory run with Australian and Aboriginal flags joined together will be, I hope, a living symbol of a new Australia, the death of decades and centuries of discrimination. I mean fundamental social and economic inequality; a disproportionately high percentage of arrest, detention, and death in prison; scandalous connection between unemployment, homelessness, and institutionalized racism; lack of educational opportunities; bloody massacres; destruction of Aboriginal identity and culture; dysfunctional families (drugs and alcohol). Most troubling of all, tens of thousands of Aboriginal children forcibly removed from their parents (the Stolen Generation); child slavery and sexual assault.

Things are indeed a-changing; legislation is improving the lot of Aboriginals; and in 1977 South Australian Premier John Olsen apologized to Aboriginal people for past wrongs, particularly the Stolen Generation. "This sad episode," he said, "has caused a scar on the face of the nation....By apologising, I hope that we can now move forward." In 1998 Philip Ruddock was appointed Minister for Reconciliation. The two flags joined together by an Aboriginal woman, hailed by thousands of Australians, may well symbolize Australia's future. Cathy's very surname foreshadows that future: Freeman, "free man."

You know, in her own way Cathy Freeman fits beautifully into Jesus' parable of the Good Samaritan; she too turns the question "Who is my neighbor?" on its head. For she too has moved the neighbor from the recipient of kindness to the giver of kindness, from the injured victim to the compassionate healer. It is the Aboriginal who holds out the hand of reconciliation to the offender, to the persecutor. Against all the odds, *she* is the one who shows mercy, shows compassion.

And what of you, of Scranton? If biblical justice is fidelity to relationships that stem from a covenant—relationships with God, with God's children, and with God's earth—then injustice is infidelity, a refusal to be faithful. In the past two hours you listed, with frankness and courage, the infidelities of your city, of your diocese, of your parishes. Till Friday morning the injustices, the discrimination, the failures in love will grace (if that's the word) the walls of our conference room. Why? Because here is where God's Word touches the human situation, takes flesh. Here is where lovely phrases like "Love one another as I have loved you" (Jn 15:12) clash with harsh reality, with hate and bitterness, with violence and revenge. Here beatitudes like "Blessed are you poor, blessed are you that hunger, blessed are you that weep" (Lk 6:20–21) come to grips with an American poverty that mangles minds and batters bodies, with one child in five aching for food, with the tears of women beaten and raped. No longer need you strain for homiletic meat; it surrounds you, assails your eyes, your ears, your nostrils.

This is not a plea to savage your congregation Savonarola style. A homily challenges and encourages. Perhaps of greatest importance for our ministry of proclamation is to recognize, with St. Paul, that "through Christ God has reconciled us to Himself and *has given us the ministry of reconciliation*" (2 Cor 5:18). To reconcile, to destroy enmity, to promote peace, such, I suggest, is our primary task. This is not to downgrade our Eucharist; for the Eucharist itself, the Church's most powerful source of grace, is the primary sacrament of reconciliation. And, wonder of wonders, to preach biblical justice is to foster reconciliation; for in the biblical sense the just are the men and women who are linked in love with God, live in loving peace with fellow humans ("neighbors"), and touch with loving reverence the earth that sustains them. A realization that the one God has in mind a universe that is one.

In imaginative moments I like to envision our vocation as part of the effort to recapture in a small way something of the original Eden, where God, humans, and material creation lived in incredible intimacy. If such is our vocation, three troubling questions challenge each of us. (1) Do the people I serve see me as a minister of reconciliation? (2) Is that the way I see my vocation? (3) If not, why not?

Fatima Renewal Center
Dalton, Pennsylvania
October 9, 2000

13

THIS IS THE FASTING THAT I WISH
Twenty-ninth Sunday of the Year (A)

- Isaiah 45:1, 4–6
- 1 Thessalonians 1:1–5
- Matthew 22:15–21

Americans live off slogans. You find slogans everywhere: on buses and subways, on TV commercials and license plates, on billboards and coins. "In God we trust." "The life you save may be your own." "No pain, no gain." "United we stand." "You only live once." "Praise the Lord and pass the ammunition." In Arizona a young rabbi with a sense of humor handed me a decorative button, "Jesus saves, Moses invests."

Today a striking slogan is crisscrossing our country—a slogan transcending religious differences and uniting political parties. The slogan is a trademark of the Children's Defense Fund, copied by the Bush administration. The slogan of a magical moment, a mounting movement, made all the more meaningful by the massacres of September eleven. The slogan? Leave No Child Behind. A must for the Catholic preacher yearning to touch God's Word to human hearts, the gospel to fragile fears. But to preach the slogan effectively, we must face intelligently and courageously three critical questions. (1) Are children actually left behind in the United States? (2) If so, where-in lies the injustice? (3) What can people of faith do about it, what ought we do?

I

First, what in hardnosed reality does it mean to say that children in the United States are being "left behind"? The answer lies in cold, passionless American statistics:

Every 20 seconds, a child is arrested.
Every 44 seconds, a baby is born into poverty.
Every minute, a baby is born without health insurance.
Every 2 minutes, a baby is born at low birthweight.
Every 4 minutes, a child is arrested for drug abuse.
Every 8 minutes, a child is arrested for a violent crime.
Every 11 minutes, a child is reported abused or neglected.
Every 19 minutes, a baby dies.
Every 2 hours and 20 minutes, a child or youth under 20 is killed
    by a firearm.
Every 4 hours, a child or youth under 20 commits suicide.
Every day, a young person under 25 dies from HIV [disease].

Other key facts just as dreadful. Of America's children,

1 in 5 was born poor.
1 in 6 is poor now.
1 in 7 has no health insurance.
1 in 8 is born to a teenage mother.
1 in 8 lives in a family receiving food stamps.
1 in 12 has a disability.
1 in 15 lives at less than half the poverty level.
1 in 24 lives with neither parent.
1 in 139 will die before first birthday.[1]

II

Thus far, just the facts; no names, no faces. But in point of fact each number registers a face, each face has a name. Therefore what? Therefore each is as human as you and I; your brother and my sister. Therefore each is a person with rights: rights that can be proven from reason, rights that have been, or should be, written into law. I mean the right to a healthy birth; to love and care from parents who have created them; to affordable housing and a safe environment; to decent clothing and nourishing food; to an education fitting them for gratifying employment and intelligent citizenship; to healthcare from conception to death. These are not privileges graciously bestowed by a benevolent state; these are natural rights that a government is obliged to acknowledge and activate. For a state to do otherwise is to act unjustly, to be unfaithful to a state's primary concern, the peace and prosperity of all its citizens—yes, its immigrants as well.

Good indeed such ethical and legal justice, but for a Catholic not enough by half. A Catholic, on Jesus' own declaration, "does not live by bread alone, but by every word that comes forth from the mouth of God" (Mt 4:4; see Deut 8:3). And a word that comes forth constantly from the mouth of God is "justice." Not simply the justice fashioned from philosophy and human law. God's Word raises justice to a higher level: fidelity to relationships, to responsibilities, that stem from a covenant. It is the justice celebrated in Psalm 72, the prayer that reflects God's will for earth's rulers, for an earthly dynasty:

> O God, give your judgment to the king,
>   your justice to the son of kings;
> that he may govern your people with justice,...
>   defend the oppressed among the people,
>   save the poor and crush the oppressor.
> He rescues the poor when they cry out,
>   the oppressed who have no one to help.
> He shows pity to the needy and the poor
>   and saves the lives of the poor.
> From extortion and violence he frees them,
>   for precious is their blood in his sight.
>   (Ps 72:1-2, 4, 12-14)

For Christians, the covenant with God was cut in the blood of Christ. This covenant makes inescapable the same three relationships that bound God's people in the Prior Testament: God, people, and earth. Love God above all earthly idols. Love every human person, enemy and friend, as a child of God, an image of Christ, especially the poor and the downtrodden. Touch the earth, material creation, all that is not God or the human person, with reverence, as a gift of God.

What does God's justice add to human justice? Neither philosophy nor the law can command love; God does. What does Jesus add to the Hebrew Testament's "You shall love your neighbor as yourself" (Lev 19:18)? The awesome command of Jesus, "Love one another *as I love you*" (Jn 15:12). The kind of love that led God's unique Son to wear our flesh, walk our earth, share our hurts and our fears, spend himself for the downtrodden, breathe his life away in agony on a criminal's cross. Little wonder that the New Testament calls Jesus "the Just One." It is he who raises our justice to his own level, where we love the unloved as Jesus loves them...and us.

But how can we claim we are living God's justice, loving as Jesus loved, when over 12 million of our children are growing up in poverty? Not the genteel poverty of the child Jesus; the poverty that maims minds and batters bodies—the poverty that kills.

III

All of which leads to a final, crucial question: What can we, people of faith, do about our children? As disciples of the Just One, what ought we to do? I suggest two areas of insertion: our government and our very selves.

Within our government a highly promising piece of legislation was introduced on May 23, 2001, by Senator Christopher Dodd of Connecticut and Representative George Miller of California: The Act To Leave No Child Behind (S. 940 and H.R. 1990). Drawn in large measure from legislation introduced separately by Republicans and Democrats in the House and the Senate, it represents a renewed commitment to our children, is expected to benefit every child in America. Specifically, it will provide children with:

- **A Healthy Start:** provide health coverage for all the more than nine million uninsured children in America, address childhood illnesses, and improve the quality of children's healthcare.
- **A Head Start:** increase funding for child care and for three- and four-year-olds in Head Start, so that *all* eligible children who need these benefits could participate; would strengthen our education system by improving teacher training and quality, increasing public-school accountability, reducing class size, and modernizing school facilities.
- **A Fair Start:** help ensure that hard-working parents have the support they need to remain employed; help them lift themselves and their children out of poverty; provide broad tax relief to low-income families currently left out of many tax programs.
- **A Safe Start:** would help to ensure that more children are in safe, nurturing, and permanent families; extend supports to families before they suffer family breakdown; encourage permanency for children who cannot stay safely at home; strengthen youth-development efforts; address other critical safety issues, e.g., gun violence, juvenile justice, and effective delinquency-prevention programs.[2]

Admirable indeed, a justice response highly ethical, splendidly legal, and in harmony with biblical imperatives. But government does not act in a vacuum; lawmakers need their constituents, need you and me. To encourage our senators and representatives to work for passage of the Act, tell them how important the provisions of the Act are for our children, for our country's future. Like the Gospel widow (Lk 18:1–8), never tire of repeating to them, "We want justice, we want justice, we want justice."[3]

Important, but not quite enough. Each Catholic family gifted with this world's goods should get personally involved, take to heart God's declaration through Isaiah:

> This, rather, is the fasting that I wish:
> sharing your bread with the hungry,
>   sheltering the oppressed and the homeless,
> clothing the naked when you see them,
>   and not turning your back on your own.
> (Isa 58:6–7)

"Your own." Somewhere near you is a child pleading for your love: food for an aching stomach, books for a mind deprived, a shoulder on which to rest. The needs are legion. Seek out one child, get to know him, then ask the just Jesus how you might share his justice, how keep his little image from being left behind.[4]

Children's Defense Fund
October 20, 2002

14
SHE WILL WEAR ME OUT
Twenty-ninth Sunday of the Year (C)

> • Exodus 17:8–13
> • 2 Timothy 3:14—4:2
> • Luke 18:1–8

Our task as preachers this Sunday is a difficult one. The theme itself, suggested by the Children's Defense Fund, is clear enough: Creating Safe and Healthy Communities for Children. Not our task to create such communities through a homily; our task to challenge and encourage our people to do so. Specifically by linking that theme to what God is saying to us in today's liturgical readings. Very simply, to relate God's Word to the practical problem. I suggest three stages, three questions. (1) What is God's Word all about? (2) What are the social issues we confront? (3) What is our response to be?

I

First, God's Word: this time a parable from the lips of Jesus. The parable has two characters, two players: a judge and a widow. The judge is a symbol of power. And this particular judge is uncommonly powerful: Not only is he a judge in a patriarchal society, a culture in which males command and females obey. This judge is afraid of no one: neither God nor people. The widow is a symbol of powerlessness. With her husband dead, she has no male to defend her, protect her, plead her cause. Some unnamed male is taking advantage of her, she wants justice, and all she can do is appeal to a coldhearted, unfeeling male judge. Not surprisingly, the judge refuses.

What does she do? Retire to her home, re-enter her kitchen, submit the way women were supposed to submit? Not this widow. She keeps after the judge, keeps pounding away at him, "I want justice. I

66

want justice. I want justice." So insistent is she that the judge finally gives in. Not because he is convinced by her arguments. No. What moves him is clear: "Because this widow keeps bothering me, I will grant her justice, that she may not continue coming for ever and wear me out" (Lk 18:5).[1]

The lesson? Perseverance; persistence. Suggested in the first reading. When the Israelites were confronted by a fierce tribe, the Amalekites, they prevailed as long as Moses held his arm aloft, with the staff of God in his hand. "But Moses' hands grew weary, so [the Israelites] took a stone and put it under him, and he sat on it. Aaron and Hur held up his hands, one on one side, and the other on the other side; so his hands were steady until the sun set. And Joshua defeated Amalek and his people" (Exod 17:12–13).

II

What are the social issues we confront? Two issues we stress this day: violence and health.

First, violence. We want safe communities for our children. In this "land of the free" the younger you are, the more vulnerable you are. In the richest country on earth roughly one out of every five children is growing up poor, hungry, ill-fed, ill-educated. Among industrialized countries the United States ranks 14th in the proportion of children in poverty, 16th in efforts to lift children out of poverty, 18th in the gap between rich and poor children, last in protecting our children against gun violence.[2] "According to the Centers for Disease Control and Prevention, U.S. children under age 15 are 12 times more likely to die from gunfire, 16 times more likely to be murdered with a gun, 11 times more likely to commit suicide with a gun, and 9 times more likely to die in a firearm accident, than children in 25 other industrialized countries combined."[3] In my own Washington, D.C., in one five-year period, 245 children died of gunshot wounds. Since 1979, more than 80,000 American children have been killed by guns— far more than all our fatal casualties in Vietnam.

If you still dream that violence to children is an occasional incident in a peaceful America, if you think it is limited to gunfire, listen to the Children's Defense Fund:

> *All American children are at risk* from the proliferation of guns which threaten all of us everywhere; from the pollution of our air, water, earth, airwaves, and Internet with smut and toxic substances; from

the breakdown of family not only from out-of-wedlock births but pervasive divorce and erosion of extended family supports; from epidemic substance abuse and from domestic violence that know no race or income limits; and from the erosion of civility evidenced by road rage, profane language, and the coarse public discourse which pervades our culture.[4]

Second, healthy communities for children? Take a striking statistic. Take, in alphabetical order, 23 industrialized countries: Australia, Austria, Belgium, Canada, the Czech Republic, Denmark, Finland, France, Germany, Hungary, Ireland, Italy, Japan, Luxembourg, the Netherlands, New Zealand, Norway, Poland, Portugal, Spain, Sweden, Switzerland, and the United Kingdom. What is striking about these countries? Each and every one of them has child safety-net policies. Specifically, (1) universal health insurance/healthcare; (2) paid maternal/parental leave at childbirth; (3) family allowance/child dependency grant. America's "fifth child" would fare better if he or she lived in any one of these countries. Why? Because the United States has none of these: no guaranteed health insurance, no income safety net, no parental leave with pay after childbirth.[5]

Safe and healthy communities for our children? In the richest nation on earth? Our healthcare would be laughable, were it not so tragic, so literally deadly. More than 11.9 million of our children are uninsured.

III

A Catholic response? A sympathetic Protestant once said to a Catholic, "If you Catholics could get your act together, you'd be dangerous." We would indeed. The potential for effective organized activity is there. I am told that there are more Catholic parishes in the United States than there are post offices. How get our act together to create safe and healthy communities for all of America's children? Bishops' pastorals are important, but not enough—if only because it is the rare Catholic who ever reads a pastoral document in its totality. What then?

Start with the family. Let each family, each "little church," become aware of, realize, some of those disturbing facts—that more than 13 million of our little sisters and brothers are at high risk from varied types of violence and from failure to take advantage of the healthcare that is available. Let our more advantaged teenagers actually feed the hungry, actually clothe the naked, actually visit the sick and the imprisoned.

In line with the widow of our Gospel, put pressure on the powerful, trouble your legislators. Tell them: "We want justice! Justice! Justice!" Tell them, time and again, that for the $68.2 billion in corporate tax breaks proposed by Congressional leaders in 1999, 5.6 uninsured children could receive health coverage every year for ten years. "We want justice!" Every year the Children's Defense Fund tracks how your members of Congress vote on children's health and education. If you're dissatisfied, organize to cry, "We want justice!" Get the CDF annual report card on how well your state is investing in your children, protecting your children. Shake a bad report in the face of your elected and appointed officials: "We want justice!" If you can, persuade them; if you can't, wear them down: "We want justice! We want justice! We want justice!"

Some years ago, at a women's protest rally, an imaginative banner read, EVE WAS FRAMED! I tend to agree. If not the original Eve, surely her daughters. Listen to these powerful lines from Marian Wright Edelman, director of the Children's Defense Fund:

> Although women constitute a majority of the population, of voters, of those in religious institutions, and of those who take primary care of children, we lack commensurate power. This must change now. Only when women, especially mothers and grandmothers, organize and stand up and say loudly to the men in power, "we will no longer look upon the killing of our children," will we stop the killing of children by guns and overcome the powerful NRA and its supporters. Only when enough mothers and grandmothers demand health care and child care and a safety net for poor women and children and stand up with our votes and voices to those in power will political leaders of all parties do right by our children. Every federal and state senator and representative and governor should be adopted by a well-informed, well-organized group of determined women and their allies with a focused agenda for children....[6]

And so we end where we began—with a woman seeking justice. But not quite the same woman. Today's woman can and must "bring a new moral dimension drawn from the insight of [her] struggles and marginality."[7] And if the Equal Rights Amendment has not made for utter equality of male and female, today's American woman is not isolated in a primeval garden or dominated by the male of the species. Today's American woman plays hardball with her male counterparts in Congress. Today's American woman is a CEO, a diplomat, a bank president, chancellor of a diocese, governor of a state, president of a university. And since 1920, American women have enjoyed (if not always employed) a powerful weapon: the power of the ballot, the right to vote. Yes, beloved sisters, if you could get *your* act together, 52% of the voting population, you'd be dangerous. For the sake of America's children—your children.

This is not simply an important political issue. Here we touch the heart of a Catholic spirituality, what we call biblical justice, *God's* sense of justice. I mean fidelity to relationships, to responsibilities, that stem from our covenant with God cut in the blood of Christ. One of these relationships is our responsibility to the more vulnerable in our society. The more vulnerable, the greater the demand on the rest of us. Time and again the Hebrew Testament summarized this responsibility as "the widow, the orphan, and the stranger." For "the orphan" substitute "the child," specifically the poor child, and you begin to understand what God expects of us today. And what is that? Never cease clamoring for justice. With your votes and your voices. In the privacy of the ballot box and through every means of modern communication. With the Gospel widow, one ceaseless cry to the powerful: "Justice! Give me, give our children, justice!" Not charity, out of the goodness of powerful hearts. No. Justice—what our children have a right, human and divine, to demand. "Give me justice...justice...justice!"

Children's Defense Fund
October 21, 2001

15
GUARD AGAINST ALL GREED
Twenty-ninth Week, Year 1, Monday

· Romans 4:20–25
· Luke 12:13–21

Ever since the terrorist bombing of the World Trade Center and the Pentagon, preachers have felt the need to link their sermons to that day of infamy. And so it is with me this afternoon. First, another stirring parable from the lips of Jesus; then a distressing set of statistics that rise from the rubble of "ground zero"; finally, what all this might say to preachers of the just word.[1]

I

First, the parable. Jesus casts in narrative form a question he had asked earlier: What good would it do you if you acquired the whole world, yet lost your very self in the process? (cf. Lk 9:25). To put flesh on that question, Jesus makes up a story. A rich farmer enjoys more crops than he has space to store them. He has a brilliant idea: Tear down the old barns, build bigger barns, barns big enough to hold not only the overflowing grain but much else of his possessions. Once the barns are built and his wealth is stored there, he will recline in his rocker, light his pipe, pat his expanding stomach, and say to himself: "Man, you've got it made. You don't have a worry in the world. You've got the world by the tail. The future is yours. So, take it easy. Eat, drink, and be merry."

The problem? In all his scheming, he has forgotten one essential: the Lord of life. The Lord who in a dream of the night addresses him with a strong word: "You fool." The Greek word means literally "You're out of your mind; you're stupid." Why? Because this very night he will die. And all he has stored up for himself will go to someone else.

71

Now all this is said in the context of a terrorizing monosyllable: greed. "Take care to guard against all greed" (Lk 12:15). This takes us from the first century to the twenty-first.

II

Greed. What is greed? A lusting for more and more, beyond all reason. It is the evil against which John Paul II inveighed in a 1987 encyclical on contemporary social concerns. He spoke of a superdevelopment

> which consists in an excessive availability of every kind of material goods for the benefit of certain social groups [and] easily makes people slaves of "possessions" and of immediate gratification with no other horizon than the multiplication or continual replacement of the things already owned with others still better. This is the so-called civilization of "consumption" or "consumerism," which involves so much "throwing-away" and "waste." An object already owned but now superseded by something better is discarded, with no thoughts of its possible lasting value in itself, nor of some other human being who is poorer. [And] the more one possesses the more one wants....[2]

If that statement is too abstract, turn to some recent statistics to bring greed down to earth.

- The richest 20% of the world's population earn 86% of the world's income, consume 80% of the world's resources, and create 83% of the world's waste. The poorest 20% of the world's population earn under 2% of the world's income.
- Globally, about a billion people are malnourished. Every day an average of 20,000 children die from hunger-related causes—about one child every six seconds. A child in the poorest countries is 10–15 times more likely to die before the age of five than a child in the U.S.
- Each U.S. inhabitant consumes each day his/her weight in "stuff" (minerals, wood products, food, energy, etc.)—just over 100 kgs [200 lbs.] per person.
- Per capita water use in the U.S.: 1,300 gallons per day—100 gallons of this in household, the remainder in agriculture and industry (it takes eight gallons of water to grow one tomato in an irrigated field). Around the world, 1.2 billion people do not have easy access to clean water.

- The U.S. consumes 25% of all fossil fuels consumed in the world. Two billion people around the world do not have access to electricity.
- Since colonial times, the U.S. has lost 50% of wetlands, 90% of prairie, 95% of virgin forests; one quarter of all large mammals are endangered, 14% of birds, 12% of plants; we have lost 33% of all topsoil through erosion.
- The U.S. and other developed countries, with a small percentage of the world's people, consume 84% of the paper. The average U.S. inhabitant consumes about 730 pounds of paper products a year; the world average is 125 pounds. 70 or more pounds per person is considered the minimal needed to insure basic literacy and communication.[3]

The United Nations, with a similarly shocking set of statistics on consumption disparities, concludes:

> Today's consumption is undermining the environmental resource base. It is exacerbating inequalities. And the dynamics of the consumption-poverty-inequality-environment nexus are accelerating. If the trends continue without change—not redistributing from high-income to low-income consumers, not shifting from polluting to cleaner goods and production technologies, not promoting goods that empower poor producers, not shifting priority from consumption for conspicuous display to meeting basic needs—today's problems of consumption and human development will worsen.[4]

III

Had enough? Let's see what this might say to us as priests and specifically as preachers of the just word. The connection with today's Gospel? Greed. This is not to imply that everyone with possessions above one's needs is greedy. Without the well-endowed, our schools and parishes, our Catholic Charities and shelters, our nursing homes and homes for the aged would not exist. But the fact remains: The overconsumption that impoverishes our present and threatens our future is due to overconsumers. And far in the forefront of overconsumers are we of the United States.

In the current issue of *America* magazine, Jesuit moral theologian David Hollenbach notes that many in the religious community have called to our attention two dimensions of the background for the

September the eleventh terrorist attacks: the economic and the polit-ical.[5] On the economic dimension he writes:

> Economically, anger over the poverty of the developing world easi-ly translates into resentment and even hatred toward those who call the shots in the globalizing economy of our day. If the West is unwill-ing to take serious steps to address the enormous economic dispar-ities between rich and poor on our globe, it is but a short step to the conclusion that Western culture is materialistic and self-centered [greedy?]. This is a breeding ground for explosive resentments that can launch terrorist attacks under the green flag of Islam.

Hollenbach goes on to quote from an address of John Paul II welcom-ing the new United States ambassador to the Holy See just two days after the terrorist attacks. The Pope declared that one of the keys to overcoming the temptation to terrorize must be a serious response to this deprivation.

> In the century now opening before us...the possibilities before the human family are immense, although they are not always apparent in a world in which too many of our brothers and sisters are suffer-ing from hunger, malnutrition, the lack of access to medical care and to education, or are burdened by an unjust government, armed conflict, forced displacement and new forms of human bondage. In seizing the available opportunities, vision and generosity are neces-sary, especially on the part of those who have been blessed with free-dom, wealth and an abundance of resources.

In brief, an adequate response to September the eleventh involves a movement away from self-centered greed, a movement to the common good, not only of the United States and Europe but of the larger world as well, especially those who lack minimally adequate economic resources. Says Hollenbach:

> The urgency of such an economic response is poignantly rein-forced by the World Bank's judgment that the Sept. 11 attacks will hurt economic growth, especially in developing countries. The bank's preliminary estimate is that as many as 10 million more people will fall into desperate poverty worldwide and that the fight against childhood diseases and malnutrition will be signifi-cantly set back. These economic realities must be addressed in any long-term effort to deal with terror.[6]

This urgency puts pressure not only on presidents and prelates, but on everyone commissioned by baptism to live and spread God's justice: fidelity to relationships, to responsibilities, that stem from our covenant with God cut in the blood of Christ. Not only love God above all human idols. Love every man, woman, and child as an image of God; love each, enemy as well as friend, like another self; love each as fully and as passionately as Jesus has loved us—love especially the poor and the impaired, the downtrodden and the dispossessed, those who share more of Christ's crucifixion than of his resurrection.

True, but the urgency weighs even more heavily on us; for by sacramental ordination we are empowered to *preach* God's justice, graced to raise the consciousness of our people, help shape them into communities of peace, of justice, of love. In concrete terms, in the context of September the eleventh, what does this demand of us?

First, unlike the rich fool, stress being over having. The parable is pellucid: Jesus "refuses to identify authentic Christian existence with the possession of material wealth, even inherited—especially when abundant. It is much more important to *be* than to *have*–to be one who listens to God's word and acts on it than to live in an unnecessary abundance of wealth."[7]

Second, we must help our people to see themselves, in God's creative design, not primarily as individuals, but as part of a world community, with responsibilities that are not limited by space or race, by belief or unbelief. In my childhood our parents often told us to eat everything on our plate; somehow it would help a starving African baby. As we grew more sophisticated, we laughed at the memory. But there was substance beneath the fantasy. We were being introduced to a significant Christian reality: Despite the distance and the color, the African child and I were brothers; we had responsibilities each to the other. And the day might come, indeed has come, when the fantasy turns into reality, and my overconsumption, my greed, is part and parcel of a hunger problem thousands of miles away.

Third, *my* overconsumption. The lust for more and more is not a characteristic reserved for non-Romans. John Paul II's encyclical *On Social Concern,* with its strong assault on greed, was not a diatribe against unbelievers, nor was it a scenario in outer space; it was addressed to his "venerable brothers" in the episcopate and to his own "dear sons and daughters." It presupposes that Roman Catholics are in large measure part of the problem.

Fourth, the encyclical implies, even declares, that we Romans ought to be, must be, part of the solution. Not only to prefer being over having; not only to avoid consumerism; but to collaborate with all men and women of good will in attacking what John Paul called the "structures of sin," injustice on institutional levels. Let me close with his appeal near the end of the same encyclical.

> I wish to appeal with simplicity and humility to everyone, to all men and women without exception. I wish to ask them to be convinced of the seriousness of the present moment and of each one's individual responsibility, and to implement—by the way they live as individuals and as families, by the use of their resources, by their civic activity, by contributing to economic and political decisions and by personal commitment to national and international undertakings—the measures inspired by solidarity and love of preference for the poor. This is what is demanded by the present moment and above all by the very dignity of the human person, the indestructible image of God the Creator, which is identical in each one of us.[8]

Bishop Molloy Retreat House
Jamaica, New York
October 22, 2001

16

INVITE THE POOR, THE CRI[PPLED,]
THE LAME, THE BLIND
Thirty-first Week, Year 1, Mon[day]

Today's Gospel message is an inv[itation]
to a banquet. Twenty centuries la[ter,]

First, the original invitation. Here is Jesus havin[g]
Sabbath at the home of a prominent Pharisee. At one point Jesus g[ives]
his host some tips on hospitality, on whom to invite to a banquet, to a
party, and whom to ignore. Not your usual guest list. There are two
groups: those invited and those not invited. In each group four types.
Who are *not* to be invited? Friends, brothers, relatives, wealthy neighbors. Who *are* to be invited? The poor, the crippled, the lame, the blind.

Why this utter reversal of all that is customary in civil society, in
social life? The big verb is "reciprocate," to pay back in kind. The
affluent four are able to repay the gracious host, and in the good society they will feel obligated to do so. They will receive an embossed
invitation, RSVP to a social secretary. The unfortunate four would
have no way of returning a six-course dinner. Some are too poor; others can't get around; still others can't even see you. Don't hold your
breath waiting for the mailman.

Now the meal is an integral part of the parable; but the parable
is not primarily about food and drink. One critical word is never men-
tioned in the parable; the unspoken word here is...love. If your gen-
erosity stems from love, you will not expect a return, recompense,

repayment in this life. Precisely because the unfortunate are unable to return your hospitality, cannot repay in kind, you are blessed in inviting them, "for you will be repaid at the resurrection of the righteous" (Lk 14:14).

Such is a Christian guest list. Not my own interests; only what is best for the other. Not those who can further my interests; only a love that moves out from self-interest to what will serve the less fortunate.

II

Move now from the first century to the twenty-first, from an invitation to a banquet to an invitation to a way of life. My stimulus here is an unforgettable day, a day of infamy, a day of terror...September the eleventh. I shall not dwell on the terror itself, on the monstrous massacre of 3,000 men and women in New York City alone. It was etched in my memory, in my bones, several weeks ago when, with half a hundred priests and deacons on a Preaching the Just Word retreat/workshop, I pilgrimed to "ground zero" and stood in stunned, reverential silence at a graveyard unique in American history. I do not excuse the terrorizing; I refuse to see therein a justified assault on an unjust capitalism. I shall not discuss whether the proper response to September the eleventh is out-and-out war. In the context of today's Gospel, I am cherishing a heartfelt hope that we in America who enjoy a disproportionate amount of the world's wealth will issue, out of love, an invitation to the poor, the crippled, the lame, and the blind of our earth. Not to a banquet; simply to a share in the riches a generous God created for all God's children.

The inequalities that divide our world, God's world, are staggering. "As the effects of globalization are creating further disparities and inequalities, around the world we are seeing an increase in violence....People are fighting for basic needs."[1] I am not claiming that America's civilization of overconsumption is what triggered the terrorism of September the eleventh. I do claim that the enormous economic disparities between rich and poor on our globe are "a breeding ground for explosive resentments that can launch terrorist attacks" such as took place "under the green flag of Islam."[2] Time and again I hear that the less developed nations dislike Americans because they envy us, envy our advanced technology, our medical breakthroughs, our economic stability, even our TV channels. Not quite. They dislike us, despise us, even hate us because, affluent as we are, we are unwilling to share, refuse to invite them to our banquet. Because in America we waste enough food each day to feed a small nation.

An ironic footnote. The United Nations estimates that seven million Afghans are in immediate need of food and shelter. The United States is dropping tons of food and other supplies from the air on the poor of Afghanistan. Out of love? Hardly. Instead, to win them over to our side. As so often, what we should be doing constantly out of profound human compassion for the poor, the crippled, the lame, and the blind, we end up doing out of self-interest.

III

Finally, what of us and the people to whom we preach biblical justice—fidelity to responsibilities that stem from our covenant with God cut in the blood of Christ? Responsibilities not only to God but to our sisters and brothers and to the earth itself. A homily cannot cover the whole field. This evening, a fundamental principle, a word on waste and indulgence, and what I dare to call a wild idea.

Begin with a basic truth from the Psalmist: "The earth is the Lord's and all it holds" (Ps 24:1). God has given us not despotism but stewardship. And a steward is one who manages what is someone else's. A steward cares, is concerned, agonizes. Stewards may not plunder or waste; they are responsible, can be called to account for their stewardship. To speak bluntly, I may not do whatever I want with whatever I own. In her typically profound and practical book *Guests of God: Stewards of Divine Creation*, Monika Hellwig insists that our consumption patterns are largely but not exclusively evident in the patterns of our waste.

> They are also seen in patterns of indulgence of every whim and inclination to luxury and pleasure to a degree that is unthinkable to most of the peoples of the earth. And they are revealed in patterns that consume resources that are scarce on a global basis, such as fossil fuels, fertilizers, arable land, fresh water and certain other mineral resources. It is time to think about styles and standards of living that fit a long-range sustainable ecology of the earth on terms of adequate access for everyone, both all the peoples of the earth now living and the generations to come. It is time to ask ourselves about our own habits of consumption, waste and waste disposal. And it is time to think in terms of the whole human family, God's family and the guests invited to God's table.[3]

"The guests invited to God's table." Yes, the poor, the crippled, the lame, and the blind. And now for my wild idea. Since not only charity but justice should "begin at home," we might well begin with our parishes (I am told that in the U.S. there are more parishes than post offices). Am I foolhardy to hope for a concerted, organized effort to ensure that in no Catholic parish will a single child go to sleep hungry, no child lack drinkable water, no child shiver in a cold home, no child be unable to read? And not only Catholic children—every small image of Christ.

Start perhaps with a single parish in every diocese. It will mushroom, I assure you. For such a project, enthusiastically supported by parishioners with varied gifts of nature and grace, cannot fail to draw down rich collaboration from the Christ who, Ignatius Loyola declared, works with us like a laborer, the Christ who commanded that we let the little children come to him.

I suspect that these last two months may have lent some credibility to my wild idea. For September the eleventh and subsequent days have brought us together in ways quite unusual. Not primarily from fear, not only from a fresh patriotism. I sense rather a coming together—rich and poor, CEO and street cleaner, Hispanic and black, cleric and lay, Catholic and Protestant and Jew and unbeliever—out of profound compassion, a realization that none of us is an island, that in our very humanness we need one another, that only together are we strong enough for goodness to overcome hellish evil.

Repayment, yes. In Jesus' words to his host, "at the resurrection of the righteous," the just (Lk 14:14). More concretely in his words to all of us: "Come, you who are blessed by my Father. Inherit the kingdom prepared for you from the foundation of the world. For *I* was hungry and you gave *me* food, *I* was thirsty and you gave *me* drink, a stranger and you welcomed *me,* naked and you clothed *me,* ill and you cared for *me,* in prison and you visited *me*" (Mt 25:34–36).

Lumen Christi Retreat House
Schriever, Louisiana
November 5, 2001

TWO MEMORIALS AND A FESTIVAL

17
LOVE'S "LITTLE WAY"
Memorial of St. Thérèse of Lisieux

- Isaiah 66:10–14
- Matthew 18:1–4

If you can reach back six or seven decades, you may remember a favorite prayer among Catholic children, a prayer as swift as it was heartfelt:

> Little Flower,
> in this hour,
> show your power.

The Little Flower, of course, is St. Thérèse of Lisieux; but the power? You might answer: Why, it's the power anyone has who now lives with God in heaven and intercedes for us on earth, begs for all sorts of graces—freedom from cancer, freedom from sin. True enough; but this morning I would rather look back, recapture the kind of power that made this girl, this young woman, this Carmelite nun so impressive in her own age and beyond. The search, I suggest, will disclose a gift that touches intimately your struggle and mine for God's justice.[1] So then, a word on Thérèse, a word on justice, a word on you and me.

I

First, a word on Thérèse. Whether as a child, or an adult, or a Carmelite nun, the word that identifies Thérèse is always a monosyllable, the monosyllable that is a synonym for Jesus. The monosyllable? Love. Here Thérèse's first Communion was critical, transformed her radically. It's true, even before her first Communion she believed that God loved her. As she expressed it in her *Autobiography*, "For a long

83

time now Jesus and poor little Thérèse looked at and understood each other." But the first Communion experience was different. "That day," she writes, "it was no longer simply a look; they were no longer two. Thérèse had vanished as a drop of water is lost in the immensity of the ocean. Jesus alone remained."[2] As her love grew, so did her wisdom powered by love. Love was not a sentimental journey, life on cloud nine. Listen to some remarkable lines from one of her poems, lines that express simply yet beautifully the link between love and sacrifice:

> Living on Love is not setting up one's tent
> At the top of Tabor.
> It's climbing Calvary with Jesus.
> It's looking at the Cross as a treasure!...
> In heaven I'm to live on joy.
> Then trials will have fled forever.
> But in exile, in suffering I want
>   To live on Love.
> Dying of Love is what I hope for....[3]

An important point to remember here: At times Thérèse uses "suffering" as a synonym for "sacrifice," but to read her writings carefully is to find her clearly distinguishing the two terms. Suffering, enduring pain and distress, "becomes sacrifice only when it is transformed by faith, hope, and love into acts of love for God." The full meaning of Christian sacrifice did not blossom in her all at once. In fact, "it took her a lifetime to be able to transform *all* her sufferings into joyous self-emptying gifts of love to God."[4]

II

Second, a word on justice. Not that justice is a favorite word with Thérèse. Still, the relationship between love and justice is incredibly intimate. The most recent collection of my homilies is titled *To Be Just Is To Love*. In that declaration I am not speaking of ethical justice—giving men, women, and children what they can claim as a right, not because they are rich or powerful, brilliant or beautiful, but simply and profoundly because they are human. I am not speaking of legal justice—where each person is given what he or she can claim as a right because it has been written into our laws. I am speaking of the justice you and I are celebrating this week. I mean biblical justice, God's justice, fidelity to relationships that stem from our covenant with God; for Christians, the covenant written in the blood of Christ. What relationships? To

God, to people, to the earth. Love God above all else, above every human idol. Love everyone, man or woman, friend or enemy, as a child of God, like another self, another I. Touch the earth, God's material creation, be it a blade of grass or nuclear power—whatever is not God or human person—with respect, with reverence, as a gift of God.

In that context we can call Thérèse just, characterize her life as a life of justice, biblical justice, God's justice. For three good reasons. (1) She sees not social classes but only one universal class, that of being a true child of God, an equality that "calls for a new look at justice," an equality that implies "an equal right to adequate food, clothing, shelter, and medical care."[5] (2) Her understanding of justice is not limited to our relationship to one another and to God. An insightful analyst of her Little Way has grasped this without speaking expressly of justice: "Thérèse's life and writings show how love is the force that connects all of creation with God."[6] All of creation. She mimics Francis of Assisi's love of all creation—not only the poor but animals and plants, natural forces, even Brother Sun and Sister Moon. (3) Thérèse's Little Way is a way of justice because it is a way without violence.

III

Third, a word on you and me. Here I find splendidly pertinent some words from Dorothy Day, who had a deep devotion to Thérèse:

> When a mother, a housewife, asks what she can do [as a stand against injustice], one can only point to the way of St. Thérèse, that little way, so much misunderstood....And this goes for the priest too, wherever he is, whether he deals with the problems of war or with poverty. He may write or speak, but he needs to study the little way, which is all that is available to the poor, and the only alternative to the mass approach of the State....Down in our own South, in the Delta regions among the striking farmers of Mississippi, this "little way" is being practiced and should be studied.[7]

What Thérèse's Little Way advocates is that the Christian live in solidarity with the poor and disenfranchised. Not only by accepting violence rather than inflicting it. Of high importance is our personal loving relationship with God. Here too Dorothy Day was following Thérèse when she wrote this startling paragraph, at first glance too much for the justice activist to swallow:

> I see around me sin, suffering, and unutterable destitution. There is misery, materialism, degradation, ugliness on every side. All I

see some days is sin. The problem is gigantic. Throughout the world there is homelessness, famine, fear, and war and the threat of war. We live in a time of gigantic evil. It is hopeless to think of combating it by any other means than that of sanctity. To think of overcoming such evil by material means, by alleviations, by changes in the social order only—all this is utterly hopeless.[8]

In that strong statement an important word is the adverb "only." I do not see either Dorothy or Thérèse rejecting action on behalf of justice. What both stressed, perhaps above all else, was a quality they saw as indispensable if evil is to be destroyed: personal sanctity. Still, Thérèse's "little acts of love" have to be translated for our own times. Dorothy Day translated them into her "little way of cooperatives and credit unions, small industry, village commune, and cottage economy."[9] She deplored a contemporary feeling of futility about what anyone's small actions could effect; yet she insisted that "we can beg for an increase of love in our hearts that will vitalize and transform all our individual actions, and know that God will take them and multiply them, as Jesus multiplied the loaves and fishes."[10]

How might you and I, ministers of biblical justice, translate for the twenty-first century the insights a young Carmelite nun revealed in the last quarter of the nineteenth century? I suggest that we focus on the two basic ideas in Thérèse's "little ways of love." The "ways" are our efforts, individually and in groups, to lessen and destroy injustice in our parishes, in our country, across our world. Concretely, I mean our struggle to lessen the poverty that plagues 33 million humans, wastes every sixth child, in the richest country on earth; our struggle to blot out the racism that has not disappeared from our land, has only taken on a more civilized face; our struggle to mend an intolerable prison situation that condemns an unprecedented two million Americans to punitive rather than restorative justice; our struggle to overturn a capital punishment that is no longer necessary for our society's protection, actually hinders the fight against crime, offends against the sanctity of all human life, can no longer be justified on ethical grounds, is inescapably in danger of killing the innocent; our struggle to face honestly our ecological issues: exhaustion of the soil, uncontrolled deforestation, global warming, consumerism, endless waste.

For us, as individuals and even in groups, the "ways" in which we can effect societal change appear to be "little." But incomparable power accrues to our little efforts if they are motivated by love: love of God, love of every human image of God, love of God's material creation. Link all our innumerable "little ways" in one gigantic, ceaseless thrust of love, and the walls of injustice will slowly but surely crumble.

Not an easy linkage, even for men ordained to serve. For "the sin of the world" has left its mark on us, in us. We have to pray each day to the Father not to be led into temptation, pray each day to be delivered from the Evil One. Unselfish love does not come easily, does not last except through grace.

That is why I take special delight in the Gospel I was privileged to proclaim to you. In the context of Thérèse's "little way," in the context of your need and mine for a little way of our own, that Gospel scene is worth recalling, worth contemplating, worth making our own within biblical justice. The disciples ask Jesus a momentous question: "Who is the greatest in the kingdom of heaven?" The kingdom of heaven here is not the kingdom in its fulness, after the Second Coming and the final judgment. The context is the present age; for what follows has to do with sin, church discipline, forgiveness. And so the question has to do, at least also, with rank in the Church.[11]

But what has Jesus' "little child" in common with Thérèse's "little way"? Ask first, how is that child a model for those who hold some rank in the Church, a model for you and me? Not because little children are supposedly innocent; rather "because of their complete dependence on, and trust in, their parents. So must the disciples be, in respect to God."[12] Such was Thérèse of the Child Jesus. For all her lofty desires, she did not think it was these desires that pleased God. As she put it in one of her letters, "what pleases him is that he sees me loving my littleness and my poverty, the blind hope that I have in his mercy....That is my only treasure."[13]

Such must you and I be as disciples of justice. What we do for justice' sake is usually quite little in itself. But motivated by love, utterly dependent on God's merciful grace, in collaboration with untold sisters and brothers of Thérèse, we can move our world slowly but surely toward God's kingdom of justice.

Sacred Heart Jesuit Retreat House
Sedalia, Colorado
October 1, 2002

18
FROM FIRST COMMUNION TO SERVICE UNTO DEATH
Memorial of St. Aloysius Gonzaga

- 1 John 5:1–5
- Matthew 22:34–40

To preach on Aloysius Gonzaga during a pastoral-liturgy convention may seem like docile compliance with Roman rubrics. But what has it to do with the link between worship and action, with "the faith that does justice"? Especially when our opening prayer set the stage for a different theme:

> Father of love,
> giver of all good things,
> in Saint Aloysius you combined
> remarkable innocence with the spirit of penance.
> By the help of his prayers
> may we who have not followed his innocence
> follow his example of penance.

It is my conviction that this innocent, penitential young man who died 410 years ago at the age of 23 might well serve as a model for young men and women who enjoy recapturing the connection between Eucharist and service, between worship and life. Sound strange? To confirm my conviction, an argument in three stages: (1) Aloysius in a painting, (2) Aloysius in real life, (3) Aloysius for us.[1]

I

First, Aloysius in a painting. In Washington, D.C., I work and play, wine and dine, in the Jesuit community of St. Aloysius Gonzaga. Adjoining our community is the Church of St. Aloysius. Over the main altar is a stunning painting remarkably restored in 1993–94. It was executed by Constantino Brumidi, an Italian-American artist who painted the frescoes in the dome of the U.S. Capitol. An interesting figure in the painting is the mother of Aloysius, modeled by the wife of Senator Stephen A. Douglas, Abraham Lincoln's rival for the presidency in 1860. But central to the painting is the boy Aloysius receiving his first Communion from the hands of a cardinal saint, Charles Borromeo.

The cardinal had met Aloysius in 1580, and when he heard that the 12-year-old boy had not yet received his first Communion, he prepared him for it, and on July 22nd gave him the body and blood of Christ for the first time. After that event (and this I urge you to keep in mind), Aloysius looked forward to Communion each week. If daily Communion had been the custom then, I have no doubt Aloysius would have received his Lord each day; for he attended Mass each day whenever possible.[2]

II

Second, Aloysius in real life. He was a prince, you know, eldest son of the marquis of Castiglione, born to pride, to power, to possessions. For almost four centuries (1328–1707) the Gonzagas were the ruling family of Mantua. Much that they did was admirable.[3] They produced able governors, built splendid churches, commissioned magnificent art, made Mantua a center of culture. But with that went rapacious rulers, unbridled power, internecine hatred, seemingly endless corruption. We discover a Niccolò d'Este with 800 mistresses, beheading a son and a second wife on a single night. We discover tyrants born out of wedlock, adored by their subjects, murdered by their subjects. "Though the Gonzaga family had no corner on high Renaissance ruthlessness and evil, by modern standards they make cardboard villains out of figures on...television,"[4] the corrupt cop, the coke king, the kid who kills for a pair of Reeboks.

Into such blood company was Aloysius born. From age five he was hustled from camp to court, from one court to another—the "education of a prince." The Medici court in Florence, for example, "was one of Italy's most magnificent, but at the same time it was one in which intrigue and deceit abounded, where daggers and poisons were the solutions to problems, and where lust and sin were made inviting."[5] In my early Jesuit days there was a tendency to ridicule in Aloysius what was called "modesty of the eyes." I must now admit it made good sense in a context where it was quite common for women to abuse little boys at the great banquets and dances.[6]

It seems Aloysius was quite gifted intellectually: highly competent in the Latin classics, even more interested in mathematics and astronomy, knowledgeable about the Spanish empire, enamored of that facet of philosophy which dealt with God—even argued in debate that the Trinity could be known from naked human reason. He had an innate talent for diplomacy; in his teens he traveled with his father on family business.

His father. Aloysius was his pride and joy. Here was the fulfillment of all his hopes, the only son fit to succeed him, to govern his estates and cities. And what did the young prince announce? "I want to become a Jesuit." His father threatened to flog him; declared that, if Aloysius joined the Jesuits, the boy would no longer be his son. Then a more seductive strategy: Forget the Jesuits! Take more lucrative roads to holiness. Look at the good a Cardinal Borromeo does. The Duke of Mantua promised him any ecclesiastical dignity in his power. Bishops and priests, uncles and cousins, members of religious orders—all were summoned to dissuade him. Nothing could, even when he was ordered out of his father's house, out of his sight. And one day late in 1585, against all the odds, Aloysius delivered to the superior general of the Jesuits, Claudius Acquaviva, a letter from his father dated November 5. It read in part:

> In the past I considered it to be my duty to refuse to this my son Aloysius permission to enter your holy Society, for I feared that owing to his youth he might embark upon his enterprise without that firm resolution which were right. Now I think that I am sure that it is God who is calling him thither....So, freely and willingly...I send him and commend him to Your Reverence, who will be to him a more helpful father than I can be....I am giving into Your Reverence's hands the most precious thing that I possess...and my chiefest hope, that I placed entirely in him, of maintaining and giving glory to my family.[7]

For our purposes here, let me select from Aloysius' Jesuit existence only its close. 1591 was a disastrous year for Italy. "Scarcity had become famine, and famine bred the plague. From the blackened country districts, pitiable caravans of starving peasants poured into Rome, already congested with its own population, that festered in its tortuous streets."[8] Hospitals were filled to overflowing; men and women were dying in the streets. Superiors gave Aloysius permission to minister to the sick and dying—reluctantly, for his health was precarious. Little reluctance in Aloysius. With intense joy he put the sick to bed, undressed them, washed and fed them. In fact, he nursed with joy the most repulsive of the patients.

There is a tradition to the effect that Aloysius contracted a fatal infection, possibly from the poor fellow a famous statue represents as carried on his shoulders. An attractive tradition, but the evidence is slim at best. More likely, sheer exhaustion, intensified by his unremitting service of the plague-stricken, took a final toll on a flesh far from robust.[9] It was his dedication that killed him, his response to the call of Christ in the crucified. During the night of June 20–21, 1591, as the octave of Corpus Christi drew to its close, "the happiest man of all the Gonzagas"[10] returned to his God.

III

Finally, Aloysius for us. What might Aloysius contribute to this conference, specifically to the link between liturgy and justice? Very little if you focus on the opening prayer of this day's liturgy, the emphasis on innocence and penance. Admirable Christian qualities, of course; but...justice?

May I offer a late-in-life insight? I have already remarked that in our Catholic tradition the most powerful source of grace for effective social action is not political savvy, not spellbinding eloquence, not episcopal encouragement. The supreme source is the Eucharist, the real presence of Christ, body and blood, soul and divinity, within you, pervading your whole person.

What motivated Aloysius, frail of body, low in energy, at times quite sickly—what motivated him to roam Rome's plague-ridden streets, seeking out the sick amid the stench of death? I do not discount his very human compassion, his Gospel love of neighbor, his horror at how uncaring the healthy could be. But I refuse to believe that any of these, for all their importance, were more powerful agents of mercy, of biblical justice, than the Christ Aloysius received so faithfully week after week from age twelve to twenty-three.

I am not suggesting that Aloysius Gonzaga was a 16th-century Virgil Michel, that he explicitly linked Eucharist and social action, that he shaped an incipient theology of liturgy and life. Still, in point of fact, of Catholic reality, his care for the uncared-for stemmed primarily from weekly worship and the consistent presence and activity of the Eucharistic Christ within him.

But what of those untold Catholics who receive Christ as often as Aloysius, more often than Aloysius, and do nothing for the poor and downtrodden, may even harbor racism in their hearts? I dare not judge them, can only suggest that they have not been listening to the Christ within them crying, "I was hungry and you gave me no food, I was thirsty and you gave me no drink, I was a stranger and you gave me no welcome, naked and you gave me no clothing, ill and in prison and you did not care for me" (Mt 25:42–43).

With a bit of brashness, let me recommend an alternative prayer, if not for the official memorial of Aloysius, at least for our living-out of the liturgy that celebrates him:

> Father of love,
> you gave us Aloysius Gonzaga
> as a model not only of innocence and penance
> but also of deep devotion to the Eucharist
> and selfless service to the sick and dying.
> Grace us, in imitation of Saint Aloysius,
> so to live our Christian lives
> that our worship and our Communion
> may spur us to ever-increasing service
> of the hungry, homeless, naked, lonely, imprisoned Christ
> all around us.

University of Notre Dame
Notre Dame, Indiana
June 21, 2001

19

THE MIGHTY ONE HAS DONE GREAT THINGS FOR ME
Solemnity of the Immaculate Conception

> • Genesis 3:9–15, 20
> • Ephesians 1:3–6, 11–12
> • Luke 1:26–38

Most Catholics, I sense, love our Lady. They celebrate her birthday each September 8th. They admire her faith when an angel asks her to mother God's Son and she replies, "Whatever you want, Lord." Families sing rapturously "O Little Town of Bethlehem" when Mary brings forth the Son of the Most High. Vowed religious women find in her their model of perpetual virginity. Refugees turn to her as she flees to Egypt to save her baby from the wrath of King Herod. Mothers weep with this "sorrowful mother" beneath the cross of her only Son, rejoice with her at his rising from the dead. And who among us does not yearn to join her in heaven, soul *and body?*

But, dear God, an immaculate conception? Three problems have troubled the centuries. (1) What can an immaculate conception possibly mean? (2) What relation does it bear to Mary's Son? (3) What significance might it have for you and me?

I

First, a basic question: What does the Immaculate Conception mean? Two meanings it does *not* have—one a bit humorous, the other highly serious. Many years ago, at a critical moment in a crucial football game, an impossible catch of a winning forward pass was called by some wag "the immaculate reception." No need to dwell on that. More seriously, the Immaculate Conception is not the Gospel just proclaimed to you: the glad tidings brought to Mary by Gabriel, "You will conceive in your womb and bear a son, and you shall name him Jesus" (Lk 1:31). This is the Virgin Birth, Jesus born of the Virgin Mary; it is not the Immaculate Conception, though many a committed Catholic confuses the two.

Then what is the Immaculate Conception? It was pithily put by Pope Pius IX when he declared on December 8, 1854:

> ...We...declare, pronounce, and define that the doctrine which holds that the Blessed Virgin Mary from the first moment of her conception was...preserved immune from all stain of original sin is revealed by God and is therefore firmly and constantly to be believed by all the faithful.[1]

At the precise moment when God infused a living soul into the flesh fashioned by Mary's parents, God's grace flooded her. She was not *freed* from "the sin of Adam," as we are by baptism. That "original sin" never touched her at all.

II

So much for the fact. But given the fact, what has Mary's immaculate conception to do with her mothering of Jesus? Why could she not have simply been like other remarkable women of the Old Testament, not conceived sinless but living exceptional lives by the ceaseless outpouring of God's grace? I mean Sarah, who bore a child to Abraham when she was advanced in years (Gen 18:11). Or Esther, who braved the anger of a king to save her people from slaughter. Or Judith, who saved her city and her nation from an invading Assyrian army and was honored by her people with the lovely hymn "You are the glory of Jerusalem, the splendid boast of our people" (Judith 15:9)[2]–titles the Church applies to Mary.

Where does the difference lie? In this: Only Mary was to give birth to Jesus, and this son of hers was to be sinless from his conception. I am not saying that God simply had to have a sinless mother for His sinless Son. I do say that it was utterly fitting, that it makes divine and human sense, that it reveals a God whose dream for our redemption never ceases to amaze us. I mean a redeemer who shares not only the very nature of God but our flesh and blood–Son of God and Son of Mary. A redeemer who came down to us not in regal robes or with angel's wings but from a woman's body. A redeemer who not only lived for us but poured out his blood for us. No, it does not surprise me that God's plan for the redemption of all humanity included a woman filled with redemption's grace from the first instant of her existence.

Some might suggest that a little dash of original sin might have made Mary more human, more like you and me. No, good friends. If it is sinfulness that measures our humanness, then Hitler and Hussein would be the most human of humans. If you want to recognize the truly human, join Mary as she wraps her infant in swaddling clothes, as in fear she flees with him to Egypt, as she loses her son in Jerusalem and asks him, "Son, why have you done this to us? Your father and I have been looking for you with great anxiety" (Lk 2:48). Stand with her beneath the cross after one of his 12 select male friends has sold him for silver, another has sworn he does not know him, and nine others have run away in panic.

Here is the sinless Mary, as human as any of her covenant sisters, living to the full for her Son the grace that marked her first moment of life.

III

All well and good—the Immaculate Conception says something important for Mary's life with Jesus. But does the Immaculate Conception touch your life and mine? It's not a matter of imitation; no one of us was conceived free from "the sin of the world" of which we sang in the *Gloria*. I submit that the Immaculate Conception should bring to mind, now and always, a tremendous truth in Catholic theology, a truth we live with each day without thinking of it.

What is that tremendous truth? This: Whatever positively advances our salvation, our progress toward God, our oneness with God, there God always takes the initiative, God always takes the first step. Example. You and I came to Holy Trinity this evening because we decided we wanted to participate actively in this liturgy, share in the core of Catholic worship, the most powerful means at the Church's disposal to sanctify us. *We* decided. But we could make this decision only because God offered each of us the grace, the spiritual power, to make it. Not that God forced us to come; God never does. The grace is simply offered. Our response is free: We can say yes or no. Equally marvelous, our yes to God is itself a graced response; God enables us to say yes...freely.

God always takes the initiative. And this is strikingly revealed in Mary's immaculate conception. In the first moment of her human existence, before Mary was able to do or say anything on her own,

God's special grace flooded her soul, kept "the sin of the world" from ever touching her and no response was possible.

As Mary grew, God still took the initiative. It was God who asked her to mother God's Son, but now God was asking for her co-operation. She did not have to say yes; but when she did, her yes was a wondrous wedding of God's grace and Mary's freedom. Such too was the life of our Lady as virgin mother: God—from the hidden years in Nazareth, through the separation of Jesus' public life, to the death watch beneath the cross—God taking the initiative, the first step. Mary responding to God's invitation in graced freedom.

Good sisters and brothers in Christ: "Mary conceived without sin" is not a strange abstraction at the edge of Catholic thinking and living. This too fits in with what you heard St. Paul say more broadly to the Christians of Ephesus: "This was according to the eternal purpose that [God] accomplished in Christ Jesus our Lord, in whom we have boldness of speech and confidence of success through faith in him" (Eph 3:11–12). In God's dream for the sinless Jesus, God shaped a woman untouched by sin. In God's dream for sinful humanity, God revealed through Mary that in our struggle against sin we are not left on our own. God always takes the initiative; God is there before we act, makes it possible for you and me "to do the right and to love goodness, and to walk humbly with [our] God" (Mic 6:8).

Holy Trinity Church
Washington, D.C.
December 9, 2002

Panel VI: "If you want peace, work for justice"

Is. 32:17: "Justice will bring about peace; right will produce calm + security"

Is. 54:13-14
"All your sons shall be taught by the Lord, & great shall be the peace of your children. (14) In justice shall you be established, far from the fear of oppression where destruction cannot come near you."

WEDDING HOMILIES

20
WHERE YOUR TREASURE IS, THERE WILL YOUR HEART BE
Wedding Homily 1

- Genesis 1:24–31
- 1 Corinthians 13:1–10, 12–13
- Luke 12:22–34

Good friends all: In the past quarter hour an extraordinary event happened here; happened to each one of you. In your excitement over Stephen and Nancy you may have missed it. What happened to you that was so extraordinary? Christ our Lord spoke to you. Not in a vision; simply through God's own Book. For when the three passages from Genesis, Paul, and Luke were proclaimed to you, the main speaker was not the reader; it was Jesus. The Second Vatican Council said so in one striking sentence: "Jesus Christ is present in his word, since it is Christ himself who speaks when the holy Scriptures are read in the church."[1]

Now these three texts have a special significance this afternoon; for they were selected by Nancy and Stephen. Selected because they speak powerfully to the life this dear couple will live together...for life. Limited by time, let me suggest why two of these passages are particularly pertinent to the life of love we are privileged to celebrate today.

I

Begin with St. Paul. A lovely passage, but we hear it so often that it turns stale. "If I speak in the tongues of mortals and of angels, but do not have love, I am a noisy gong or a clashing cymbal. And if I have prophetic powers, and comprehend all mysteries and all knowledge, and if I have all faith, so as to remove mountains, but do not have love,

I am nothing. If I give away all my possessions, and if I hand over my body so that I may boast, but do not have love, I gain nothing" (1 Cor 13:1–3; NRSV). Now bring that love song down to concrete reality, rephrase it in contemporary syllables, and what am I saying? What are Nancy and Stephen saying? If I can speak with the rolling thunder of Jesse Jackson, if I can preach with the passion of Martin Luther King Jr.'s "I Have a Dream," but do not love, I am only a harsh, terribly loud noise raping our planet. If I can tell you, predict to our world, what the new millennium will be like, if like another Einstein I can disentangle the deepest mysteries of science, if I have a faith as strong as Jesus' faith, strong enough to move the Rockies, but do not love, I am nothing, a cipher, zero. If I give everything I own to the poor, if I rot in prison a political prisoner for three decades like Africa's Mandela, but do not love, it will do me no good whatsoever; it's nothing but waste.[2]

But what kind of love is this? What is St. Paul talking about? Not a business contract; not a list of what Stephen and Nancy must do or not do if the contract is not to be broken. Paul put it pithily in his letter to the Christians of Rome: "God's love has been poured out in our hearts through the Holy Spirit that has been given to us" (Rom 5:5). The gift you first received, Nancy and Stephen, when baptismal waters flowed over your foreheads, that gift will be deepened immeasurably when you murmur "I do" to each other. The gift is God's presence within you, God giving Himself to each and both of you without restraint, "poured out in" you says Paul. Nor is that all. Gifted with God's own love, aware of God' s love within you, you have the power to "pour out" your love, love each other somewhat as God loves you. I mean, without restraint, unselfishly, incredibly aware of the other, of the one who is your "treasure," therefore your "heart" (Lk 12:34). Very simply, the God who *is* Love imparts to you something of God's own nature, the Holy Spirit, the Spirit of love. Such is God's wedding gift to you.[3]

It is this gift that enables St. Paul to declare what sounds so unrealistic: "Love is patient, kind, not jealous, not pompous, not inflated, not rude, does not seek its own interests, is not quick-tempered, does not brood over injury, does not rejoice over wrongdoing but rejoices with the truth. Love bears all things, believes all things, hopes all things, endures all things" (1 Cor 13:4–7). Yes indeed, but only in the power of the God who is alive and active within you.

II

Turn now to the passage you borrowed from Genesis, the first book of the Hebrew Testament, the very first chapter. The background? God's creative activity in earth and sea and sky, sun and moon, beasts and birds. Before God looks over creation, sees how good all of it is, God climaxes all this with a startling sentence, "Let us make humankind in our image, according to our likeness." And so it happens: "God created humankind in the image of God....Male and female God created them" (Gen 1:26–27).

Two sentences, Nancy and Stephen, that should spark your life together, keep you from ever taking each other for granted. You might even tape them to your refrigerator, above each day's schedule. First, each of you came into this world not simply a delightful infant; you entered our space "like God." How can that possibly be? For centuries we curious creatures called theologians have struggled to understand what it means to be like God. One explanation among several makes special sense to me, makes rich sense for today's celebration. You and I are like God because we have the capacity, the freedom, to love. To love God, to love one another. The First Letter of John is strong on this:

> Whoever is without love does not know God, for God is Love....In this is love: Not that we have loved God, but that God loved us and sent His Son as expiation for our sins. Beloved, if God so loved us, we also must love one another....If we love one another, God remains in us, and His love is brought to perfection in us.
>
> (1 Jn 4:8–12)

That gift, the freedom to love somewhat as God loves, was wondrously enriched when God said, "It is not good for the man to be alone. I will make a suitable partner for him" (Gen 2:18). For God did not shape just one image to reflect the divine, to mirror God's goodness, God's compassion, God's self-giving. No, "Male and female God created them" (Gen 1:27). Our imaginative God shaped not one human but two. Similar, but not the same.

This is of high importance for your life together, crucial for any marriage. You are indeed similar. Both of you are family people, touchingly devoted to those who gave you life, closely linked in love to your extended families. Both of you are blessed with siblings who, for some strange reason, think you are "the greatest" since sliced bread. You share a faith in God that fortifies you, a Eucharistic Christ who week after week nourishes you with his own flesh and blood. Each of you finds the other adventurous and courageous, accepting and forgiving, supportive and encouraging. You are delightfully comfortable with each other, honest with each other, trusting of each other; you even enjoy the other's humor. And with a bow to God's humor, both of you have been infected with the virus of a devotion to Jesuits for which there is no known cure.

Yes, you are similar...but not the same. From blue eyes and green, you will at times look out at your world, at people and problems, in different ways, even come to contradictory conclusions. For which I say, "Thank God!" For neither of you is a clone of the other. Marriage, what Scripture calls "two becoming one body" (Gen 2:25), does not mean Stephen becomes another Nancy, or Nancy another Stephen. God shaped each of you in such a way that through your love each of you might become more and more like God, not more and more like each other. Helped, of course, by the other, but never absorbed into the other, Nancy never ceasing to be Nancy, Stephen never ceasing to be Stephen. In this connection, the distinguished Protestant theologian Karl Barth was right on target when he warned us, in looking at man or woman, not to change *is* into *ought,* not to transform indicatives into imperatives. For

> real man and real woman would then have to let themselves be told:
> Thou [Stephen] shalt be concerned with things (preferably
> machines) and thou [Nancy] with persons! Thou [Stephen] shalt
> cherish the mind, thou [Nancy] the soul! Thou [Stephen] shalt fol-
> low thy reason and thou [Nancy] thy instinct! Thou [Stephen] shalt
> be objective and thou [Nancy] subjective! Thou [Stephen] shalt
> build and thou [Nancy] merely adorn; thou [Stephen] shalt conquer
> and thou [Nancy] cherish, etc.! This is commanded thee! This is thy
> task! By exercising one or the other function, thou shalt be faithful
> to thyself as man or woman! This is quite impossible. Obviously we
> cannot seriously address or bind any man or woman on these lines.
> They will justifiably refuse to be addressed in this way.[4]

Yes, despite all the gifts you share, all that you love to be and do together, you differ in much. Whether it's politics or sports, finances or food, art or music, liturgy or labor, if you simply agreed totally on everything, I would be surprised, disappointed, yes fearful. Very simply, help each other to develop into the person God wants, to be Godlike each in your own God-given way. Remember, male and female God created you. For all its importance, anatomy is not destiny.

III

Thus far I have spoken of your love for each other. A potential problem here. Psychology and Christian tradition both warn us that a love which is turned totally inward, a love which does not reach outward, is in danger of dying. I shall never cease insisting how splendidly symbolic is the recessional of a wedding. When Stephen and Nancy move down the aisle as husband and wife to the strains of Beethoven's "Joyful, Joyful We Adore Thee," it will mean more than a welcome signal that the reception is near at hand. The recessional is a movement from church to world, from altar to people, from Christ crucified on Calvary to Christ crucified at the crossroads of our country, yes within sight of our Capitol. A word in explanation.

Stephen and Nancy: God has gifted you in wondrous ways—love beyond telling from parents and grandparents, stimulus from siblings, minds that opened to God's creation at Holy Cross and the University of Massachusetts, support from ever so many friends, work that excites and pleasures you. You are gifted indeed. Still, God's gifts are given not to be clutched possessively but to be shared generously. Shared not only with dear ones such as surround you today, those who know you and like you. I mean also the less fortunate, those who share more of Christ's crucifixion than of his resurrection. I dare not predict with certainty who these might be; I leave it to the Lord to show you as time unrolls. But I do commend to your love and care America's children. Why? Because of all God's images they are the most vulnerable. In the richest country on earth every sixth child is living below the poverty line, living in a kind of hell. Some basic facts:

> Every 44 seconds, an American baby is born into poverty. Every minute, a baby is born without health insurance. Every 2 minutes, a baby is born at low birthweight. Every 11 minutes, a child is reported abused or neglected. Every 2 hours and 20 minutes, a child or youth under 20 is killed by a firearm.[5]

This in a land that among industrialized countries is first in military technology, first in military exports, first in Gross Domestic Product, first in the number of millionaires and billionaires, first in health technology, first in defense expenditures, but 11th in the proportion of children in poverty, 16th in efforts to lift children out of poverty, 18th in the gap between rich and poor children, 23rd in infant mortality, last in protecting our children against gun violence.[6]

Have I left Nancy and Stephen? Not for a moment. I suspect that, wherever God's love leads you in the years to come, you will find some of the 16 million children who are in danger of being left behind in our political planning. They ask so little of us: braces for crooked teeth, food for this hungry family, a shoulder for a lonely child to rest on, medicine for the uninsured, day care expenses; the needs are beyond counting. Bring hope to the eyes of one hopeless child, bring love to one little image of God who has never experienced love's touch, and, I promise you, your own love will grow a hundredfold. And in such outreach of love never forget these startling words of Jesus at our final judgment: "I was hungry and you gave me food, I was thirsty and you gave me drink, a stranger and you welcomed me, naked and you clothed me, ill and you cared for me....Whatever you did for one of these least brothers and sisters of mine, you did for me" (Mt 25:35–36, 40).

Dear Stephen and Nancy: It is indeed an awesome love you have embraced. Come now, and as you pledge this love solemnly to each other, to God, and to your acre of God's world, know that this sacrament is God's own pledge: "I will be with you always." Yes, always.

Church of St. Aloysius Gonzaga
Washington, D.C.
May 12, 2001

21
THIS IS A DAY THE LORD HAS MADE
Wedding Homily 2

- 1 Corinthians 12:31b–13:1-3, 8–13
- Romans 12:9-13
- Matthew 25:31-40

Good friends all: Just proclaimed to you were three passages from Scripture, from the New Testament. The feeling among many Christians is that such passages are proclaimed because in a wedding between Christians it would be "nice" to include "the Good Book," a gracious nod to our God. Moreover, where two Catholics are the featured actors, Rome does insist on such readings. But today the more important fact is that the passages you heard from St. Paul and from Jesus were carefully chosen by Gwen and Carlos. Why? Because these segments of Scripture speak powerfully to this dear couple about the life they will share as long as both shall live.

Since the words proclaimed have now vanished from our hearing, it would be worth our while to go back and see why Carlos and Gwen were so taken by these texts, why they hear therein God speaking to them—speaking in fact to all of you who are married or hope to be.

I

First, what in the passage from St. Paul's letter to the Christians of Corinth in Greece spoke so eloquently to Carlos and Gwen? Here a bit of background can help. Paul has just spoken of special gifts that some members of the Church have. Some are apostles, others prophets; some teach, others work wonders; some are healers, others administrators; some speak in various languages. Important gifts indeed, but swiftly Paul adds, "But I shall show you a still more excellent way [of life]" (1 Cor 12:31). And then Paul launches into that extraordinary tribute to love which begins, "If I speak in human and angelic tongues but do not have love..." (1 Cor 13:1–3). Let me put his hymn of praise in contemporary language:

If I can utter words with the eloquence of Martin Luther King Jr. or in the poetic flights of Maya Angelou, but do not have love, I am simply making loud noises, whistling down the wind. If I can predict just when and where bin Laden's terrorists will strike next, if I can solve the mysteries of cell structure, if I know all there is to know about everything, if I have the kind of faith Jesus said can move the Rockies from the West to the East, but do not have love, I am nothing, a cipher, zero. If I give away the billions that would make me richer than Bill Gates, if I sacrifice my body for a critical cause—peace, justice, reconciliation—but do not have love, I gain nothing, it's all in vain, without value, is good for nothing.

What St. Paul has done is to put all God's gifts to the Church—lofty offices, special graces, high honors, memorable achievements—in perspective, the proper place they have in the whole picture. Apply it to today's celebration, and what is Paul saying? All that Carlos and Gwen will achieve in their life together—in law and medicine, whatever and wherever—will make sense, will have value, will be worth recording only if what they do they do out of love.

Strong language? Yes, of course. Christianity is not a Sunday morning cure for a week's tensions. Christianity is not a foxhole for the fearful, a crutch for the weak in spirit. To live the Christian life is to love—above simply everything else, above the papal tiara, above the bishop's mitre, above power and possessions, above fame and fortune. And that is why the marriage of Gwen and Carlos is so grand a gift to all of us today. They live in love, they will vow to live in love, and they want their love to be the driving force behind all they are, all they do, all they possess, all they achieve.

For that reason, in tune with the Psalmist, we can all sing, "By the lord has this been done" (Ps 118:23). Not primarily by Carlos and Gwen, not by their parents, not by you and me. It is the Lord who has made this day, the God who, the First Letter of John declares, *is* Love (1 Jn 4:8), the God from whom all human love descends. That is why we can obey the Psalmist when he sings, "This is [a] day the Lord has made; let us rejoice in it and be glad" (Ps 118:24).

II

When Gwen and Carlos chose for their second biblical reading a small section of St. Paul's letter to the Christians of Rome, they were bringing the love he described so lyrically to the Christians of Corinth into everyday reality. Here again some background can help. Paul has just reminded his hearers—as he reminds us—that Christians, "though many, are one body in Christ, and individually members of one another" (Rom 12:5). Now he insists that such an intimate oneness makes demands on the Christian community. The general principle? "Let [your] love be sincere," genuine, not hypocritical (v. 9). What does this involve concretely? "Be devoted to one another with mutual affection, outdo one another in showing honor, be fervent in spirit, rejoice in hope, endure in affliction, persevere in prayer, contribute to the needs of God's dedicated people, rejoice with those who are rejoicing, mourn with those who are mourning" (vv.10–15).

What St. Paul is telling us is what Catholic tradition and contemporary psychology stress. The love of a man and a woman that does not move outward, a self-giving that does not reach beyond themselves, is a love in danger of dying. Today I am thrilled to find St. Paul's exhortation fulfilled in spades. For Carlos has written, "Gwen's sincerity is contagious." What exactly is that sincerity? It is revealed in so many ways. In their movement toward God together— Carlos from doubt to faith, Gwen from certainty to deeper understanding. Listen to Carlos: "I have learned more of faith from our experience together as a couple than in the rest of my life so far. I cherish her values, her love for her friends, her faith in God and belief in the Catholic Church, the way she treats those she loves, and her desire to help (and fix) all the problems in the world. Gwen has a deep commitment to those around her and to the poor and suffering."

Yes, they first met at an airport bus stop as total strangers—until Carlos smiled. But, says Gwen, "It is not only the girl at the bus stop at whom Carlos smiles, with whom Carlos converses. It is the checkout clerk, the small child in a hospital, the homeless man at the corner, the tired woman lugging groceries. His smile never fails to bring one in return, and more often than not, a story with it."

Do you wonder that I hear St. Paul clapping his hands in joyful approval? For in Carlos and Gwen he sees realized his insight into what the one body of Christ implies. No one can say to any other, "I do not need you" (see 1 Cor 12:21–26). Not pope to peasant, not cleric to lay, not rich to poor, not brilliant to retarded. Not Carlos to the checkout girl.

III

All this leads happily to the Gospel chosen with such care from many possibilities. Jesus gives us an unusual glimpse into the future that awaits each and all of us. At the Last Judgment, our life for eternity will be determined by our response to what he expected of us on earth. And what will Jesus expect? He phrases it in a startling way. Not how long you and I prayed; not whether we fasted on Good Friday; not even how well we kept the Ten Commandments. No. Jesus will say to those on his right, "*I* was hungry and you gave me food, *I* was thirsty and you gave me drink, *I* was a stranger and you welcomed me, *I* was naked and you clothed me, *I* was ill and you cared for me, *I* was in prison and you visited me" (Mt 25:35–36).

How does this affect the love of Carlos and Gwen? How does it touch your love and mine? In a single simple sentence Jesus made it lucidly clear: "Whatever you did for one of these least brothers [and sisters] of mine, you did for me" (v. 40). How is this possible? Because Jesus identifies in a special way with the hungry, the homeless, and the housebound, with the impoverished, the immigrant, and the imprisoned. Not because they are holier than the well-fed, the richly-housed, and the hale and hearty; holier than the wealthy, the established, and the free. Only because they are in greater need, because they share more of Jesus' crucifixion than of his resurrection.

Carlos and Gwen, in your wondrous wedding of medicine and law, you will have rich opportunities to touch your love for each other, your love for others, to unnumbered humans in dreadful need. Is Jesus still hungry? I commend to you our children. In the richest country on earth, every fifth child is growing up below the poverty line, many with the poverty that kills. I mean those whom the president of Covenant House called "God's lost children,"[1] the hundreds of thousands of runaway youngsters who sleep on America's streets each night, cold, hungry, frightened, looking desperately for someone who cares. I mean the hungry child who cannot afford a meal; the illiterate child who cannot read, a cold child yearning for a warm bed. I mean the children in your own Washington, D.C., many of them preparing not their futures but their funerals, because in a single year over two hundred died from gunfire.

Jesus a stranger? I commend to you our immigrants. A century ago, the moving words on the pedestal of the Statue of Liberty revealed how Americans felt: "Give me your tired, your *poor,* your huddled masses yearning to breathe free." Today, perhaps 300,000 immigrants live in detention, in confinement. Not for terrorism. Simply lack of space in facilities owned and operated by the U.S. Immigration and Naturalization Service. The result? Sixty percent of detainees are currently housed in city and county jails, routinely housed with inmates held on criminal charges.

Jesus naked? I commend to you our homeless veterans, men and some women who once offered their lives for us. On any given night, more than 275,000. Over the course of a year, more than half a million—one of every four homeless males. What to do? Add your personal attention to the Homeless Veterans Comprehensive Assistance Act[2] enacted by the Senate and House. You might even invite a homeless veteran to dinner and a bed.

Jesus ill? I commend to you a hospital of your choice, perhaps the loneliest bed a human can occupy. Or else a man or woman housebound, where no one ever rings the bell. It is something akin to Jesus' agony in the garden, with the apostles asleep around him.

Jesus in prison? I commend to you our country's prison situation. A system horribly broken. Two million Americans are behind bars—one of every 125 people in the United States. A disproportionate number of blacks and hispanics, in common with white inmates in that they are poor, addicted, uneducated, and jobless.

Touch even one of these with your love, and I promise you: Your love for each other will multiply beyond all expectation.

Gwen and Carlos: No homilist can tell you exactly how you are to share your love with the less fortunate. What I do know is that you have started what you call a "life team," that you work effectively together, that you want your professional lives to make a difference in the lives of others, to imitate the Jesus who declared, "The Spirit of the Lord is upon me, for [the Lord] has anointed me. He has sent me to preach good news to the poor, to proclaim release for captives and sight for the blind, to send the downtrodden away relieved" (Lk 4:18). Above all, I know that the driving force of all you do is your love: your profound love for God, for each other, for your dear ones, and for the afflicted who surround you. You know far better than I the gifts with which a gracious God has graced you: loving parents without whom this day would not have dawned; devoted siblings who believe you are the best thing since penicillin; fast friends who delight to walk with you; an education difficult to parallel; a joyful faith you have come to share through troublous times and a fair amount of stress. Much has been given you—not to clutch feverishly but to share generously.

Come then, Gwen and Carlos, and in the presence of God and God's people, pledge for ever the love that already binds you together.

St. Luke the Evangelist Church
Westborough, Massachusetts
July 5, 2002

22
THREE LOVES: GOD, EACH OTHER, THE OTHER
Wedding Homily 3

- Song of Songs 2:8–10, 14, 16a; 8:6–7a
- Colossians 3:12–17
- Matthew 5:1–16

Good friends all: In your understandable joy over Tina and Paul, you may have missed something equally joyous. You see, during the past quarter hour God has spoken to each of you. If you hesitate to believe me, listen to the Second Vatican Council: "[Christ himself] is present in his word, since it is he himself who speaks when the holy Scriptures are read in the church."[1] Three passages were proclaimed to you, passages from God's own Book, passages plucked carefully by Paul and Tina. Why? Because through these inspired words God is saying something highly important for every couple joining hands and hearts for life. Concretely, three loves: God, each other, and the other. So then, lean back (but not too comfortably) and listen to Christian marriage from a confirmed bachelor.

I

The first set of inspired words stems from a highly unlikely source. The Song of Songs is a song about love—ideal human love.[2] Ideal in the sense that this love is total, is passionate, is sexual. Why proclaimed here, in a church, in sacred space? Because in a single remarkable sentence the Song tells us that such love "is a flame of the Lord" (8:6b).[3] It is a sharing in the model for every love, the incredible love that exists in the Trinity, the divine love Father, Son, and Holy Spirit enjoy with one another.

We know very little about love within the Trinity, for the Trinity is shrouded in mystery. But this we do know: God not only loves; God *is* Love. Inspired by God, the First Letter of John declares it: "God is Love" (1 Jn 4:8). Love is not just a quality God has; love is what God *is*. Hard to grasp, I grant, because this is not our experience of love. We love, we are loving people. But God? Love is God's very nature; another name for God is Love.

And in that love Tina and Paul share. Listen to the same letter of John: "Beloved, let us love one another, because love is of God; everyone who loves is begotten of God and knows God" (4:7). God's love has become part of this dear couple, whether they are aware of it or not. It is the most profound way they image God, mirror God's unique Son, our Lord Jesus Christ.

Tina and Paul, basic to your life together is a realization to be taped not to your refrigerator but on your hearts: *Your* love is a flame of the Lord. It simply means, it is God—Father, Son, and Holy Spirit—who sparked the flame to begin with. Not coincidence but a loving Providence brought you together on a Saturday night at the Chesapeake Bay, brought you together another Saturday night—where else, in God's humor, but a pub in Greenwich Village? And it is God who above all human efforts will keep your love aflame, prevent its dying, crumbling into ashes. If you ever need proof that your love is a sharing in God's love, fix your eyes on a cross outside Jerusalem: God's own Son pouring out his life so that you might live in love. Not some abstraction called humanity. No, every man, every woman. You, Tina and Paul. Yes, God's Son gave his life that *you* might live in love. "Greater love than this," Jesus himself declared, "no one has" (Jn 15:13).

II

The second set of inspired words: If the Song of Songs swept you up on a divine ideal—"Love is a flame of the Lord"—St. Paul reminds you that you keep this flame of the Lord burning bright on a tough, often hostile earth.[4] St. Paul's first piece of advice is broad enough not to trouble you deeply: "Clothe yourselves with compassion, kindness, humility, gentleness, and patience" (Col 3:12). After all, these are day-to-day Christian virtues, not all that difficult. But then St. Paul tosses in the "zinger": "Just as the Lord has forgiven you, so you must forgive one another" (v. 13).

If I were asked to suggest in one word the most critical of marital problems, I would say "forgive." Why? Apart from forgiveness

Christianity is a mockery, Bethlehem and Calvary make no sense. You and I listen not only to Jesus' first words from the cross, "Father, forgive them" (Lk 23:34). We listen to a crib and a cross that are themselves mute cries for forgiveness. The cross echoes in blood Jesus' parables of forgiveness: the prodigal son, the good shepherd. We recall, all too facilely, Jesus' strong warning, "If you do not forgive others, neither will your Father forgive your transgressions" (Mt 6:15).

> The problem with forgiveness has been that of all acknowledged good acts, it is the one we are most suspicious of. "To err is human, to forgive supine," punned S. J. Perelman. In a country where the death penalty has been a proven vote getter in recent years, forgiveness is often seen as effete and irresponsible. Sometimes it even seems to condone the offense, as noted centuries ago by Jewish sages who declared, "He that is merciful to the cruel will eventually be cruel to the innocent."[5]

No, good friends, to forgive is still divine. Divine because forgiveness begins with God. It is God who in the Hebrew Testament ceaselessly forgives His people when they shatter His commandments, violate their covenant, lust after false gods. It is God who responds to His people when they complain that God has forsaken them, has forgotten them:

> Can a mother forget her infant,
>   be without tenderness for the child of her womb?
> Even should she forget,
>   I will never forget you.
> See, upon the palms of my hands I have written your name.
>   (Isa 49:15–16)

And without forgiveness marriage is a relentless struggle for the upper hand. If you care to see life without forgiveness, turn to the "soaps" on TV. See the shoulders shrugged, the backs turned, the silences more cutting than words. One of the most majestic letters in the New Testament declares, "Do not let the sun set on your anger" (Eph 4:26). I would say, "Never go to bed angry, back to back like bitter enemies."

But to forgive is not a simple exchange of words: "I'm sorry" and "I forgive you." There is so much more to forgiveness. St. Paul indicated that when he added, "Over all these [compassion, kindness, humility, gentleness, patience] put on love, the bond of perfection" (Col 3:14). The deepest, most meaningful forgiveness stems from love. Take the ills that plague our world: the terrorism of September 11, the hostility in Northern Ireland, the bloodshed in the Middle East—there is so little hope for forgiveness because there is so little love. In a smaller but not insignificant way, each family, each married couple, is a microcosm of our larger world, is literally "a little world," "a world in miniature." Theologians have called a Christian family "a little church," the Church in miniature.

Tina and Paul, forgiveness will come more easily if you refuse to forget what you have written about each other. Says Paul of Tina:

> She is smart, funny, ambitious, accomplished, eager to please, supportive, loving, trusting and trustworthy, thoughtful, kind, sharing, sweet-natured, tenacious, [a] genuinely good person, a generous spirit. Even if she is slightly worked up about something, she bounces back into shape and knows right from wrong. She is witty, slightly sly and clever. She is not good at telling lies, has virtually no "poker face." This is good. It is indicative of her underlying moral compass, which unfailingly points to true north.
>
> Tina is willing to accept a fair point during a disagreement. Our political discussions can be vigorous, but they are also respectful and seek a common understanding, even if we don't agree. She is mildly tempestuous, has good instincts that she doesn't always trust. She has more growth potential than she could possibly imagine right now, and in many ways has just begun to grow into who she really is. Inside and out, Tina is adorable, she is beautiful, and she is cute, even when she's exceedingly tired. I am a lucky, lucky man.

And Tina about Paul:

> Why do I want to spend the rest of my life with Paul? His kindness and love, his spirit and zest for life, his loyalty and compassion, his intelligence, curiosity and wonder of life, his sense of humor and keen wit. But I think what draws me to him the most is his moral compass. He knows who he is, what he believes in, and what he thinks is important and moral. He has a distinct view of right and wrong, but a respect and appreciation for the grey in life and that not all of life's lessons are simple or easy. He helps me see that it is often through life's complexities that one truly grows.
>
> I see marriage as a partnership in every sense of the word. It is going through the joys and sorrows of life with your best friend by your side, knowing there is someone you can always depend on. It is the wonder of growing, learning, and exploring life with a very special person. It takes passion, communication, and commitment. I am so proud to be spending the rest of my life with this wonderful man.

Two wondrously complementary approaches to marriage. Here is marriage at its finest, because its expectations are stimulated by

God's grace—concretely, as St. Paul phrased it, "because God's love has been poured out in [their] hearts through the holy Spirit that has been given to [them]" (Rom 5:5).

III

The third set of inspired words selected by Tina and Paul stems from Jesus' himself in the Gospel of Matthew: "You are the light of the world. Your light must shine before others, that they may see your good deeds and glorify your heavenly Father" (Mt 5:14, 16). Why "good deeds"? Not only that God may be glorified. Also, on a very practical level, because of an insight from an experienced woman psychologist:

> A love that is not for more than itself will die—the wisdom of Christian tradition and the best we know from psychology both assure us of this truth. It is often very appropriate at the early stages of a relationship that the energy of romance and infatuation exclude the larger world from our vision. But over the long haul an intimate relationship...which does not reach outward will stagnate.[6]

"A love that is not for more than itself will die." To remain aflame, your love must reach out to others. Not only to parents and siblings; not only to friends you already cherish. Your love must reach out—reach out together—to the less fortunate who surround you. One strong suggestion. The director of the Children's Defense Fund, Marian Wright Edelman, made one type of outreach poignantly demanding. In an essay entitled "It's Time!" she wrote in part:

> *It's time!* It's time to build a mighty movement to Leave No Child Behind in the richest and most powerful nation on earth....
> *It's time!* The wealthiest time in American history. A $10 trillion American economy. A projected multi-trillion dollar federal budget surplus over the next 10 years. Number one in billionaires and millionaires. The top Gross National Product in the world....
> *It's time!* An era of stunning American intellectual, technological, and scientific achievement....We've sent humans to the moon, spaceships to Mars, cracked the genetic code, amassed tens of billions of dollars from a tiny microchip, and discovered cures for diseases which give hope to millions....
> *It's time!* Unrivaled American military leadership in a globalizing world....Our president proposes spending $618,000 a minute, $6.25 billion a week, and $27 billion a month to maintain our military defenses....

> The wealth of [the] four richest Americans exceeds that of
> 14 million American families combined, exceeds the revenues of
> 24 state governments with 42 million citizens, and could lift 12
> million children out of poverty five times over.[7]

My suggestion? Get involved in the ongoing project Leave No Child Behind. In Congress is an Act to Leave No Child Behind. It gives the President, Congress, and all Americans the opportunity to ensure every child health insurance, end child poverty and hunger, get every child ready for school, have every child reading by fourth grade, provide after-school and summer programs, ensure each child a decent afford-able home, protect every child from abuse and violence. The Act is too comprehensive to be passed as a whole; but parts have passed, such as food stamps and tax relief;[8] others are in progress, such as child care. What is important is for us, for American families, to prod our repre-sentatives to continue acting to save our children.[9]

Even more personally, I have a dream. I imagine every Christian family in the United States looking after one deprived child. In an America where the younger you are the poorer you are; not far from any of us is a child aching for nourishing food or limping along on a home-made crutch, a child without health insurance or a shoulder to rest on, a child sexually or physically abused or HIV-positive and crying for compassion, a teenager drug-addicted. The needs are legion, but legion too are the families gifted with the blessings of God's good earth.

Paul and Tina, in a short while you will waltz down the center aisle of this basilica as man and wife, to the strains of (appropriately, I think) Handel's "Arrival of the Queen of Sheba." That recessional, that walk together, will be superbly symbolic. For it will represent, it will express, a movement. Not primarily a movement to a liquid recep-tion. More profoundly, a movement from church to world, from altar to people, from Christ crucified on Calvary to Christ crucified at the crossroads of our towns and cities. It will represent your outreach to a whole little world that yearns to share in your love—especially the "lit-tle ones" of whom Jesus said, "to such as these the kingdom of God belongs" (Lk 18:16).

Basilica of St. Josaphat
Milwaukee, Wisconsin
June 1, 2002

SPECIAL OCCASIONS

23
FREE AT LAST!
Celebration of Martin Luther King Jr. Day

- Colossians 3:12–15
- Matthew 5:1–12

Somewhat like the three wise men from the East, we too have recently left the Christmas crib. The song of the angels may still be ringing
in our ears, "On earth peace to those on whom God's favor rests" (Lk
2:14). The peace of Christ. The peace you and I struggle to bring to
our war-torn violent earth. This evening's liturgy, the Mass for Peace
and Justice, brings to mind the well-worn words of Paul VI, "If you
want peace, work for justice." The prophet Isaiah had sensed that
much earlier: "Justice will bring peace; right will produce calm and
serenity" (Isa 32:17; see 54:13–14). On this day when we are focusing
on biblical justice, let's pause for a quarter hour to see why the pope's
pithy phrase makes such Christian sense.[1] Three stages to my develop-
ment. A word on justice; a word on peace; a word on the connection
between justice and peace.

I

First, recall what you heard this morning so "passionately" from
Scripture. The justice we prize above all is not the justice our human
reason is justifiably proud to have excogitated: Give every man,
woman, and child what they deserve, what they have a strict right to
demand, because it can be proven from philosophy or has been written into law. Oh yes, that justice is precious. With it, we can claim certain rights: the right to a job, a living wage, healthcare, adequate food,
decent housing, to be treated with respect. Scripture itself talks along
those lines. "The innocent and the just you shall not put to death, nor
shall you acquit the guilty. Never take a bribe, for a bribe blinds even

119

the most clear-sighted and twists the words even of the just" (Exod 23:7–8). Without it, civilization is impossible; life on earth would degenerate into a jungle, where might makes right and the prize goes to the swift, the smart, the savage.

Still, where justice is concerned, God has not left us to our own resources, to the reasoning powers with which we are born. God has revealed to us an even higher level of justice. That justice is fidelity to relationships that stem from a covenant—in the Christian case, the covenant cut in the blood of Christ. The operative word here is "relationships." Three: to God, to fellow humans, to the earth. It is no longer a question only of what we deserve. It goes beyond what people can claim as a right. Love God with all you are, with every fiber of your being. Love every human person as a child of God, an image of God; love him, love her, like another self—especially the poor and the downtrodden, the despised and the powerless; yes, the enemy. And touch each "thing," each facet of God's material creation, earth and sea and sky, with reverence, with respect, as a gift of God. Use God's things to build up relationships, not destroy them—from a jug of wine to nuclear energy, from bread shared generously to luxuries clutched feverishly. It is John Paul II's bold assertion: Christians must "realize that their responsibility within creation and their duty toward nature and the Creator are an essential part of their faith."[2]

Where lies the difference between justice human and justice divine? A momentous monosyllable: love. Neither ethical justice nor legal justice can command love. God's justice does. All the way back in Deuteronomy: "You shall love the Lord, your God, with all your heart, and with all your soul, and with all your strength" (Deut 6:5). All the way back in Leviticus: "You shall love your neighbor as yourself" (Lev 19:18).[3] And Jesus is even more inclusive than Leviticus: "You have heard that it was said, 'You shall love your neighbor and hate your enemy.' But I say to you, love your enemies" (Mt 5:43). "This is my commandment: Love one another as I love you" (Jn 15:12).

II

Turn now to peace. What was ancient Israel's vision of peace? A state of bounty and well-being that stemmed from God; included in it were concord and harmony, order and security and prosperity. In time, peace became the mark of the messianic kingdom. For the prophets, the messianic king sent by God would be "Prince of Peace" (Isa 9:5), would "proclaim peace to the nations" (Zech 9:10). Jewish religion was not indifferent to the good things of earth; these fell under God's gifts, were part and parcel of peace.

On Jesus' lips, peace at its most profound is associated with salvation. Because Jesus has forgiven her sins, a sinful woman can "go in peace" (Lk 7:50). Because a hemorrhaging woman's "faith has saved" her, Jesus can tell her to "go in peace" (Lk 8:48). Jesus' farewell to his disciples, "Peace I leave with you, my peace I give to you" (Jn 14:27), is not the absence of war or a tenuous truce between enemies; not an end to psychological tension; not a sentimental feeling of well-being. Peace is our oneness with God now and into eternity. Jesus' peace is the gift of salvation.

Basically, Jesus' peace means that God is alive in us. "In a little while," he told his disciples, "the world will no longer see me, but you will see me, because I live and you will live. On that day you will realize that I am in my Father and you are in me and I in you" (Jn 14:19-20). That is why he could say to his disciples and to us, "Do not let your hearts be troubled or afraid" (v. 27). To borrow Paul's swift summary, "Christ himself is our peace" (Eph 2:14).

In the Catholic version, we are concerned with both levels of peace. Peace on a human level alone—concord, harmony, order, security, prosperity—for that too is a gift of God. And peace on a deeper level, a profound oneness with God—Father, Son, and Holy Spirit dwelling within us—a oneness that can exist, must exist, even when life is tough, when the going is rough, when human living is not very human and not much alive.

III

My final question: How does biblical justice bring about biblical peace? Instead of a tortuous logical argument, let me set before you a man who lived and died for what we are talking about, the man we honor each year on this day, a martyr for peace through justice.

Justice? Martin Luther King Jr. summed up his life's purpose during his daring speech "I Have a Dream" in the 1963 March on Washington.[4] From the steps of the Lincoln Memorial he encouraged and challenged hundreds of thousands of protesters.

> We have also come to this hallowed spot to remind America of the fierce urgency of now. This is no time to engage in the luxury of cooling off or to take the tranquilizing drug of gradualism. Now is the time to make real the promises of democracy. Now is the time to rise from the dark and desolate valley of segregation

to the sunlit path of racial justice. Now is the time to lift our nation from the quicksands of racial injustice to the solid rock of brotherhood. Now is the time to make justice a reality for all of God's children.

But his struggle for justice was not to be accompanied by bitterness, hatred, violence.

Let us not seek to satisfy our thirst for freedom by drinking from the cup of bitterness and hatred. We must forever conduct our struggle on the high plane of dignity and discipline. We must not allow our creative protest to degenerate into physical violence. Again and again, we must rise to the majestic heights of meeting physical force with soul force.

And in his dream justice would lead to what we have called peace.

This is our hope. This is the faith that I go back to the South with. With this faith we will be able to hew out of the mountain of despair a stone of hope. With this faith we will be able to transform the jangling discords of our nation into a beautiful symphony of brotherhood. With this faith we will be able to work together, to pray together, to struggle together, to go to jail together, to stand up for freedom together, knowing that we will be free one day. This will be the day, this will be the day when all of God's children will be able to sing with new meaning:

> My country, 'tis of thee, sweet land of liberty, of thee I sing.
> Land where my fathers died, land of the pilgrims' pride,
> From every mountainside, let freedom ring!

Martin Luther King ended his dream for justice with his hope for peace.

And when this happens, when we allow freedom to ring, when we let it ring from every village and every hamlet, from every state and every city, we will be able to speed up that day when all of God's children, black men and white men, Jews and Gentiles, Protestants and Catholics, will be able to join hands and sing in the words of the old Negro spiritual:

> Free at last! Free at last!
> Thank God Almighty, we are free at last!

"When all of God's children will be able to join hands." Peace through justice.

Good brothers in Christ: Martin Luther King's dream of peace through justice was a magnificent beginning. Although he received the Nobel Peace Prize in 1964, his effectiveness was limited: limited by challenges to his leadership, limited by the self-defense and black-nationalism message of Malcolm X, limited by the "Black Power" of Stokely Carmichael, limited by his criticism of American intervention in Vietnam. Much remains to be done. King is indeed a symbol of peace through justice, but, like Jesus, "a sign that [is still] contradicted" (Lk 2:34). A symbol, a sign, that should speak to you and me in powerful, even frightening syllables.

Where King confronted racism, you and I can add to it injustices galore. You have just now rehearsed the hurts of your people; they will surround you, fill your conference room walls, the rest of this week. I would simply ask you to broaden your horizons, expand your vision, beyond your parish, across our country, throughout its cultures. Concretely, let me swiftly mention three national issues.

First, each of us should feel anguish over, protest, and bring to the pulpit the hunger of America's fifth child. For in the richest country on earth the younger you are, the poorer you are. Every fifth child is growing up below the poverty line. And the Children's Defense Fund reminds us, "All American children are at risk from the proliferation of guns..., from the pollution of our air, water, earth, airwaves, and Internet with smut and toxic substances; from the breakdown of family..., from epidemic substance abuse and from domestic violence that know no race or income limits...."[5]

Second, we who preach justice for peace cannot ignore our immigrants: 200,000 in detention, 60 percent of them housed in city and county jails, routinely housed with inmates held on criminal charges. I still agonize over a detainee center described for me by a Jesuit friend: "There are no windows; [immigrants] never breathe fresh air or see the light of day except through one skylight. One woman has been there for almost three years. It would break your heart to see them. They have such a lost and hopeless look on their faces."

Third, preaching justice for peace, we dare not ignore our prison system. We lock up two million Americans, one out of 125 people in the U.S.; 48 percent black, 18 percent Hispanic. What do they have in common with the whites? They are poor, addicted, undereducated, and jobless. Our sentencing is more and more punitive: no more parole on the federal level, minimum-sentencing legislation, in California "three strikes and you're out." Two thirds of our prisoners return to jail; victims are not healed from their wounds; and our communities are no safer. Please, my brothers, look into a growing movement: restorative justice. In harmony with biblical justice, its aim is to heal.

My brothers in Christ: The justice issues that crowd our culture are dismayingly many. No homily can solve a single injustice. But a homily can, a homily should, raise issues, raise awareness, stimulate our people to come together, talk together, act together. As a sympathetic Protestant told one of our Preaching the Just Word team, "If you Catholics could get your act together, you'd be dangerous."

Literally for Christ's sake, let's get our justice act together.

Holy Name Retreat Center
Houston, Texas
January 15, 2001

24

IF YOU HAVE FAITH....
The Radio Mass of Baltimore

- Habakkuk 1:2–3; 2:2–4
- 2 Timothy 1:6–8, 13–14
- Luke 17:5–10

Three swift movements to my homily: a day of infamy, a life of faith, and several suggestions.

I

We are agonizingly aware that on the eleventh of September terror struck America from the skies. Terror we had never expected, never experienced. Not only were the twin towers of America's business reduced to rubble; not only was the symbol of America's military might set aflame. More than 3,000 men and women perished suddenly, frighteningly—their flesh often scattered beyond recapturing. And fear swept over our land, from rock-ribbed Maine to sun-drenched California.

But there was another side to terror, the aftermath, a response on a different level. For the rest of the week, untold millions packed America's churches, heads bent in homage or arms raised in supplication. Candlelight processions dotted America's campuses. Government officials and politicians of all styles crowded Washington's National Cathedral. Catholic bishops in the District of Columbia moved from a meeting hall to Mass in the basilica nearby.

Why? Some of us were chillingly afraid, and needed courage. Others were mourning dear ones destroyed, and needed comfort. Some survivors were still in shock, and knew not where else to turn. And yet, through all this disarray and confusion, what I sensed was a more-or-less conscious response to the challenge of Jesus in today's

Gospel, "If you have faith the size of a mustard seed, you would say to this mulberry tree, 'Be uprooted and planted in the sea,' and it would obey you" (Lk 17:6).

II

Faith....A wondrous monosyllable. What is this faith, a pinch of which, can compel a tree to uproot itself and be transplanted in the sea? What is this faith that millions believe can bring courage to the despairing, consolation to the desolate, peace to the terrorized?

One facet of faith is something of a head trip: You accept as true what God has revealed to us in Christ. This you regularly do in the Sunday Creed. You believe in one God the Father, Creator of all that is. You believe that God's Son took our flesh, lived for us, died for us, and rose from the dead. You believe in the Holy Spirit, giver of life. You believe in one, holy, catholic, and apostolic Church. You believe that baptism forgives your sins. You believe that death is not the end of life, only a fresh beginning for ever.

Important indeed. God speaks to you and you say yes. But remember what the New Testament Letter of James warned us: "You believe that God is one. You do well. Even the demons believe that and tremble" (Jas 2:19). Intellectual knowledge alone is not enough to save you or me.

The faith that saves? Another single syllable: trust. I mean, giving yourself totally, heart as well as mind, flesh as well as spirit, into God's hands. It is Jesus in Gethsemane's garden: "Father, if you are willing, take this cup away from me; still, not my will but yours be done" (Lk 22:42). Utter trust. No matter how dark the skies, how severe the temptation to hurl the question, "Why, God, why?" The trust of young Mary, asked to bear God's son in flesh, not knowing what was to come; no angel told her about Calvary. The trust of Abraham, asked to leave kin and country and go he knew not where—knew only that it was God who called. Whatever you want, Lord.

You may be surprised that God allowed six million Jewish men, women, and children and countless numbers of Gypsies, political dissidents, communists, homosexuals, mental patients, and physically disabled individuals to perish under the Nazis, permitted world wars, this year permitted three thousand persons to perish horribly in New York, Washington, and Pennsylvania. Surprised, but still trusting. Such is the faith that moves not mulberry trees but God's very Self.

III

What might all this say to us? Several suggestions.

First, the Radio Mass is not a one-way street. We the reasonably healthy are not simply bringing the gospel to you who are housebound or hospitalized. You bring a special gift to us. Your trust in God is important for us. You may well say with St. Paul in a single sentence, "I rejoice in my sufferings for your sake, and in my flesh I am filling up what is lacking in the afflictions of Christ on behalf of his body, which is the Church" (Col 1:24). In your union with the suffering Jesus, you help to bring the fruits of his passion to life in our lives. Your hurts, your pains, your loneliness need never be a waste, as long as your trust in God, your complete offering of all you are and all you endure, is a ceaseless "Sacred Heart of Jesus, I place my trust in you."

Second, your ability to trust stems in large part from this Eucharist. For our Catholic tradition assures us that the Eucharist is "the source from which all [the Church's] power proceeds."[1] All of us must remember that trusting does not mean we feel good or can prove that God is good. In critical moments we need to remember that our celebration of the Eucharist is "in memory of Jesus Christ *who on the night before he died,* turned to God and praised and thanked Him out of the depths of his distress."[2]

Third, trust comes not from proving but from loving. The ways of God are not our ways. And life is too complex to try to prove that everything makes human sense: an infant born HIV-positive; a child with Down syndrome; a young man killed by a drunken driver; a family destroyed by a tornado; World War II; 3,000 killed by terrorists in one morning. God's question to us is insistently Jesus' question to Peter, "Do you love me?" (Jn 21:15–17). If any reason for loving is needed, kneel before a crucifix and recall the First Letter of John: "The way we came to know love was that [Jesus] laid down his life for us" (1 Jn 3:16). "In this way the love of God was revealed to us: God sent His only Son into the world so that we might have life through him. In this is love: not that we have loved God, but that He loved us and sent His Son as expiation for our sins" (1 Jn 4:7–10). Dare we ask the crucified Jesus, "Do you really love me?"

The faith that moves not mulberry trees but God's very Self is a living faith. And a living faith is a loving faith—loving God in the midst of hate and horror, of death and destruction. Loving every human being, enemy as well as friend, as an image of God—loving each as Jesus has loved us.

No, I cannot tell you why God did not prevent September the eleventh. All I know is that a God who loved us so much that He became one of us, loved us so much that He died for us, loved us so much that He promises we shall live with Him for ever—such a God deserves to hear from us, yes from every bed of pain, what he heard from Peter, "Lord, you know everything; you know that I love you" (Jn 21:17).

The prayer of every Christian, in transporting joy and profound sorrow, now and at the hour of our death, is Jesus' own last prayer: "Father, into your hands I entrust my spirit" (Lk 23:46).

Trust. Always, trust.

Chapel of Grace
St. Ignatius Church
Baltimore, Maryland
October 7, 2001

25
LET THE LITTLE CHILDREN COME TO ME
Homily for the Baptism of an Infant

• Mark 10:13–16

For me, one of the most moving scenes in all four Gospels is the story you have just heard from Mark:

> People were bringing children to Jesus [Luke says "even infants" (18:15)] that he might touch them, but the disciples rebuked them. When Jesus saw this he became indignant and said to them, "Let the children come to me, do not prevent them; for the kingdom of God belongs to such as these. Amen, I say to you, whoever does not accept the kingdom of God like a child will not enter it." Then he embraced them and blessed them, placing his hands on them.
>
> (Mk 10:13–16)

I am aware that Jesus was not baptizing the little ones, was not even talking about baptism.[1] Still, his tender care for children, even for the tiniest, his blessing, and especially his insistence that we let the little ones come to him—all this can legitimately be transferred to this sacred hour in this lovely chapel. In what way are we letting Emma Grace Joan Maria come to Jesus? Let me speak of yesterday, of today, and of tomorrow.

I

Yesterday. By "yesterday" I mean July the second, 2001, at 3:15 in the afternoon. It was then that Cathleen and Frans took newborn Emma into their arms for the first time. But not just Cathleen and Frans. Jesus, with his Father and his Holy Spirit, was right there with you, welcoming Emma to his earth. Not that Emma wasn't alive for

months before; Cathleen can bear eloquent witness to Emma's alive-
ness during those unique months when Emma was growing within her.
Months when Jesus was delighting in every movement. But there is
something special about an infant opening her eyes to her father and
mother. Especially when there was Jesus murmuring to her, "Welcome
into my world, dear Emma, the world I walked for 33 years, the world
I made for such as you, the world I came to redeem." For Jesus, each
infant opening his or her eyes on this world is a debut, literally a coming-out party. A coming-out to Jesus. At that moment Jesus could have
said to her what God the Father said to Israel centuries ago:

> Thus says the Lord, who created you and formed you:
> "I have called you by name; you are mine....
> You are precious in my eyes and I love you."
>
> (Isa 43:1, 4)

II

Move now from yesterday to today. This day Emma, already
beloved of God, beloved of Jesus, comes to Jesus in an even deeper
relationship. But isn't it enough for Emma simply to be loved by
Jesus? It would be, except that a generous Jesus wants to do more. In
several remarkable sentences St. Paul told us, simply yet profoundly,
what that "more" is. First, he tells us that Emma is being "baptized
into Christ," will be "clothed with Christ," will "belong to Christ"
(Gal 3:27, 29). We get a better idea of what this means when a child
is not simply sprinkled with water but is totally immersed into the
water. The Greek for "baptize" means dip, wash, plunge, immerse,
drench. Then it is that we see what St. Paul meant when he wrote,
"We were buried with [Christ] through baptism into death, so that,
just as Christ was raised from the dead to the glory of the Father, we
too might live a new life" (Rom 6:4). Very simply, what we do in baptism represents symbolically the death, burial, and resurrection of
Christ. Emma descends into the baptismal font, is covered with its
waters, and emerges into a new life. In that act Emma goes through
the experience of dying to sin, being buried, and rising, as did Christ.
Baptism identifies Emma with the glorified Christ, enabling her "to
live actually with the life of Christ himself."[2] Could Emma speak for
herself, she would be entitled to say with St. Paul, "I live, no longer I,
but Christ lives in me" (Gal 2:20).

Wondrous indeed, and yet it is not all; there is still more to Emma's baptism. Again St. Paul puts it pithily: "In one [Holy] Spirit we were all baptized into one body" (1 Cor 12:13). What is that body? The community of Christians, the Church of Christ. It is not merely a society of human beings; it is what St. Paul calls the body of Christ. He compares it to the physical body each of us humans has. "As a [human] body is one though it has many parts, and all the parts of the body, though many, are one body, so also Christ. For in one Spirit we were all baptized into one body...and we were all given to drink of one Spirit. Now you are Christ's body, and individually parts of it" (1 Cor 12:12–13, 27).

Yes, of this body of Christ, this body of which Christ is the Head, this community of Christians, Emma will be as much a part as each of us who now surround her.

III

Which leads to...tomorrow. This incredible gift of God lays a heavy responsibility on so many of us. You see, we never asked Emma's permission, never asked if she wanted to be a member of this body, wanted to be a Catholic Christian, wanted to walk in the ways of Christ. Cathleen and Frans are convinced that membership in the Catholic Church—believing what we believe, worshiping as we worship, living the gospel of Christ, loving as Jesus loved—is easily the best birthday gift they can offer her, a gift that will draw her gratitude when she reaches what we optimistically call "the age of reason."

But will she be grateful? So much depends on what Emma sees, what she experiences, as she grows from infancy into childhood, into adolescence, into young womanhood. In a special way, what she sees, what she experiences, in the Christian community. If Emma is to grow into Christ, those who surround her in the States and in the Netherlands will be crucial.

In America will she experience in us men and women who love God with all their heart and soul, all their mind and might? Will she experience believers who have a deep devotion to the Christ who died and rose for them, have a personal relationship with him that is their strength when the dark clouds gather, their joy when "life is beautiful"—remember Roberto Benigni in the film *La vita è bella*? Will she find in Catholics who touch her life men and women who live what Jesus declared, "Unless you eat [my] flesh and drink [my] blood, you do not have life within you" (Jn 6:53)? Or will she be disillusioned because in this country of her baptism only three out of ten Catholics receive the Bread of Life as little as twice a month?

To what will Emma return in a Netherlands that is one-third Catholic? A community of grace that cherishes every man and woman as a child of God, as an image of God, loves not only friends but enemies? Will those who love her be open like Jesus to the stranger, open to the immigrant, open to those who are different—the way they look, talk, think, smell? Will she see in her Catholic community a special love for the children who, unlike Emma, grow up poor—a poverty that mangles the mind, batters the body, and shatters the spirit?

Not knowing the future, I have more hopes than answers. I do know that today a wondrous adventure opens up. For Emma of course; for Cathleen and Frans, for a smaller Frans and for Kate. But also for all of us who surround Emma today. It is our adventure to respond to the command of Jesus, "Let the little children come to me." Not simply to *let* Emma come to him, not hinder her, but more importantly to be her companions on the way. Distance may separate us physically from Emma time and again. But remember the miracle of our Christian community: From one end of the earth to the other, we are one body, because the same Holy Spirit lives in us and holds us together. The good we do in D.C., the Christlife we lead, the love we lavish, the prayers we send aloft, the memories we cherish—all these will touch the life of Emma in Amsterdam. This body of Christ—what early theologians called the "We" of Christians—is an internet Bill Gates might envy. In Christ Jesus we are incredibly one. One with one another, and all with Emma—today, tomorrow, and into eternity. We are blest.

Chapel of St. Ignatius
Holy Trinity Church
Washington, D.C.
August 5, 2001

26
'TIS GRACE HATH BROUGHT ME SAFE THUS FAR
Seven Decades a Jesuit

· Genesis 6:5-8; 7:1-5, 10
· Mark 8:14-21

These recent weeks I have been musing dreamlike over my seven Jesuit decades. Time and again I was struck by a line from that ever so popular hymn "Amazing Grace." Eight monosyllables: "'Tis grace hath brought me safe thus far." Grace. Not some vague abstraction. Rather, God's ceaseless presence in my life: inspiration for my mind, love for my heart, courage for my will. For all of this the proper response is the way the Preface of the Latin Mass begins: "Vere dignum et iustum est...." "It is utterly fitting and a matter of justice, O God, always and everywhere to give you thanks and praise." In thanksgiving and praise, let me touch on three areas where grace has enriched me beyond what I could have imagined. I mean, in St. Paul's words, "where sin increased, grace overflowed all the more" (Rom 5:20). The three areas overlap, but they can be distinguished by their special emphases. One man's experience, but I trust it may speak to all who hold Woodstock dear and its "way of proceeding."

I

My spiritual journey. Basically, Ignatian spirituality. Here, for lack of space, just three influences on my spirituality.

First, Ignatius' conviction that he had a direct encounter with God. Karl Rahner has put these words on the lips of Ignatius:

I was convinced that first, tentatively, during my illness at Loyola, and decisively, during my time as a hermit in Manresa I had a

133

direct encounter with God....I knew God, nameless and unfath-
omable, silent and yet near, bestowing Himself upon me in His
Trinity. I knew God beyond all concrete imaginings. I knew Him
clearly in such nearness and grace as is impossible to confound or
mistake....I experienced God Himself, not human words describ-
ing Him....This experience is grace indeed, and basically there is
no one to whom it is refused.[1]

Second, Ignatius' conviction in the closing contemplation of the
Spiritual Exercises, "How To Love Like God."[2] God, specifically Christ,
is present everywhere, working like a laborer for me in all creatures
on the face of the earth. In startlingly concrete language Ignatius compelled me to revamp a narrow theology which implies that, when the
risen Jesus rose to his Father, this earth somehow lost him, save for a
vague something called sanctifying grace and a mysterious presence
under the appearances of bread and wine. Ignatius forces us to sur-
render a spirituality that looks up to heaven for God's grace. No, it is
Christ who each moment gives being billions (yes, billions) of stars;
gives life to more than four thousand varieties of roses; gives intelligence to a student shaping an idea, a surgeon transplanting a human
heart, an architect sending a skyscraper soaring; gives love to a man
and a woman so as to live in steadfast oneness.

Third, a late realization: The *Spiritual Exercises* are not a head
trip. My whole being should react to reality. Not simply define sin: an
offense against God. Smell the stench of sin. Ignatius' high purpose is
to see us struck, surprised, stunned by what we experience, from the
ecstasy of Eden unspoiled, through sin's rape of the earth and earth's
dwellers, to the forsakenness of the crucified Christ and our rebirth
in his rising from the rock. I am convinced that Ignatius would res-
onate to Lonergan's insistence that without feelings

> our knowing and deciding would be paper thin. Because of our feel-
> ings, our desires and our fears, our hope or despair, our enthusiasm
> and indignation, our esteem and contempt, our trust and distrust,
> our love and hatred, our tenderness and wrath, our admiration, ven-
> eration, reverence, our dread, horror, terror, we are oriented mas-
> sively and dynamically in a world mediated by meaning.[3]

II

My intellectual journey. Basically, the world of ideas. I have
described myself as a three-headed creature—perhaps more accurately,
a Jesuit with three distinct but related graces. My Jesuit education

fashioned a scholastic, a traditional Thomist, essentially a knower. It was a way of thinking that, for all its disadvantages, at its best revealed to me two ways of desiring knowledge. One way is to desire it as a perfection of myself, and that is the way philosophers on the whole desire it. The other way is to desire knowledge not merely as a perfection of myself, but because through this knowledge what I love becomes present to me—God, people, things—and that is the way saints desire it.

My Scholasticism was broadened by contemporary philosophers. Teilhard, Kierkegaard, Marcel, Buber, Whitehead—all expanded the width of my human experience. Whitehead told me that nothing can be omitted: experience drunk and sober, sleeping and waking, self-conscious and self-forgetful, intellectual and physical, religious and skeptical, anxious and care-free, happy and grieving, in the light and in the dark, normal and abnormal.[4]

With all this, why did I go back 15 centuries and more to the Fathers of the Church? Study of the Fathers served to bridge the gap that had been created between theology and spirituality. Theology was a search not only for the truth of God, but also for God's very Self. And the search was carried on not by reason alone, not simply by that particular activity of intelligence whereby one can infer new propositions from previous propositions. The whole person comes into play, is put to work on God's revelation, because it is the whole person that must respond to the revealing God. Not only does knowledge have love for its finality. Love deepens knowledge; and at their most profound, knowledge and love become one, because knowledge is union.

And very importantly, I shared the early Christians' rich experience of the Church as community. In Karl Delehaye's striking phrase capturing the spirit of earlier theologians, "The Church is the great We of the faithful."[5] It is not something the Fathers simply believed; they preached it in season and out; they lived it.

III

My pastoral journey. Basically, the world of people. I had indeed been preaching since ordination in 1941. But five decades later, 1991, my whole background—classics and patristics, philosophy and theology, teaching and preaching, writing and editing—came to a focus: living and preaching the just word, proclaiming biblical justice. I mean fidelity to relationships that stem from our covenant with God cut in the blood of Christ. Love God above all human idols; love every human being, friend and enemy, as an image of God however flawed; touch all of God's material creation—earth and sky and sea—with reverence, as a gift of God, a reflection of divinity.

Why so crucial? Because that's where it's at, all of it: relationships. Whether in the Blessed Trinity or in our wounded humanity, with millions in Washington, D.C., or with a handful of "Survivors" on a forsaken isle, life = relationships. A shivering, exhilarating awakening: Not only survival but salvation takes place within a single all-embracing community. Here is the heart of homiletics; this above ethics and law is what I must preach. In the crucifixion of Christ and his resurrection, that single community, the kingdom of God, is once again possible: God, men and women, nature in intimate communion. God's dream, a single community, in which God and all creation live in a harmony that sin cannot substantially corrupt, an interdependence that is an essential facet of salvation's story.

Do you wonder that I am even more excited about preaching, about living, in 2001 than I was in 1941?

A final grace I pray, a grace still to come, this too borrowed from "Amazing Grace": "and grace will lead me home." Not too soon, I hope.

Woodstock Theological Center
Washington, D.C.
February 13, 2001[6]

27

DRY BONES, I WILL BREATHE
SPIRIT INTO YOU
Mass of the Holy Spirit

- Ezekiel 37:1–14
- Ephesians 3:14–21
- John 14:15–17, 25–29

How might a homilist pay fitting tribute to Lady Loyola on her 150th birthday?[1] A problem; for a homily is not a history, a liturgy is not a lecture—not a catalogue of names and dates. Not that names are unimportant. An Evergreen Memorial is for ever stamped with Ahern and Abromaitis, Beatty and Bunn, Canning and Cleophas, Doehler and Donohoe and Duffy-Boyle, Gorman and Grady, Kelly and Kirwin, Lacy and Early, McEneany and McNierney, Nachbarh and Novotny, Sellinger and Scheye, Varga and Wise and Wiesel...and hundreds more.

If not names to celebrate, then what? Six weeks ago I thought I had the answer. Loyola's glory lay in three areas: your world of learning, your world of loving, your world of living. And all three infused with the incomparable power of the Holy Spirit. Two weeks of research, of selection and organization, the anguish and thrill of creativity, and with a blissful sigh I laid my masterpiece to rest.

And then? Then dawned September the eleventh (911, the code call for crisis), the day that may have changed America, and Loyola, for ever. The morning when a hellish terror not only leveled the World Trade Center and part of the Pentagon, but also altered how we think, how we love, how we live. And so I shall retain what I call the "upside" of Loyola's 150 years—how the Holy Spirit has profoundly transformed and continues to transform your world of learning, of loving, of living; but at each point I shall issue a challenge that stems from September's day of infamy.

137

I

First, Loyola's world of learning. You see, the life of the mind is perilously impoverished if knowledge is sought simply for its own sake, if knowledge does not lead to wonder. Not only questioning: I wonder if Israel should reoccupy the West Bank. No, in the grasp of wonder, I marvel; I'm surprised, amazed, delighted, enraptured, in awe. It is Mary pregnant with Jesus by God's Spirit: "My soul finds delight in God my Savior" (Lk 1:47). It is Magdalene about to touch her risen Jesus: "Teacher!" (Jn 20:16). It is doubting Thomas discovering in the wounds of Jesus "My Lord and my God!" It is Michelangelo striking his sculptured Moses: "Speak!" It is Alexander Fleming fascinated by a radically new class of antibiotics revolutionizing medicine, America thrilling to the first footsteps on the moon. It is Mother Teresa cradling a retarded infant of God in the rubble of West Beirut, cradling a crippled old image of God in the excrement of Calcutta. It is the wonder of a first kiss.

Such should be, such has often been, Loyolans' reaction to the life of learning. Not a new methodology for biology or psychology; simply awe in the presence, in the experience, of the multifaceted, myriad miracle that is reality, all that is real. I mean amazement at what breadths and depths there are to being alive: awe over the architectural artistry of the ant and the grace of a loping panther; awe at the blinding speed of a white marlin and the majestic flight of the bald eagle; awe before the inspired imagery of Shakespeare, the fantastic measures of Tchaikovsky's *Nutcracker,* the transforming insight of Einstein—yes, awe at the beating heart of each unique fetus.

With such wonder Loyolans may hope to touch the pinnacle of knowledge. For, as philosopher Jacques Maritain discovered, the height of human knowing is not the concept, the idea; it is the experience—where you and I feel God; yes, *feel* God.

There is still more. In the Catholic vision, knowledge is not primarily a way to make a million. Why are you gifted with knowledge? To use it with the wisdom that stems from the Spirit, so as to continue what God has begun, become co-creators with God in shaping this world the way God wants it shaped. A fine theologian summed it up with humor: "We are not merely stewards working for an absent landlord. Our God is working...and inviting us to join in that work."[2] "Words," a pre-eminent Presbyterian preacher declares, "are our godly sharing in the world of creation, and the speaking and writing of words is at once the most human and the most holy of all the businesses we engage in....The ultimate purpose of language...is so that humanity may speak to God."[3]

Such is the role of the Holy Spirit in your life of learning. Not to infuse new information in you; not to pass examinations for you. The Spirit's role is Ignatius Loyola's high purpose in his *Spiritual Exercises:* to see you struck, surprised, stunned by the wonder of it all. Not stunned into silence. Moving from awe to action, moving together with God's rich grace to edge your acre of God's world a little closer to God's own dream for it.

All well and good; I do not retract it. But has September the eleventh affected your world of learning, of wonder, challenged it in any way, expanded it? Concretely, have you been forced to appreciate the ordinary in your experience? I mean the wonder in being able to breathe, to walk and talk, to smile and laugh, to pray and play, the wonder in just being alive? Have friendships become more precious, bitterness less common? Is your God more real to you, even if you must hurl at heaven an anguished cry, "Why, God, why?" In the midst of such widespread grief, the horrible hurt in so many hearts, where do you find your joy? In helping September's bereaved to bear their burdens, or escaping a nation's tears with such trash as Jerry Springer's "Wet, Wild, and Naked"? What have you learned—about yourself, about people, about God?

II

Turn now to Loyola's world of loving. For all the importance it attaches to learning, to the mind, Loyola is not simply a head trip. Loyola is at its best when understanding takes hold not only of discursive reasoning but of the whole person—heart and soul, emotions and passions, imagination. Simply, when knowledge is not divorced from love. Not love TV-style; not the one-night stand. No, the effort of love's imagination to find Christ *everywhere*, in every thing that exists, in each person alive.

Unreal? Not at all. What the Holy Spirit lets you discover is the ceaseless presence of Christ to your earth, the Incarnation not only in Nazareth two millennia ago but in your midst this very moment. The Holy Spirit compels us to revamp a narrow theology which implies that, when the risen Jesus rose to his Father, this earth somehow lost him, save for a vague reality called sanctifying grace and a mysterious presence under what looks like bread and wine. The Holy Spirit sparks a spirituality that does not simply look up to heaven for God's grace, for God's love. No, the Holy Spirit brings you back to Ignatius Loyola's *Spiritual Exercises* that close with a contemplation on "Learning To Love as God Loves." Ignatius asks us: "Consider how God [here actually Christ[4]] works and labors for me in all creatures upon the face of the earth, that is, he behaves as one who labors."[5] The image is bold when you think of the risen Jesus—working like a laborer. Bold indeed but justified if you take it out of heaven and bring it down to earth.

Stretch your Christian imagination. How is it that billions of stars (yes, billions) can fly the sky more speedily than rockets, the Rockies still rise in breathless splendor, oil gushes from the fields of Alaska? Because an all-powerful Christ gives them *being*. Not once for all; at each moment, at this moment. How is it that more than four thousand varieties of roses can grow and perfume our earth, giant redwoods stalk the California sky? Because an imaginative Christ gives them *life*. How is it that your Irish setter can smell the game beyond your ken, gulls scavenge your ocean, the shad ascend the waters? Because a sensitive Christ gives them *senses*. How is it that a student can shape an idea, a surgeon transplant a human heart, an architect send a skyscraper soaring, a man or woman live deliriously in death-less oneness with the other? Because a still human Christ gives them *intelligence and love*. How can you believe that the Son of God died a bloody death for you, confidently expect to live for ever, give yourself unreservedly to God and your sisters and brothers? Because a living Christ infuses *faith* in you, fills your flesh with *hope*, inflames your very bones with a *love* not of this world.

And all this Christ does not from some majestic throne in heaven. He reminds Ignatius of a skilled, enthusiastic worker—very much alive, always in touch with his creation, terribly in love with all he shapes. Alive at each moment of each creature's existence, at each moment of your existence. Indeed, this world is charged with the presence of Christ, with the labor of Christ.

To see a living Christ at work in every thing and every person is a gift of the Holy Spirit. It is a way of linking love to intelligence. For it helps you to see that "nothing human is merely human. And no enterprise, no matter how secular, is merely secular. We live in a universe of grace."[6] To grasp this is a giant step towards loving somewhat as God loves: loving not only God but all of God's creation. In the midst of so much that is evil or simply dull, my whole being captivated by a world wherein Christ is at work—Christ laboring for me.

Again, all well and good. But how has September the eleventh touched your world of loving? I realize that a natural reaction to terrorism is rage—anger, justified anger, over inhuman destruction beyond our experience or expectation. I am not a pacifist, but I must ask you to consider at a profound level whether the unrestrained cry for vengeance, the new desire for mandated assassination of enemy leaders, less concern over collateral killing of the innocent, even the presidential rallying cry "Dead or alive"—how does all this fit into Jesus' "You have heard that it was said, 'You shall love your neighbor and hate your enemy,' but I say to you, love your enemies, and pray for those who persecute you, that you may be children of your heavenly Father" (Mt 5:43–45)? If we are actually "at war," does this mean that for victory's sweet sake, for the life of our land, "anything goes"? If not, where do we draw the line, refuse on moral grounds to ape the enemy? Where does justice end and injustice begin?

Here, I submit, is a struggle for Loyola's soul. Here I struggle with you.

III

Third, turn to Loyola's world of living, the world of social realities. I mean the life that moves beyond your individual selves to community, people interacting, impacting one another, depending on one another. The Jesuit educational ideal is not the intellectual mole who lives almost entirely underground, surfaces occasionally for fresh air and a Big Mac, and burrows back down to the earthworms before people can distract him. A Jesuit college is where young men and women who may one day profoundly influence America's way of life touch, some for the first time, the ruptures that sever us from our earth, from our sisters and brothers, from our very selves. Not simply in an antiseptic classroom, important though the class is for understanding. Even more importantly, experience of *rupture*: experience not only of ecology but of an earth irreparably ravaged, not only abstract poverty but the bloated stomachs of the hungry, not only the words "child abuse" but the vacant stare of the child abused, not only a book on racism but the hopelessness or hatred in human hearts.

It is precisely here, and splendidly here, that God has breathed a new spirit into dry bones; here the Holy Spirit has given new life to contemporary Loyola. I marvel that six out of every ten students are living examples of Jesus' critical test for Christian living: "I was hungry and you gave me food, I was thirsty and you gave me drink, I was a stranger and you welcomed me, I was naked and you clothed me, I was ill and you cared for me, I was in prison and you visited me. [For] whatever you did to one of these least brothers [and sisters] of mine, you did for me" (Mt 25:35–36, 40).

Frankly, you amaze me and you delight me. Ten days with the poor in border communities of Mexico; weekends with the homeless in Baltimore; Christmas in April with the elderly poor and disabled homeowners; Spring Break Outreach to the disadvantaged throughout the eastern United States; living and working with the poor in El Salvador; your partnership in Beans and Bread; your involvement in environment, in healthcare, in AIDS. Perhaps most moving, your outreach to the most vulnerable in our land, our children. And, blessing of blessings, an administration enthusiastic, and faculty integrating community service into 49 courses.

You know, without your rich service, without you and such as you across the country, the Society of Jesus could not live the contemporary mission declared to us by the 1975 General Congregation of the Jesuits: "The mission of the Society of Jesus today is the service of faith, of which the promotion of justice is an absolute requirement."[7] Required not simply for ourselves....

> Especially we should help form our Christian students in such a way that, animated by a mature faith and personally devoted to Jesus Christ, they can find him in others and, having recognized him there, they will serve him in their neighbor. In this way we shall contribute to the formation of those who by a kind of multiplier-effect will share in the process of educating the world itself.[8]

Not another course, to be relegated to history after your last exam. If anything at Loyola is a preparation for life, here it is. For life is a matter of relationships—not only in the Blessed Trinity but in the whole of earthly living. Your holiness and mine, our reality as human beings, as men and women shaped in God's likeness, is measured by three relationships: to God, to people, to the earth. Love God above all else; love every other like another self; touch God's things, material creation, with reverence, as a gift of God.

Again, all well and good. And once again September the eleventh rears its ugly head. For what I have just described is justice, and what so many of you are living is God's justice. But God's justice, right relationships, confront you with terrorism. Not simply the terrorism from abroad; with that, the terrorism next door, the terrorism from within. I mean the terror the Children's Defense Fund described last year:

> All American children are at risk from the proliferation of guns which threaten all of us everywhere; from the pollution of our air,

water, earth, airwaves, and Internet with smut and toxic substances; from the breakdown of family not only from out-of-wedlock births but pervasive divorce and erosion of extended family
supports; from epidemic substance abuse and from domestic violence that know no race or income limits; and from the erosion
of civility evidenced by road rage, profane language, and the
coarse public discourse which pervades our culture.[9]

In your admirable efforts to establish right relationships—especially in
the context of September the eleventh—how do you touch, react to,
the terrorisms next door?

Good students and friends of Loyola: I am impressed, delighted,
in awe at all that the Holy Spirit has been shaping this century and a
half, and with uncommon urgency these past three decades. In brief,
what Ignatius yearned to see in you: contemplatives in action.
Contemplatives: women and men who day in and day out look long and
lovingly at the real,[10] are lost in wonder at so much that speaks to you
of God, deeply disturbed by man's inhumanity to man, our rape of
God's good earth. *In action:* impelled by the Spirit of God within you
to continue the mission Christ declared his own: "The Spirit of
the Lord is upon me; for the Lord has sent me to bring glad tidings
to the poor, proclaim liberty to captives and sight to the blind, let the
oppressed go free" (Lk 4:18).

Yes, impressed, delighted, in awe. Still, at this critical moment in
America's story, in Loyola's story, I must ask you to ponder deeply in
your hearts, to enter ongoing conversations, on the challenges today's
terrorism hurls at your learning, your loving, and your living. To that
end, I ask you to pray from your hearts, pray with me, a prayer that
often slips too glibly from our lips. "Come, Holy Spirit, fill the hearts
of your faithful—fill our hearts—and enkindle in them the fire of your
love. Send forth your Spirit, O Lord, and you will renew the face of
the earth."

Reitz Arena
Loyola College in Maryland
October 21, 2001

28
GOD'S JUSTICE AND AMERICA'S SIXTH CHILD
Children's Defense Fund
National Conference 2001

- Deuteronomy 15:7–11
- Mark 9:35–37; 10:13–15

I shall begin, and I shall end, with a man and a woman. In-between I shall speak of God's justice and America's sixth child.

I

I begin with a man and a woman. A Jew and a Jewess. A man from God's people rescued from the slavery of Egypt, and a woman who lived while Jesus was alive. The man is Joshua, the successor of Moses, chosen by God to lead God's people into the Promised Land. Listen to the Hebrew Testament as it describes how Joshua caused the walls of Jericho to fall:

> Now Jericho was in a state of siege because of the presence of the Israelites, so that no one left or entered....And [Joshua] ordered the people to proceed in a circle around the city, with the picked troops marching ahead of the ark of the Lord. At this order they proceeded with the seven priests who carried the ram's horns before the Lord blowing their horns, and the ark of the covenant of the Lord following them;...and for six days in all they did the same.
> On the seventh day, beginning at daybreak, they marched around the city seven times in the same manner....As the horns blew, the people began to shout. When they heard the signal horn, they raised a tremendous shout. The wall collapsed and the people stormed the city and took it.
> (Josh 6:1–20)

And I begin with a woman. She emerges from a parable on the lips of Jesus (Lk 18:1–8). The parable has two characters, two players: a judge and a widow. The judge is a symbol of power. And this particular judge is uncommonly powerful. Not only is he a judge in a patriarchal society, a culture in which males command and females obey. This judge is afraid of no one: neither God nor people. The widow is a symbol of powerlessness. With her husband dead, she has no male to defend her, protect her, plead her cause. Some unnamed male is taking advantage of her, she wants justice, and all she can do is appeal to a cold-hearted, unfeeling male judge. Not surprisingly, the judge refuses.

What does the widow do? Retire to her home, re-enter her kitchen, submit the way women were supposed to submit? Not this widow. She keeps after the judge, keeps pouncing away at him: "I want justice. I want justice. I want justice." So insistent is she that the judge finally gives in. Not because he is convinced by her arguments. Not in the slightest. What moves him is clear: "Because this widow keeps bothering me, I shall deliver a just decision for her, lest she finally come and strike me" (v. 5)–literally, "lest she come and give me a black eye."

II

Now let go of Joshua and the widow; we shall return to them. For the present, focus on the single word that consumed both of them: justice. But not just any justice; God's justice.

You see, when a fearless prophet named Micah declared to Israel, "What does the Lord require of you but to do justice?" (Mic 6:8), he was not imposing on God's people simply or primarily a good, earthly ethics: Give to every man, woman, and child what each person has a strict right to demand, because he or she is a human being, has rights which can be proven from philosophy or have been written into law. What, then, was the justice God wanted to "roll down like waters" (Amos 5:24)? In a single word, fidelity. Fidelity to what? To relationships, to responsibilities, that stemmed from their covenant with Yahweh. What relationships? To God, to people, to the earth. (1) Love God above all else, above every creaturely idol, above power and money and fame. (2) Love every human person like another self, another I, as if you were standing in his or her shoes, especially the paper-thin shoes of the downtrodden. (3) Touch the earth, things, all that is not God or the human person, with reverence, with respect, with awe, as a gift of God, a trace of divinity.

It is the Israelite tradition on justice that sparked the ministry of Jesus. He summed it up in the synagogue at Nazareth: "The Spirit of the Lord is upon me, because [the Lord] has anointed me to bring glad tidings to the poor. He has sent me to proclaim liberty to captives and recovery of sight to the blind, to let the oppressed go free" (Lk 4:18). That ministry he proclaimed pithily in a new commandment, a breath-taking command he laid on us not long before he was crucified for us: "Love one another as I have loved you" (Jn 15:12).

The point of all this? If biblical justice is fidelity to relationships, then biblical injustice is a refusal of relationships: a refusal to love God above all else, a refusal to love my sisters and brothers like other selves, a refusal to touch the things of God with reverence and respect. In focusing today on our children, two justice issues cry agonizingly for our attention: violence and health.

First, violence. We want safe communities for our children. In this "land of the free" the younger you are, the more vulnerable you are. In the richest country on earth roughly one out of every six children is growing up poor, hungry, ill-fed, ill-educated. Among industrialized countries the United States ranks 11th in the proportion of children in poverty, 16th in efforts to lift children out of poverty, 18th in the gap between rich and poor children, last in protecting our children against gun violence."[1] According to the Centers for Disease Control and Prevention, U.S. children under age 15 are 12 times more likely to die from gunfire, 16 times more likely to be murdered with a gun, 11 times more likely to commit suicide with a gun, and 9 times more likely to die in a firearm accident, than children in 25 other industrialized countries combined.[2] In this very capital of the United States, in one five-year period, 245 children died of gunshot wounds. Between 1979 and 1998, nearly 84,000 American children were killed by guns—more than all our battle fatalities in Vietnam.

If you still dream that violence to children is an occasional incident in a peaceful America, listen to our own Children's Defense Fund:

> Although a majority of child deaths are homicides, two out of every five young firearms deaths are the result of suicide or an accidental shooting. Thirty-three percent of young people killed by guns take their own lives....This is particularly notable when considering that federal law requires individuals to be at least 21 years old to purchase a handgun, and more than 20 states have some minimum age requirement for the possession of rifles and long guns....Unfortunately, in most cases...the weapons come from...[the home of the victim or the home of a friend or relative].[3]

Second, healthy communities for children? Take a striking statistic. Take, in alphabetical order, 23 industrialized countries: Australia, Austria, Belgium, Canada, the Czech Republic, Denmark, Finland, France, Germany, Hungary, Ireland, Italy, Japan, Luxembourg, the Netherlands, New Zealand, Norway, Poland, Portugal, Spain, Sweden, Switzerland, and the United Kingdom. What is striking about these countries? Each and every one of them has child safety-net policies. Specifically, (1) universal health insurance/healthcare; (2) paid maternal/parental leave at childbirth; (3) family allowance/child dependency grant. America's "sixth child" would fare better if he or she lived in any one of these countries. Why? Because the United States has none of these: no guaranteed health insurance, no income safety net, no parental leave with pay after childbirth.[4]

Safe and healthy communities for our children? In the richest country on the face of the earth? Our healthcare would be laughable, were it not so tragic, so literally deadly. Nearly 11 million of our children are uninsured. Eleven million images of God.

III

Now back to Joshua and the widow. But not quite the same two people. I mean today's Joshua circling today's Capitol, today's woman clamoring insistently for justice now. I mean your ceaseless cry to the politically powerful in the words you heard from the Hebrew Torah, from the book of Deuteronomy: "If one of your kinsmen in any community is in need in the land which the Lord, your God, is giving you, you shall not harden your heart nor close your hand to him in his need. Instead, you shall open your hand to him and freely lend him enough to meet his need. When you give to him, give freely and not with ill will; for the Lord, your God, will bless you for this in all your works and undertakings" (Deut 15:7-8, 10). I ask you to remind the politically powerful how Jesus rebuked his disciples when they tried to keep children from bothering him: "Let the children come to me; do not prevent them, for the kingdom of God belongs to such as these" (Mk 10:14).

Let me become chillingly concrete. When you are raising your voices for your children, you are not on your knees begging for charity. Your heads held high, you are demanding justice. What your children have a strict right to demand. "Give me justice! Give me justice! Give me justice!" Facing the White House, I dare to declare: "Mr. President, when our country has a surplus into the trillions, you do not seek first to divide the pie, so that everybody gets a piece, beginning with the richest. No, you look first to those who need it most. Not the children of the very affluent; the children of the lowly poor.

How do I know this? Because this is the justice God demanded of God's kings. Read, reflect on, Psalm 72—a prayer for God's king, for God's representative on earth:

> O God, give your judgment to the king,
>> your justice to the son of kings;
> That he may govern your people with justice,
>> your oppressed with right judgment,....
> That he may defend the oppressed among the people,
>> save the poor and crush the oppressor....
> He rescues the poor when they cry out,
>> the oppressed who have no one to help.
> He shows pity to the needy and the poor
>> and saves the lives of the poor.
> From extortion and violence he frees them,
>> for precious is their blood in his sight.
>
> (Ps 72:1–4, 12–14)

A priority for the poor, particularly for poor children, such is not political America today. Poverty is not a prime example of compassion linked to conservatism. Unhappily, our children do not enjoy a lobby comparable to those that spend billions for guns in the home, for tobacco smoke in the lungs, for salmonella in school hamburgers, for arsenic in our drinking water, for carbon dioxide in our air. Three weeks ago I was gifted with a brand new knee courtesy of Medicare. Now I can walk the ways of Washington weeping for the uninsured: the crippled kid too poor for a brace, the youngsters swallowing lead poisoning in their rundown shacks, the baby born with HIV.

And still, my friends, you are far from powerless. I see in each of you, and in millions more like you across our country, a rebirth of Joshua and of the Gospel widow. In my dream I see new Joshuas gathering together not soldiers in arms but infants in their carriages, adolescents on their crutches, teenagers in their ragged Reeboks, and marching in terrifying thousands around your Capitol seven times as Andy Young did in the 1960s, clamoring with all the passion of the widow, "Justice! Give us justice! Justice for these children of God! Don't you hear the children crying?"

And when you can no longer walk, talk! Your voices are powerful: e-mail and air mail; phone and FedEx. Teach your little ones to scrawl one word, seven forceful letters: j-u-s-t-i-c-e. Send it to your servants in Senate and House, in the very White House itself. They will listen, if there are enough of you—if not out of compassion, then from self-preservation.

Yours too is the power of prayer—prayer that not only rises like incense to heaven, but can penetrate the smoke-filled cloakrooms of Congress. Believe it! A mass of committed Christians and Jews, yes Hindus and Buddhists, can topple the walls of injustice, can free our sixth child from an oppressive slavery. Not by our naked humanity; in the power of a God for whom nothing, absolutely nothing, is impossible. All God asks is that we love—love one another as God loves us—even unto crucifixion.

To sum up, I make bold to ask you three questions; I would appreciate your response, loud and clear. (1) Are you convinced that in our country every sixth child is suffering serious injustice? (2) Do you believe that, in the power of God, you and your sisters and brothers can correct, even destroy, such injustice? (3) Are you willing, are you resolved, like the widow in the Gospel, to keep crying for children's justice, to keep struggling for children's justice, even if necessary to suffer crucifixion for children's justice?

Go forth, then, and in the power of God see to it that no child is left behind!

Washington Hilton and Towers
Washington, D.C.
April 19, 2001

29
TERROR NEXT DOOR
A Homily on Extreme Fear in Our Midst

- 1 Corinthians 1:26–31
- Mark 13:12

Terror, *Webster's Unabridged* informed me four decades ago, is "a state or instance of extreme fear, fear that agitates body and mind." Being normally inquisitive, I recently made use of the Internet search engine Google which found 616,000 entries for terrorism. Being reasonably intelligent, I am aware of terror on national and international levels: bombing of the federal building in Oklahoma City, bombing of the American embassies in Nairobi and Dar es Salaam; radical leftist organizations like the Japanese Red Army, Germany's Red Army Faction, Italy's Red Brigades; ethno-nationalist terrorist movements like the Abu Nidal organization, the IRA, the Basque separatist group ETA; the Holocaust; the World Trade Center; the Pentagon; and Flight 93. I am aware that some such groups are motivated by a religious imperative, even appeal to their scriptures to justify their actions—what has been aptly called "holy terror."

As a tiny contribution to an extensive issue, I dare to suggest that terrorism, like charity, may well begin at home. I shall go on to suggest, as a Catholic Christian, what our Scriptures and our theologies have to say on this matter. I shall conclude with some personal observations and recommendations.

I

Without neglecting terror abroad, I shall stress terror at home. Not home as our national community as a whole. I mean home as the family, the neighbor next door, a judge, gun violence, uncaring politicians, the local constabulary, immigrants, our prison situation, death row, child sexual abuse—whatever individual, group, or situation incites fear by its action or its very presence—fear that agitates body and/or mind.

Family. You know, to be young is to be confused and confusing. In the moving screenplay *The Forty Blows,* François Truffaut showed us 13-year-old Antoine Doinel at once terrified and rather proud of a mother who conceived him out of wedlock, wanted to abort him, doesn't really like him very much, is always bawling him out "for nothing...for little things." His father is "all right, I guess. But he's a bit of a coward because he knows my mother's unfaithful, but he says nothing so that there won't be any fights at home." Antoine works out of one troublesome situation only to fall into another, is constantly ridden by anxiety. He runs away because he cannot face the anger at home, is sent to a center for juvenile delinquents because his father can no longer endure him. "Do whatever you want with [Antoine]; take him away, put him in the country somewhere. We can't figure him out. He needs some real punishment."[1] Terrorism indeed.

Our neighbors. Example? "The Elephant Man" of stage and screen. When a compassionate surgeon, Frederick Treves, first saw him, John Merrick was 20. He was terribly misshapen, "the most disgusting specimen of humanity" Treves had ever seen. Giant nodes extended his head like masses of dough; its circumference was no less than his waist. Another mass of bone protruded like a pink stump from his mouth, making of it only a slobbering aperture, turning speech into torture. From his back hung sack-like masses of flesh covered by a kind of loathsome cauliflower skin; from his chest, a bag of flesh "like a dewlap suspended from the neck of a lizard." A hip disease had left him permanently lame, unable to walk without a stick.

When Treves came upon him, Merrick was a circus freak, exploited for his ability to shock, to make people throw up; he had no other way to live. "He was shunned like a leper," Treves recalled, "housed like a wild beast, and got his only view of the world from a peephole in a showman's cart." Terrorism indeed.

Treves housed Merrick in the London Hospital, with his own bed-sitting room and a bathroom. Merrick, he discovered, was highly intelligent, acutely sensitive, romantically imaginative. The cruelty of his fellows had not embittered him. The transformation began when a young widow entered his room, wished him good morning, and shook his hand. Merrick sobbed uncontrollably; apart from his mother, she was the first woman who had ever smiled at him, ever touched his hand. From then on he lost his shyness, loved to see his door open and the world flock to him, from actress Madge Kendal to the

Princess of Wales (the future Queen Alexandra). He died at 28, having told Treves, "I am happy every hour of the day."[2]

More frightening still "next door." A friend in Reading, Pennsylvania, tells me a nauseating incident in that city. A man took from school the eight-year-old child of his former girl friend; took her by telling the teacher that the mother had forgotten that the child had a doctor's appointment. He called the mother, told her he had the child, that she could have the child back if she (the mother) would only talk to him. She agreed; but he fled. More than a week later the child was found in a shallow grave; she had been suffocated and/or drowned with a chain around her neck. Terror indeed.

Legal terror. In Texas it is not uncommon for a defendant to remain in jail for months before ever seeing a lawyer. "In recent years the Texas Court of Criminal Appeals has upheld death sentences in at least three cases in which the defense lawyers slept during trial. The trial judge in one case reasoned though the Constitution requires that a defendant be represented by a lawyer, it 'doesn't say the lawyer has to be awake.'"[3] Terror indeed.

Gun violence. In my own backyard, Washington, D.C., in a single five-year period, 224 children were killed by gunfire. Some were deliberate targets, others just happened to be there, at least one lay in a cradle. In consequence, children in our nation's capital were planning their own funerals: how they wanted to look, how be dressed, where be waked. They simply did not believe they would be around very long. Little wonder that our children have been planning for the worst, as if their own murders are inevitable, as if their own dreams will surely be just as cruelly cut short.[4] Terror indeed. And it is but one aspect of child terror.

> *All American children are at risk* from the proliferation of guns which threaten all of us everywhere; from the pollution of our air, water, earth, airwaves, and Internet with smut and toxic substances; from the breakdown of family not only from out-of-wedlock births but pervasive divorce and erosion of extended family supports; from epidemic substance abuse and from domestic violence that know no race or income limits; and from the erosion of civility evidenced by road rage, profane language, and the coarse public discourse which pervades our culture.[5]

Terror indeed.

Uncaring politicians. Among industrialized countries, the United States ranks first in military technology, first in military exports, first in Gross Domestic Product, first in the number of millionaires and billionaires, first in defense expenditures, but 14th in the proportion of children in poverty, 16th in efforts to lift children out of poverty, 18th in the gap between rich and poor children, 22nd in infant mortality, last in protecting our children against gun violence.[6] Terror indeed.

The local constabulary. From Los Angeles to New York City, blacks and Hispanics walk in fear of the police who are sworn to protect them. An unarmed African American is savagely beaten by police arresting him; unarmed Amadou Diallo is shot 41 times by police who think he is going to shoot them.[7] Terror indeed.

Immigrants. A century ago we Americans were proud to proclaim the "world-wide welcome" inscribed on a tablet in the pedestal of the Statue of Liberty:

> Give me your tired, your poor,
> Your huddled masses yearning to breathe free,
> The wretched refuse of your teeming shore.
> Send these, the homeless, tempest-tost to me,
> I lift my lamp beside the golden door.

As I write (December 2000), not only are Americans resisting immigration for economic reasons; within U.S. immigration policy, detention of immigrants reveals horror stories. In 1999 there were 200,000 immigrants in varying lengths of detention; by the end of 2001, it is estimated, there will be over 302,000. For lack of bed space in facilities owned and operated by the U.S. Immigration and Naturalization Service, 60 percent of detainees are currently housed in city and county jails. Once there, they are routinely housed with inmates held on criminal charges. In remote areas contact with attorneys is difficult, language always a problem. In San Pedro, California, a husband and wife were held in separate units for 16 months, never allowed to visit each other or write directly; while in custody, they lost their home; their three children, the oldest 15, were left to fend for themselves in Los Angeles.

Listen to a Jesuit friend of mind, Thomas L. Sheridan, retired professor of theology, who helps the Jesuit Refugee Service at a detainee center in Elizabeth, New Jersey: "There are no windows; [immigrants] never breathe fresh air or see the light of day except through one skylight. One woman has been there for almost three years. It would break your heart to see them. They have such a lost and hopeless look on their faces." Terror indeed.

Our prison situation. Two decades ago, Fr. Michael Bryant started as the District of Columbia jail's full-time minister. At that time he believed that the U.S. justice system was fair, impartial, and balanced. After listening to thousands of men and women in that jail, he now recognizes that "our system of criminal justice is not fair, is not impartial, and is not balanced."[8] Blacks make up only 13% of our national population, Hispanics 9 or 10%; yet 48% in prison are black, 18% Hispanic. What problems do they have in common with white inmates? They are poor, addicted, undereducated, and jobless. Our sentencing is more and more punitive: no more parole on the federal level, "three strikes and you're out" in California, minimum sentencing legislation. Two thirds return to prison. Terror indeed.

Death row. Few of the informed deny that innocent persons have been executed; the only real question is how many. As far back as 1987 a study in the *Stanford Law Review* identified 350 cases in the 20th century in which innocent people were wrongly convicted of crimes for which they could have received the death penalty. Of that number perhaps as many as 23 were executed; New York led the list with eight.[9] Time and again I imagine the horror, the terror on the faces of those persons moments before a lethal injection. Terror indeed.

Child sexual abuse. I was startled to learn that in the United States one of every four girls and one of every six boys are sexually abused before the age of eighteen. I was horrified to learn that "More cases of child abuse are never reported than are ever tried in court."[10] Terror indeed.

II

Given these examples of terror, how ought we react precisely as Christians? As a Catholic Christian and theologian, with a profound involvement in the Hebrew Testament and the New Testament, I find it important but inadequate simply to condemn all such terror as unjust on ethical and legal grounds. Important because without the efforts of ethical and legal justice to treat people as they deserve, life on earth would turn into a jungle, where might makes right, and the prize goes to the swift, the smart, and the strong. Inadequate because neither philosophy nor the law, neither human reason nor the U.S. Supreme Court, can command a four-letter word that raises us above the beast. I mean...love. No one can lay this burden on humans save the God who shaped us, the God whose very name is Justice, the God who gives a more profound meaning to justice than all our earth-bound excogitations could ever conceive. This leads me to the heart of my message: biblical justice.

A splendid Scripture scholar has left us a fine working definition of biblical justice: "fidelity to the demands of a relationship." Behind this, he pointed out, lay a whole way of life.

> In contrast to modern individualism the Israelite is in a world where "to live" is to be united with others in a social context either by bonds of family or by covenant relationships. This web of relationships—king with people, judge with complainants, family with tribe and kinfolk, the community with the resident alien and [with the] suffering in their midst and all with the covenant God—constitutes the world in which life is played out.[11]

The operative word here is "relationships." All life, even and primarily the life of the triune God, is summed up in relationships. For us on earth, the relationships are basically three: to God, to people, to the earth. Love God above all else; love every human person as a child of God, as an image of God, as a brother or sister, like another self; touch "things," earth and sea and sky, whatever is not human, with reverence, with respect, as a gift of God.

My point? Terrorism is a reaction to relationships. Perceived relationships. Often, indeed, a skewed, distorted perception. Examples? When the leadership in Iran perceives the United States as Satan, the Evil One. When a fair number of Protestants used to see in Revelation's "Babylon the Great, the mother of harlots and of the abominations of the earth" (Rev 17:5) the pope or the Roman Catholic Church as a whole. When a serial killer strangles a number of prostitutes because they befoul his perception of woman. When the Nazis exterminated six million Jews as inferior humans, a peril to Aryan purity. When the U.S. Supreme Court declared that slaves were property.

Here indeed is terrorism; for a perverted perception of proper relationships leads to injustice in action: unnumbered millions killed, wounded, or missing in World War II; the mistrust, suspicion, even hatred generated by centuries of religious misunderstanding and intolerance; totalitarianism and concentration camps.

On the other hand, even an accurate perception of right relationships raises its own problems, can lead to terror. To make relationships right, individuals, groups, and nations have risen up in protest, occasionally with violence. Assume, for the sake of argument, that a just war is possible—the American Revolution, World War II against Germany and Japan. How can you kill your enemy and still claim to love him? How can you bomb Dresden mercilessly, drop an atom bomb on Hiroshima that left 202,000 dead of radiation,[12] and claim a right relationship with Germans and Japanese? And for all our good intentions in Vietnam, we could not prevent a massacre of innocent civilians at My Lai. My Lai itself is indefensible. And yet, ironically, to destroy terrorism, must we not at times terrorize? To restore right relationships, must we not at times redefine the love that lies at the basis of biblical justice?

On an individual level, justified anger can lead to undesirable relationships. Take the reaction to poverty-stricken Limerick expressed in a memoir by Malachy McCourt: "I was a smiley little fella with a raging heart and murderous instincts. One day I would show THEM—yes, you rotten f-ing arsehole counter-jumping stuck-up whore's-melts nose-holding tuppence-ha'penny-looking-down-on-tuppence snobs. I'll go back to America where I was born and I'll fart in yer faces. And I did."[13]

Historically, right relationships often take time to develop. In America it remained for the Quakers of the 17th century to speak out against slavery as a moral wrong, an injustice, a serious flaw in relationships. It took radical abolitionists like John Brown to invade the South to free the slaves. Not until 1865, when the 13th Amendment to the Constitution was adopted, were all slaves freed. Even then, it took the Supreme Court to the middle of the 20th century to impose what the Sermon on the Mount had been unable to achieve: no racial discrimination in housing, education, public accommodations, and employment. The turning point: when a black woman, Rosa Parks, refused to give up her bus seat to a white passenger. The cutting edge: when Martin Luther King Jr. led hundreds of thousands of blacks and whites on a March on Washington, his dream of the day when all persons would be judged not by their color but by their character. And still we struggle.

The words "my sisters and my brothers" leap facilely to our lips. The reality is all too frequently written in blood. Not unexpectedly, Jesus was right on target in a somewhat different context: "Brother will hand over brother to death..." (Mk 13:12).

III

Finally, what of us, privileged to proclaim God's justice from the pulpit? It is not our task to solve complex issues in a short sermon. It is our task to help form consciences, to lay out issues with clarity, to suggest or even at times declare where the gospel applies. For we cannot be content with glittering generalities, abstract principles. We need the courage for concrete directives, not only on issues of faith but also with regard to sociopolitical action by Christians in the world. What can we do, what can we say, to help establish right relationships in situations that make for terror? Several examples.

Start with one haunting symbol of the gulf that severs the haves and the have-nots, the gulf that provokes the extreme fear we call terror, the gulf that is a seedbed of violence and crime. I mean hunger. The president of Bread for the World has put the situation bluntly:

> The world has already made progress against hunger. There are fewer undernourished people in the developing world today than there were 25 years ago, despite the population explosion. But more than 800 million people around the world still suffer from chronic hunger, and hunger has increased in Africa. And among the industrialized countries, the United States is the only nation that still puts up with widespread hunger: 31 million people in the United States still struggle to put food on the table.[14]

What can we do? We don't need new programs. Since 1996, millions have lost government assistance, especially food stamps. "If just the Food Stamp Program were as strong now as it was in 1996, in today's economy we'd have half as many hungry people as we do."[15] Our task? To pressure government to provide greater access to nutritional food through domestic programs that already exist. Such pressure is effective. Churches in Birmingham, Alabama, worked so effectively on their representative in Congress, Spencer Bachus, that during a hearing of the House Banking Committee on debt relief this Southern Baptist held up an address by John Paul II and said, "I've never read much by Catholics before, but I don't know how any Christian could read this and not think we ought to write off these debts. If we don't reduce this debt, people in poor countries are going to be suffering for the rest of their lives. And I think we are going to be suffering a lot longer than that."[16]

This, we must tell our people, is not simply human compassion, admirable as such compassion is. This is biblical justice, the justice of God, that Jesus will stress at the Last Judgment with his shattering declaration to those on his left, "*I* was hungry and you gave *me* no food." For "what you did not do for one of these least ones, you did not do for me" (Mt 25:42a, 45). Inadequate we indeed are as individuals to feed a hungry country; but as the Body of Christ, millions upon millions of committed Christians graced with the good things of God's earth, we can feed every hungry Christ from Maine to California. That is why I dare say to all Christians what a sympathetic Protestant said to a Roman Catholic, "If you could get your act together, you'd be dangerous."

Take another example that makes for extreme fear, for terror: our penal system. We can add our voices to those that want to replace the retributive model of justice, basically a model that punishes, with the restorative, based on biblical justice, with a view to healing. The restorative model, which brings the offender and the victim together with mediators and representatives of the court, has begun to show promise in New Zealand, was used in South Africa by the Truth and Reconciliation Commission, and can point to early stages in about 600 U.S. jurisdictions. Relationships are re-established, sorrow is expressed, even forgiveness is possible.[17]

And so it is with each instance, each situation, of terror. Our task as preachers of biblical justice? Raise awareness. Persuade our people to live four precepts fashioned by theologian Bernard Lonergan: (1) *Be attentive.* Know the data, the facts. It is Jesus' insistence, "Take care what you hear" (Mk 4:24). (2) *Be intelligent.* Rid yourself of prejudices, of myths, of "This is what everybody says." (3) *Be reasonable.* Marshal the evidence, examine the opinions, judge with wisdom. Here community co-operation must replace the Lone Ranger. (4) *Be responsible.* Do something; act on the basis of prudent judgments and genuine values.[18]

How do Christian men and women of biblical justice get that way? In close union with Christ our Lord. How shall we change our world, its rugged individualism, its excessive consumerism, its growing violence, its deep-rooted racism—yes, the terrorism in our culture? *We* shall not do it; *God* will do it, or it will not happen. And still, God will normally do it *through us.* Through men and women whose dynamism for change is not their own naked humanity but the power of God. God needs us, but only because God wants to need us, wants humanity to co-operate with divinity in the love that saves a child, a family, a community, the world God's Son loved unto crucifixion. But remember, even our co-operation is grace, is a gift. If you are embarrassingly aware of your very human weakness, listen to St. Paul as he addresses not only the Christians of Corinth but today's Christians as well (1 Cor 1:26–31):

> Consider your own calling, brothers and sisters. Not many of you were wise by human standards, not many were powerful, not many were of noble birth. Rather, God chose the foolish of the world to shame the wise, and God chose the weak of the world to shame the strong, and God chose the lowly and despised of the world, those who count for nothing, to reduce to nothing those who are something, so that no human being might boast before

God. It is due to Him that you are in Christ Jesus, who became for us wisdom from God, as well as righteousness, sanctification, and redemption, so that, as it is written, "Whoever boasts, should boast in the Lord" (*see* Jer 9:23).

And you might add to God's call Paul's awareness of a gift that accompanies each call: "I have the strength for everything through Him who empowers me" (Phil 4:13).[19]

30
DON'T BE AFRAID TO BE AFRAID
A Pentecost for Priests

- Acts 2:41
- John 20:19–23

As you go forth from this retreat/workshop, I would ask you to meditate with me on three aspects of your experience here. Begin with the past, with remembrance. Move on to the future, with apprehension. Close with the present, a Christian answer to apprehension.

I

Begin with remembrance.[1] Begin with a remarkable sentence in the Acts of the Apostles. Luke is speaking of the original Christian community, summarizing what constituted it a community. Four realities. "They devoted themselves to the teaching of the apostles and to the communal life, to the breaking of the bread and to the prayers" (Acts 2:42).

Similarly for you. Five days ago you came together from different areas of the archdiocese and formed a small community. How? (1) Like the earliest Christian community, you listened together to the teaching of the apostles, to the Word of God. Specifically, you absorbed God's justice from the Hebrew Testament and from the lips of *ho dikaios*, "the Just One," Jesus the Christ. Briefly, right relationships: to God, to people, to the earth. (2) Like the earliest Christians, you lived a communal life: talked and listened to one another, ate and drank together, smiled and laughed, enjoyed old friends and rejoiced in new friends. (3) Like the Christians of old, you broke together the Bread of Life and consumed the cup of salvation, newly aware that the most powerful source your people have for living the just word is the Eucharist. For the Eucharist is the very presence of the Just One in the people gathered,

160

in the Word proclaimed, in the Body and Blood received. (4) You shared in "the prayers": the Prayer of the Church, the meditations, the scrutiny, and the reconciliation.

Such has been your exceptional experience of community—a microcosm of God's dream for a single family on earth. A fresh realization that salvation, your salvation and your people's, is achieved within a single triadic community: a triune God, humans of every color and kind, and material creation. Do I love God above all created idols? Do I love every human person, friend or enemy, as Jesus loved and still loves me? Do I touch each "thing"—from a blade of grass to nuclear power—with reverence, with respect, as a gift of God?

II

So much for remembrance; turn now to the future. For all your joy in this community experience, it is difficult to face the future without a feeling of fear, without some apprehension. Why? If only because you are leaving a well-knit community to live within communities that not only are multiethnic but harbor many of the injustices that have decorated the walls of your conference room this week. You are increasingly fewer, and the issues, the needs, the wrongs are so many and so fearful.

Precisely here, however, as with the original apostles, Jesus appears with a single monosyllable: "Peace" (Jn 20:19, 21). In our language, "Don't be afraid." Perhaps more realistically, "Don't be afraid to be afraid." Through ordination you have been commissioned to live out Jesus' own program proclaimed in the Nazareth synagogue:

> The Spirit of the Lord is upon me,
>   for [the Lord] has anointed me
>   to bring glad tidings to the poor.
> He has sent me to proclaim liberty to captives
>   and recovery of sight to the blind,
>   to let the oppressed go free.
>
> (Lk 4:18)

The natural reaction is to be stunned, disturbed, disheartened at the magnitude of the task. The antidote? "As the Father has sent me, so I send you" (Jn 20:21). Powerful words, encouraging words. As God the Father sent his only Son, just so God's Son sends you.

III

Sent by Jesus. That sending should calm your fears, for the sending involves a rich promise. As with the apostles, so with you. Jesus has breathed into you his Holy Spirit (Jn 20:22). Two days ago Raymond Kemp related to you how in the Holy Land Scripture scholar Carroll Stuhlmueller warned a group of pilgrim priests, "Don't underestimate the power of Satan." I agree. I would simply add a complementary injunction, "Don't underestimate the power of the Holy Spirit."

This morning you are sent forth once again to move mountains. I mean, to move minds, to change hearts, to fashion communities of peace, of justice, of love. But not by your own native powers: a high IQ, a remarkable rhetoric, a pleasing personality. That way lies an ancient, still vigorous heresy called Pelagianism. No, only by the power of the Holy Spirit lodged within you. Oh yes, your efforts—your blood and sweat and tears—are important, because Christ has chosen to act through you. But the grace, the conversion, the change in mind and heart, all of that comes from above, from a Christ who has promised to remain with us. Not only under the appearances of bread and wine, but in his very own "Spirit of truth, whom the world cannot accept, because it neither sees nor knows Him; but you know Him, because He remains with you and is in you" (Jn 14:17).

Good brothers, don't underestimate the power of the Spirit. And don't underestimate the power of the cross. I mean what St. Paul meant: "Christ crucified, a stumbling block to Jews and foolishness to Greeks, but to those who are called...Christ the power of God and the wisdom of God" (1 Cor 1:23-24).

Christ's cross, and yours as well. Your very limitations, your apparent failures, let Christ use them. Calvary looked for all the world, *to* all the world, like an abysmal failure. Yet it is the cross that redeems the world. "By your holy cross you have redeemed the world." Do you really believe that? Then don't simply preach it; live it!

So then, good brothers in the priesthood of Christ, go forth with confidence, trusting not in yourselves but in the power of the Spirit and in the power of the cross.

Sacred Heart Jesuit Retreat House
Sedalia, Colorado
October 4, 2002

31
ALIVE IN CHRIST, ALIVE WITH US
Memorial Mass for Joseph John Burghardt

- Acts 2:14, 22–33
- 1 Peter 1:17–21
- Luke 24:13–35

What brings us here today? Yesterday's memories...today's realities...tomorrow's hopes.

I

Yesterday's memories. A man, a son, a husband, a father, a cousin. A man. As pointed out by his son Christopher at his father's funeral, Joe is a man remembered as proprietor and sole employee of "Joe's Taxi," known in northern Jersey for delivering Benedictine nuns and *New York Times* right on schedule, a man remembered for being astute enough to marry a woman who would cater to his gourmet taste buds, a man whose dexterity on a piano's keyboard was as precise as his memory of the statistics of both Big East basketball and his beloved Red Sox, a man as committed to his duty in a voting booth as in a church pew, a man who above all loved his family.

A son. Joe, the son of a German man and a Polish woman who not only set up a home but also generated an ethic—a way of looking at life—that has strengthened each new generation of this family. This ethic focused on God amid much hard work and good humor.

A husband. I believe we can say Joe lived what St. Paul demanded of Christians in Ephesus: "Husbands, love your wives, even as Christ loved the Church" (Eph 5:25). To outsiders it appeared that Joe and Celeste strove for "roots and wings" not only for their children but also for each other. To insiders the breadth of respect that these two have had and continue to have for each other is remarkable in longevity and rich in depth.

A father. Jennifer, Christopher, Danielle—all living witnesses to Joe's paternal care that showed itself with the Burghardt emphasis on God and education. God at the heart of the family, education the tool to enable each child to create a good, self-sufficient life but all the while not losing sight of the needs of others. Joe exemplified his fatherhood not only by what he said but by how he lived. Again and again and again he showed his care and concern for others.

A cousin. The Burghardt history of leaving Germany in the 1780s and relocating to Padew, a village in Austria-Hungary where curiously the family maintained many of its German roots while assimilating much of the Polish church heritage and culture surrounding them, made the Burghardts marvelously multicultural. Some married Polish partners and the melting pot soon was filled with new foods. A Burghardt *pierogi*–what a curious notion! More than a century after Jacob, the first Burghardt to trek with his tribe to Padew, many family members set up new life in the United States. None of us knows much about the generation before the one that ventured to Ellis Island and Boston, but cousins gathering from time to time have woven the Burghardts together as a thread connecting the extended family.

II

Today's realities. No matter our Christian belief in resurrection, there are today's cruel realities. When Celeste wakes up, Joe is not beside her in bed. When Danielle or Jennifer wants fatherly advice, neither can simply pick up the phone and ask Joe for his insights on the problem of the day. Christopher has become the new patriarch of the family at a much younger age than he would have liked. There are grandchildren yet to be born who will never hear Joe's laughter or count on his steadfast support. All have suffered a loss for which there is no substitution.

Each of you knows what Joe brought into your life and now there is so much that, at least in a physically recognizable form, Joe will *not* be there for—the birth of Danielle and Jonas' first baby, the graduations of Christopher and Michelle's children, the first prom dates of Jennifer and Rick's youngsters. It is clear that the loss of Joe necessarily is the loss of dreams that included him. Shattered dreams are among life's most painful agonies.

One of the fondest hopes of two people in love is growing old together. Not only has that peaceful dream been torn from you, Celeste, but a kind of nightmare has been thrust on you. You are now both mother and father, both grandmother and grandfather, all this without Joe at your side. These are exhausting thoughts.

III

Such are some of today's realities. So where are our hopes? This is where our faith comes to the fore. Joe's body has been taken from us; it is dead. True indeed and tragic—but Joe's soul, which gave life to his body, is alive. His soul did not die, will not die, cannot die. *Joe is alive!*

All of us pray to saints: to St. Anthony to find something we have lost or misplaced, to St. Jude for hopeless cases, to St. Teresa of Avila for wisdom. Why? Because they are *alive.*

Joseph John Burghardt is as alive as Anthony, as alive as Jude, and as alive as Teresa. On Christmas Eve, Roman Catholics in Eastern Europe set a place at table for those in the family who have died. This sign evidences the belief, a certainty if you will, that these persons are still very much alive and involved with their family not only at Christmas but every day.

As Catholics we should be convinced Joe is in contact with all the Burghardts who have gone before us: not only with his father John but with those who had the courage to move across an ocean on arduous voyages, embracing much of the same determination of the Burghardts who earlier left their legacy in Germany to settle in Austria-Hungary. And let's not forget the women who had to be as strong as their husbands to build solid families during times of emigration, through times of epidemics, amid times of poverty and prosperity. Joe is alive, not in isolation in outer space but in contact with all these Burghardts. Nor should we be surprised when we sense that Joe has a pretty good idea of what is going on in Sparta, in Arlington, in Mount Laurel, and in Hingham.

Where are our hopes in all this? Remember what genuine hope is. It is not a feeling but a sincere confidence that something *will* take place. For instance, that after today's tears will come tomorrow when we will reshape our dreams and do so with the confidence that Joe, who is alive, *is* with us today and will be with us in years to come. That grandchildren who will never meet him on earth will hear stories of his goodness and gain strength from that heritage. That we will live in the anticipation of bodily resurrection and look forward to a glorious Burghardt reunion.[1]

Sparta, New Jersey
April 10, 2005

NOTES

Homily 1

1. *The Catholic Study Bible,* ed. Donald Senior et al. (New York: Oxford University Press, 1990) 886, note on Isa 7:14.
2. This homily was delivered to the Jesuit community of St. Aloysius Gonzaga, Washington, D.C., at one of its regular liturgy evenings.

Homily 2

1. For details see *The Spiritual Exercises of Saint Ignatius Loyola: A Translation and Commentary,* ed. George E. Ganss, S.J. (St. Louis: The Institute of Jesuit Sources, 1992), nos. 101–107, pp. 56–57.
2. For details see ibid., nos. 235–37, p. 95.
3. This homily was delivered at a home Mass for members of the extended Flanigan family.

Homily 3

1. The tradition goes back to the second-century apocryphal *Protoevangelium of James* 18.1; to Justin Martyr's *Dialogue with Trypho* 78; and to Origen's *Against Celsus* 1.51.
2. The Greek word here translated "lodge" is *katalyma;* not an inn, "but should be understood as a public caravansary or khan, where groups of travelers would spend the night under one roof" (Joseph A. Fitzmyer, S.J., *The Gospel according to Luke (I–IX)* (Garden City, N.Y.: Doubleday, 1981) 408.
3. This homily was preached to Augustinians of the Eastern Province during a Preaching the Just Word retreat/workshop.

4. Actually, a frequent Old Testament expression indicating awe and seriousness in the service of God.
5. John Battle, "The Coming Struggle in Afghanistan," (London) *The Tablet,* Dec. 15, 2001, 1172–73, at 1172.
6. A report from Rome by Robert Mickens, "Pope Voices Alarm at a World on the Brink of Chaos," ibid. 1793–94, at 1793.
7. Paulist Press (New York/Mahwah, N.J., 2001).

Homily 4

1. Here and later I am borrowing, with a partially different approach, some material from an earlier homily, "For Your Penance, Look Redeemed," published in my collection *Tell the Next Generation: Homilies and Near Homilies* (New York/Ramsey: Paulist, 1980) 44–48.
2. The same Greek verb, *teleō,* is translated "accomplished" and "finished" in the two texts quoted. I see no substantive difference in meaning.
3. See Jean Leclercq, *Le défi de la vie contemplative* (Gembloux: Duculot, 1970) 360–61, 367–68.
4. New York: Harper & Row, 1969.
5. From the "Rules of Modesty" (human and Christian decorum in the life of a Jesuit).

Homily 5

1. Vatican II, Constitution on the Sacred Liturgy, no. 10.
2. Mark Searle, "Serving the Lord with Justice," in Mark Searle, ed., *Liturgy and Social Justice* (Collegeville, Minn.: Liturgical, 1980) 23–24.
3. Robert Hovda, "The Mass and Its Social Consequences," *Liturgy* 80 (June–July 1982) 2–3, 5–6, at 6.
4. See Searle, "Serving the Lord with Justice" (see n. 2 above) 25–26.
5. Marco DiCicio, O.F.M., "What Can One Give in Exchange for One's Life? A Narrative-Word Study of the Widow and Her Offering, Mark 12:41–44," *Current in Theology and Mission* 25 (1998) 441–49, at 446.
6. Joseph A. Fitzmyer, S.J., *The Gospel according to Luke (X–XXIV)* (Garden City, N.Y.: Doubleday, 1985) 1321.
7. John R. Donahue, S.J., *What Does the Lord Require? A Bibliographical Essay on the Bible and Social Justice* (revised and expanded; St. Louis: Institute of Jesuit Sources, 2000) 28.

Homily 6

1. Gerard Manley Hopkins, "The Wreck of the *Deutschland,*" stanza 35, *The Poems of Gerard Manley Hopkins,* ed. W. H. Gardner and N. H. MacKenzie (4th ed.; London: Oxford University Press, 1975) 51–63, at 63.

2. This homily was delivered at a home Mass for members of the extended Flanigan family.

Homily 7

1. This homily was preached to a small group of relatives and friends of Jerry Colbert, producer of the National Memorial Day Concert, shortly before the concert itself.
2. Raymond E. Brown, S.S., *The Gospel according to John (xiii–xxi)* (Garden City, N.Y.: Doubleday, 1970) 744.
3. For a fine discussion of the various opinions on what "one" means, see Brown, ibid. 774–79.
4. The data that follow are taken from the "Questions and Facts" section of the Web site of the National Coalition for Homeless Veterans. See http://www.nchv.org/background.cfm#questions.
5. I am aware of the conviction of some scholars that "the least" brothers and sisters, the sufferers, are Christians, probably Christian missionaries whose sufferings were brought upon them by their preaching of the gospel. The criterion of judgment for "all the nations" (Mt 25:32) would be their treatment of those who have carried to the world the message of Jesus which ultimately meant acceptance or rejection of Jesus himself. I am using the more traditional interpretation.
6. Here Jesuit theologian Bernard Lonergan is masterful with his four "transcendental precepts": Be attentive, be intelligent, be reasonable, be responsible. See his *Method in Theology* (New York: Herder and Herder, 1972).

Homily 8

1. Figures from *The State of America's Children Yearbook 2000* (Washington, D.C.: Children's Defense Fund, 2000) xv.
2. Ibid.
3. See ibid. xiv–xv.
4. For greater detail see my homily "God's Justice and America's Sixth Child," homily 28 in this volume.
5. From 2002 American Community Survey Profile; see electronic version, http://www.census.gov/acs/www/Products/Profiles/Single/2002/ACS/Narrative/380/NP38000US0840.htm.
6. The information here has been graciously supplied by Ryan D. White, director of Parish Social Ministry, Catholic Charities, Diocese of Beaumont.

Homily 9

1. This homily was preached to permanent deacons of the Diocese of Little Rock, Arkansas, and their wives, during a mini-retreat/workshop Preaching the Just Word.

2. What follows is based on an account by Michael Wojcik, "Officer Tells Why He Forgave Shooter," in the archdiocesan paper *St. Louis Review,* Jan. 26, 2001, 2.
3. John R. Donahue, S.J., "A World without Enemies?" *America* 184, no. 4 (Feb. 12, 2001) 30–31, at 30.
4. David Van Biema, "Should All Be Forgiven?" *Time* 153, no. 13 (April 5, 1999) 54–58, at 55.

Homily 10

1. The New American Bible translates "Let justice surge like water."
2. Philip Land, S.J., "Justice," *The New Dictionary of Theology,* ed. Joseph A. Komonchak, Mary Collins, and Dermot A. Lane (Wilmington, Del.: Michael Glazier, 1987) 548–55, at 548–49; italics in text.
3. John R. Donahue, S.J., *What Does the Lord Require? A Bibliographical Essay on the Bible and Social Justice* (Studies in the Spirituality of Jesuits 25/2: March 1993; St. Louis: Seminar on Jesuit Spirituality, 1993) 20–21.
4. John Paul II, "Peace with All Creation," *Origins* 19, no. 28 (Dec. 14, 1989) 465–68, at 468.
5. Elizabeth A. Johnson, "Community on Earth as in Heaven: A Holy People and a Sacred Earth Together," Santa Clara Lectures 5, no. 1 (Santa Clara, Calif.: Santa Clara University, 1998) 13.
6. Editorial, "Neglected Diseases," *America* 186, no. 17 (May 20, 2002) 3.
7. From *The State of America's Children Yearbook 2001* (Washington, D.C.: Children's Defense Fund, 2001) xxxi. For many more distressing statistics, see ibid. xxviii–xxxii.
8. This homily was preached to Jesuits of the Wisconsin Province on the first full day of a Preaching the Just Word retreat/workshop.
9. Decree 4 of the 32nd General Congregation of the Society of Jesus (Dec. 2, 1974–Mar. 7, 1975) 48.2, see electronic version, http://www.creighton.edu/CollaborativeMinistry/our-mission-today.html.

Homily 11

1. It is only just to mention here that not all translators of Mt 5:10, as well as 5:6, translate the Greek *dikaiosynē* as "justice." For example, the New American Bible reads "righteousness," and the explanatory note in *The Catholic Study Bible* edited by Donald Senior et al. (New York: Oxford University Press, 1990) tells us that righteousness "here, as usually in Matthew, means conduct in conformity with God's will." In a note on v. 6, Daniel Harrington, S.J., says, "Righteous refers first to God's justice and then to human relationships and behavior" (*The Gospel of Matthew* [Sacra pagina 1; Collegeville, Minn.: Liturgical, 1991] 79).
2. See Josephus, *Antiquities* 18, 5, 2, nos. 16–19.

3. Here the meaning "just" for *dikaios* is best restricted to "innocent."
4. Pertinent here is the fact that this homily was preached on the first full day of a retreat/workshop for Jesuits of the Detroit Province.
5. Decree 4 of the 32nd General Congregation of the Society of Jesus (Dec. 2, 1974–Mar. 7, 1975) 48.2–49.3, see electronic version, http://www.creighton.edu/CollaborativeMinistry/our-mission-today.html.
6. Ibid. 53.7.
7. From a homily delivered by Father Arrupe at the Ateneo de Manila, Quezon City, Republic of the Philippines, on the feast of St. Ignatius, July 31, 1983, commemorating the fourth centenary of the arrival of the Jesuits in the Philippines; in *Recollections and Reflections of Pedro Arrupe, S.J.,* tr. Yolanda T. De Mola, S.C. (Wilmington, Del.: Michael Glazier, 1986) 128.
8. Address of John Paul II opening the deliberations of the Third Assembly of Latin American Bishops at Puebla de los Angeles, Mexico, Jan. 28, 1979.
9. See Dietrich Bonhoeffer, *The Cost of Discipleship* (rev. ed.; New York: Macmillan, 1963) 45–48.
10. Robert M. Morgenthau, OpEd, "What Prosecutors Won't Tell You," *New York Times,* Feb. 7, 1995.

Homily 12

1. I have taken this account from Gary Smith, "Torch Song," *Sports Illustrated* 93, no. 12 (Sept. 25, 2000) 40–43, at 43, changing his past tenses into present tenses for rhetorical effect.
2. Quoted by Tim Layden, "The Start of Something Big," ibid. 93, no. 13 (Oct. 2, 2000) 40–47, at 47.
3. Ibid.
4. Joseph A. Fitzmyer, S.J., *The Gospel according to Luke (X–XXIV)* (Garden City, N.Y.: Doubleday, 1985) 884.
5. See T. W. Manson, quoted by Fitzmyer, ibid.
6. Fitzmyer, ibid.
7. This homily was delivered to priests of the Diocese of Scranton during a Preaching the Just Word retreat/workshop.
8. Josephus, *Antiquities* 20, 6, 1, nos. 118–23.

Homily 13

1. These statistics are taken from Marian Wright Edelman's Foreword, "It's Time!" in *The State of America's Children Yearbook 2001* (Washington, D.C.: Children's Defense Fund, 2001) xxx–xxxi.
2. This summary is taken from http://www.cdfactioncouncil.org/the-act/; for supplementary information, see http://www.childrensdefense.org/pressreleases/default.asp.

3. As this manuscript goes to press, I would no longer encourage people to lobby their senators and representatives to vote for this legislation *unless* it is accompanied by other legislation to increase significantly monies to schools to help realize these goals. Unfunded good intentions can be worse than no legislation.
4. Homilies such as this sample were preached in various churches in the United States on October 20, 2002.

Homily 14

1. "Wear me out": The Greek verb has its roots in prize-fighting—"so that she may not give me a black eye!"
2. Figures from *The State of America's Children Yearbook 2000* (Washington, D.C.: Children's Defense Fund, 2000) xv.
3. Ibid.
4. Ibid. xiv–xv; emphasis mine.
5. See ibid. xiv.
6. Marian Wright Edelman, "Why We Must Build a 21st Century Movement To Leave No Child Behind and What You Can Do," *The State of America's Children Yearbook 2000* (Washington, D.C.: Children's Defense Fund, 2000) xxiv.
7. Ibid.

Homily 15

1. This homily was delivered on the first full day of a Preaching the Just Word retreat/workshop for preachers at Bishop Molloy Retreat House, Jamaica, Long Island, N.Y.
2. John Paul II, *On Social Concern,* no. 28 (Washington, D.C.: United States Catholic Conference, n.d.) 48–49.
3. The items above are taken from "Brethren Witness: Care for Creation," electronic version, http://www.brethren.org/dov/DOVPak/Omega2.pdf.
4. From http://www.globalissues.org/TradeRelated/Consumption.asp.
5. David Hollenbach, S.J., "Responding to the Terrorist Attacks: An Ethical Perspective," *America* 185, no. 12 (Oct. 22, 2001) 23–24.
6. All the quotations on the economic dimension are borrowed from Hollenbach, ibid. 23.
7. Joseph A. Fitzmyer, S.J., *The Gospel according to Luke (X–XXIV)* (Garden City, N.Y.: Doubleday, 1985) 969.
8. John Paul II, *On Social Concern* (n. 2 above) no. 47 (USCC 96).

Homily 16

1. Anup Shah, "Effects of Over-Consumption and Increasing Populations," electronic version, 2001, www.globalissues.org/WhatsNew/.

2. David Hollenbach, S.J., "Responding to the Terrorist Attacks: An Ethical Perspective," *America* 185, no. 12 (Oct. 22, 2001) 23–24, at 23.

3. Monika K. Hellwig, *Guests of God: Stewards of Divine Creation* (New York/Mahwah, N.J.: Paulist, 1999) 96.

Homily 17

1. This homily was delivered during a five-day retreat/workshop, Preaching the Just Word, to priests of the Archdiocese of Denver, Colorado.

2. *Story of a Soul: Autobiography of St. Thérèse of Lisieux,* trans. John Clarke, O.C.D. (2nd ed.; Washington, D.C.: ICS Publications, 1976) 77.

3. *The Poetry of St. Thérèse of Lisieux,* tr. Donald Kinney, O.C.D. (Washington, D.C.: ICS Publications, 1995) 17, verses 4 and 15.

4. Ann Laforest, O.C.D., *Thérèse of Lisieux: The Way to Love* (Franklin, Wis.: Sheed & Ward, 2000) 21.

5. Ibid. 113.

6. Ibid. 38.

7. Quoted from *The Catholic Worker,* December 1965, by Laforest (n. 4 above) 1, 2, and 7. Original Dorothy Day piece is available in electronic version; see http://www.catholicworker.org/dorothyday/.

8. Quoted in William D. Miller, *Dorothy Day: A Biography* (San Francisco: Harper & Row, 1982) 431.

9. See Laforest (n. 4 above) 112.

10. Dorothy Day, *Loaves and Fishes* (Maryknoll, N.Y.: Orbis Books, 1997) 176.

11. See *The Catholic Study Bible,* ed. Donald Senior et al. (New York: Oxford, 1990) The New Testament, p. 38, endnote re: Mt 18:2.

12. Ibid., endnote re: Mt 18:3.

13. Letter 186; see *St. Thérèse of Lisieux: General Correspondence,* Vols. 1 and 2, tr. John Clarke, O.C.D. (Washington, D.C.: ICS Publications, 1982 and 1988).

Homily 18

1. This homily was delivered during the 2001 Pastoral Liturgy Conference sponsored by the University of Notre Dame's Center for Pastoral Liturgy. The theme of the conference was "Liturgy and Justice."

2. See Joseph N. Tylenda, S.J., *Jesuit Saints & Martyrs: Short Biographies of the Saints, Blesseds, Venerables, and Servants of God of the Society of Jesus* (2nd ed.; Chicago: Loyola, 1998) 186–89, at 187.

3. In the rest of this second section I am reproducing factual material from my homily "Happiest Man of All the Gonzagas," in my collection *Let Justice Roll Down Like Waters: Biblical Justice Homilies throughout the Year* (New York/Mahwah, N.J.: Paulist, 1998) 149–53, at 150–51.

4. William Hart McNichols, S.J., "Saint Aloysius: Patron of Youth," in *Aloysius,* ed. Clifford Stevens and William Hart McNichols (Huntington, Ind.: Our Sunday Visitor, 1993) 37–41, at 39.

5. Tylenda, *Jesuit Saints & Martyrs* (n. 2 above) 187.

6. See McNichols (n. 4 above) 39.

7. Translation as in C. C. Martindale, S.J., *The Vocation of Aloysius Gonzaga* (New York: Sheed and Ward, 1945) 128–29.

8. Ibid. 217.

9. On this see P. Molinari, S.J., "St. Aloysius Gonzaga," in *Companions of Jesus: Profiles of the Jesuit Saints and Beati* (2nd ed.; Rome: Gregorian University, 1984) 73.

10. The phrase stems from Scipio Gonzaga, one of the cardinals who frequented Aloysius' bedside during his last days; quoted in Martindale, *Vocation* (n. 7 above) 222.

Homily 19

1. Pius IX, bull *Ineffabilis Deus,* Dec. 8, 1854 (tr. *The Teaching of the Catholic Church as Contained in Her Documents,* originally prepared by Josef Neuner, S.J., and Heinrich Roos, S.J., edited by Karl Rahner, S.J., translated from the original German by Geoffrey Stevens [Dublin: Mercier, 1967] no. 325).

2. Exegetes differ on whether Judith was a real person or a symbol (her name in Hebrew means simply "Jewess") of the Jewish people who overcame their formidable enemy through trust in God.

Homily 20

1. Second Vatican Council, Constitution on the Sacred Liturgy, no. 7.

2. Here I am reproducing, with a slight change, a paragraph from my homily "You Cannot Love Like Jesus Unless...," in my collection *Christ in Ten Thousand Places* (New York/Mahwah, N.J.: Paulist, 1999) 199.

3. See Joseph A. Fitzmyer, S.J., *Romans* (Anchor Bible 33; New York: Doubleday, 1993) 398.

4. Karl Barth, *Church Dogmatics: A Selection* (New York: Harper and Row, 1962) 201.

5. Marian Wright Edelman, "It's Time!" *The State of America's Children Yearbook 2001* (Washington, D.C.: Children's Defense Fund, 2001) xxx.

6. Ibid. xxii.

Homily 21

1. Mary Rose McGready, *God's Lost Children: The Shocking Story of America's Homeless Children* (California: Covenant House, 1991).
2. For electronic version of H.R. 2716, as amended, see http://veterans.house.gov/legislation/107/hr2716s.html.

Homily 22

1. Second Vatican Council, Constitution on the Sacred Liturgy, no. 7.
2. The Song has also been interpreted as a portrayal and praise of the mutual love between the Lord and His people.
3. Such is the interpretation suggested by Scripture scholar Roland E. Murphy, O.Carm., "Canticle of Canticles," *The New Jerome Biblical Commentary*, ed. Raymond E. Brown, S.S., Joseph A. Fitzmyer, S.J., and Roland E. Murphy, O.Carm. (Englewood Cliffs, N.J.: Prentice-Hall, 1990) 29:24, p. 465.
4. I am aware that some scholars regard the Letter to the Colossians as the work of some pupil or follower of Paul.
5. David Van Biema, "Should All Be Forgiven?" *Time* 153, no. 13 (April 5, 1999) 54–58, at 55.
6. See Evelyn Whitehead and James D. Whitehead, "Christian Marriage," *U.S. Catholic* 47, no. 6 (June 1982) 9.
7. Excerpted from Marian Wright Edelman, "It's Time!," Foreword to *The State of America's Children Yearbook 2001* (Washington, D.C.: Children's Defense Fund, 2001) ix–xxxii, at ix–x.
8. Aspects of both were passed in May 2002.
9. The Act is listed as S. 940 and H.R. 1990. As this manuscript goes to press, it is clear that much more money must be allocated to schools in order for the goals of this legislation to be realized.

Homily 23

1. This homily was preached during a Preaching the Just Word retreat/workshop for Passionists of the Western Province at Holy Name Retreat Center, Houston, Texas.
2. John Paul II, "Peace with All Creation," Jan. 1, 1990, English text in *Origins* 19, no. 28 (Dec. 14, 1989) 465–68, at 468.
3. In the present context the word "neighbor" is restricted to "fellow countrymen."
4. Quotations are taken from the electronic version of the text, www.stanford.edu/group/King/.
5. *The State of America's Children Yearbook 2000* (Washington, D.C.: Children's Defense Fund, 2000) xiv–xv.

Homily 24

1. Second Vatican Council, Constitution on the Sacred Liturgy, no. 10.
2. The Bishops' Committee on Priestly Life and Ministry, National Conference of Catholic Bishops, *Fulfilled in Your Hearing: The Homily in the Sunday Assembly* (Washington, D.C.: United States Catholic Conference, 1982) 27.

Homily 25

1. Jesus' remarks on children in this passage are stimulated by the qualities he insists are necessary if one is to enter the kingdom of God: receptivity to the gospel and total trustful dependence on God (see Mt 18:3–4).
2. Joseph A. Fitzmyer, S.J., "The Letter to the Romans," *The New Jerome Biblical Commentary*, ed. Raymond E. Brown, S.S., Joseph A. Fitzmyer, S.J., Roland E. Murphy, O.Carm. (Englewood Cliffs, N.J.: Prentice-Hall, 1990) 51:64, p. 847.

Homily 26

1. Karl Rahner, S.J., *Ignatius of Loyola*, with an Historical Introduction by Paul Imhof, S.J. (London and New York: Collins, 1979) 11–13. The translation, by Rosaleen Ockenden, was made on the German original, *Ignatius von Loyola* (Freiburg i. B.: Herder, 1978). I have reproduced this translation in my text with several minor changes.
2. See *Spiritual Exercises*, no. 236.
3. Bernard J. F. Longeran, S.J., *Method in Theology* (New York: Herder and Herder, 1972) 31.
4. See Alfred North Whitehead, *Adventures of Ideas* (New York: Free Press, 1967) 226.
5. Karl Delehaye, *Erneuerung der Seelsorgsformen aus der Sicht der frühen Patristik* (Freiburg i. B., 1958) 135.
6. This homily was originally preached at the Woodstock Theological Center in February 2001. Later the same year this was published in the October 15 issue of *America* magazine (Copyright 2001). With slight changes, the homily is reprinted here with permission of America Press.

Homily 27

1. This homily was delivered during a Mass of the Holy Spirit not only opening the 2001–2002 school year at Loyola College in Maryland but also celebrating the 150th year of the college's existence. The factual information for the first 135 years in this homily depends largely on Nicholas Varga, *Baltimore's Loyola, Loyola's Baltimore 1851–1986* (Baltimore, Md.: Maryland Historical Society, 1990).

2. Edward Collins Vacek, S.J., "Work," *The New Dictionary of Theology,* ed. Joseph A. Komonchak, Mary Collins, and Dermot A. Lane (Wilmington, Del.: Michael Glazier, 1987) 1098–1105, at 1102.

3. From a 1983 address by Frederick Buechner celebrating the rededication of the library at New York City's Union Theological Seminary.

4. I am aware that in this contemplation Ignatius speaks explicitly of "God," not of Christ. But, as Hugo Rahner states emphatically, "In full accordance with Ignatian theology, the 'creator and Lord' of this contemplation is Christ, the incarnate Word, who in virtue of what he is and of what he does, dwells in all creatures and 'behaves as one who works'..." (*Ignatius the Theologian* [New York: Herder and Herder, 1968] 134).

5. *Spiritual Exercises,* no. 236; translation mine.

6. Ronald Modras, "The Spiritual Humanism of the Jesuits," *America* 172, no. 3 (Feb. 4, 1995) 10, 12, 14, 16, and 29–32. Modras is a lay professor of theological studies at the Jesuit St. Louis University.

7. Decree 4 of the 32nd General Congregation of the Society of Jesus (Dec. 2, 1974–Mar. 7, 1975) 48.2, see electronic version, http://www.creighton.edu/CollaborativeMinistry/our-mission-today.html.

8. Ibid. 109.60.

9. Children's Defense Fund, *The State of America's Children Yearbook 2000* (Washington, D.C.: Children's Defense Fund, 2000) xiv–xv.

10. So has contemplation been insightfully defined by Discalced Carmelite William McNamara.

Homily 28

1. Figures from *The State of America's Children Yearbook 2001* (Washington, D.C.: Children's Defense Fund, 2001) xxii.

2. See ibid.

3. Ibid. 107.

4. See ibid. xxix.

Homily 29

1. See *The Adventures of Antoine Doinel: Four Screenplays by François Truffaut* (New York: Simon and Schuster, 1971) passim.

2. Quotations from Ashley Montague, *The Elephant Man: A Study in Human Dignity* (New York: Dutton, 1979) 14–16, 18, 22, 29, 34, 63–64, 77.

3. Bob Herbert, "Criminal Justice," *New York Times,* OpEd, June 24, 1999, A31. The paragraph is actually a quotation from Stephen Bright, director of the Southern Center for Human Rights.

4. See the editorial "Children Too Ready To Die Young," *Washington Post*, Nov. 3, 1993, A26.
5. Children's Defense Fund, *The State of America's Children Yearbook 2000*, (Washington, D.C.: Children's Defense Fund, 2000) xiv–xv.
6. Ibid. xv.
7. From various newspaper accounts.
8. "The U.S. Penal System: Restorative and/or Retributive Justice?" a panel discussion co-ordinated by Raymond B. Kemp, *Woodstock Report*, no. 61 (March 2000) 3–10, at 4; see also p. 5.
9. See Robert M. Morgenthau, "What Prosecutors Won't Tell You," *New York Times*, OpEd, Feb. 7, 1995, A25.
10. Statistics, electronic version, are taken from the Web site of the Child Abuse Prevention Council of Sacramento, Inc.: http://www.capcsac.org/statistics.
11. John R. Donahue, S.J., "Biblical Perspectives on Justice," in *The Faith That Does Justice: Examining the Christian Sources for Social Change*, ed. John C. Haughey, S.J. (Woodstock Studies 2; New York: Paulist, 1977) 68–112, at 69. More recently, Donahue has stated that his "earlier reflections should be supplemented by the reflections of J.P.M. Walsh" in the latter's *The Mighty from Their Thrones: Power in the Biblical Tradition* (Philadelphia: Fortress, 1987). See Donahue, *What Does the Lord Require? A Bibliographical Essay on the Bible and Social Justice* (Studies in the Spirituality of Jesuits 25/2: March 1993; St. Louis: Seminar on Jesuit Spirituality, 1993) 20–21; see also the revised and expanded edition of the latter work (St. Louis: Institute of Jesuit Sources, 2000) 24–25.
12. Estimates as of 1990 in the Japanese section of the Library of Congress, Washington, D.C.
13. Malachy McCourt, *A Monk Swimming: A Memoir* (New York: Hyperion, 1998) 2.
14. David Beckman, "Let's Cut Hunger in Half," *U.S. Catholic* 66, no. 1 (January 2001) 24–27, at 24.
15. Ibid.
16. Quoted ibid. 26.
17. See the November 15, 2000 Statement of the Catholic Bishops of the United States, *Responsibility, Rehabilitation, and Restoration: A Catholic Perspective on Crime and Criminal Justice* (Washington, D.C.: United States Catholic Conference, 2000).
18. See Bernard J. F. Lonergan, S.J., *Method in Theology* (New York: Herder and Herder, 1974) esp. 14–15, 55, 238–42, 357, 363.
19. This homily was written specifically for inclusion in the volume *Surviving Terror: Hope and Justice in a World of Violence*, ed. Victoria Lee Erickson and Michelle Lim Jones (Grand Rapids, Mich.: Brazos Press, 2002) 249–57, 332–33. With minor changes this homily is reprinted here with the permission of Brazos Press, a division of the Baker Publishing Group.

Homily 30

1. This sermonette/meditation was delivered on a number of occasions as a "sending forth" at the close of a Preaching the Just Word retreat/workshop—usually in the present form to ordained priests.

Homily 31

1. It is only fair to state that this homily had for co-author Katharyn L. Waldron. Her contributions are especially, but not solely, evident in the sections that deal with Burghardt family history.

Comprehensive Index for Homily Books by Walter J. Burghardt, S.J.

compiled by
Fr. Brian Cavanaugh, T.O.R.

Reference Key:	TNG	*(Tell the Next Generation, 1980)*
	LSJ	*(Sir, We Would Like to See Jesus, 1982)*
	PYW	*(Still Proclaiming Your Wonders, 1984)*
	GOC	*(Grace on Crutches, 1986)*
	ENH	*(Lovely in Eyes Not His, 1988)*
	TCL	*(To Christ I Look, 1989)*
	DBC	*(Dare to Be Christ, 1991)*
	CMC	*(When Christ Meets Christ, 1993)*
	SWB	*(Speak the Word with Boldness, 1994)*
	LFL	*(Love Is a Flame of the Lord, 1995)*
	JRD	*(Let Justice Roll Down Like Waters, 1998)*
	TTP	*(Christ in Ten Thousand Places, 1999)*
	TBJ	*(To Be Just Is to Love, 2001)*
	LJE	*(Let Jesus Easter in Us, 2005)*

LITURGICAL SEASONS:

Advent Season:	TNG, pp. 25, 30
Advent: 1st Sun. (A)	LSJ, p. 17; DBC, p. 5
1st Sun. (B)	GOC, p. 19; CMC, p. 15
Vespers 1st Sun. (B)	JRD, p. 5
1st Sun. (C)	CMC, p. 20
2nd Sun. (A)	PYW, p. 19; ENH, p. 5; SWB, p. 3; TBJ, p. 5
2nd Sun. (B)	LSJ, p. 23; TCL, p. 21
2nd Sun. (C)	PYW, p. 25; TCL, p. 27
3rd Sun. (A)	LSJ, p. 29; ENH, p. 11
3rd Sun. (B)	LFL, p. 5
3rd Sun. (C)	LSJ, p. 33
3rd Mon. (Yr. 2)	LJE, p. 3
4th Sun. (A)	SWB, p. 8
4th Sun. (C)	TTP, p. 7
Christmas:	TNG, p. 34, LJE, p. 6
Solemnity of BVM,	
Mother of God:	TBJ, p. 12
Epiphany, Mon. (Yr. 2)	LJE, p. 10

Lenten Season: TNG, pp. 19, 44, 49
Ash Wednesday: GOC, p. 27
Sat. after Ash Wed.   DBC, p. 13
    1st Sun. (A)   ENH, p. 19
    1st Sun. (B)   PYW, p. 33; TCL, p. 35; TBJ, p. 17
    1st Sun. (C)   SWB, p. 14
    1st Mon. (Yr. 1)   JRD, p. 10
    2nd Sun. (A)   LSJ, p. 41; DBC, p. 16; SWB, p. 19; JRD, p. 15
    2nd Sun. (C)   DBC, p. 22
    2nd Mon. (Yr. 1)   TTP, p. 12
    3rd Sun. (A)   GOC, p. 31; ENH, p. 26; TTP, p. 17
    3rd Mon. (Yr. 2)   TTP, p. 22
    4th Sun. (A)   TTP, p. 28
    4th Sun. (B)   CMC, p. 33
    4th Sun. (C)   LSJ, p. 46; DBC, p. 29
    4th Mon. (Yr. 1)   CMC, p. 38; TTP, p. 34
    4th Mon. (Yr. 2)   LJE, p. 15
    5th Sun. (A)   GOC, p. 37; ENH, p. 32; TBJ, p. 23
    5th Sun. (B)   GOC, p. 43; PYW, p. 39; TBJ, p. 30
    5th Sun. (C)   PYW, p. 45
Palm Sunday: TNG, p. 52
Palm Sunday (A)   GOC, p. 49; DBC, p. 35
Palm Sunday (B)   GOC, p. 54; PYW, p. 51; TCL, p. 41
Palm Sunday (C)   PYW, p. 55
Holy Week: TNG, p. 78
Holy Monday (Yr. 1)   TBJ, p. 36; TBJ, p. 41
Holy Thursday   TNG, p. 58; PYW, pp. 61, 67; JRD, p. 132
Good Friday: LSJ, p. 52; GOC, pp. 59, 65; TBJ, p. 47
                7 Last Words: LFL, pp. 17, 22, 26, 30, 34, 37, 41

Easter Season:
    Vigil (C)   ENH, p. 41
    Easter Sun. (C)   LJE, p. 25
    2nd Sun. (A)   GOC, p. 73; DBC, p. 45
    2nd Sun. (B)   TCL, p. 49; TBJ, p. 55
    2nd Sun. (C)   PYW, p. 77; DBC, p. 51; TTP, p. 38
    2nd Mon. (C)   SWB, p. 25
    2nd Mon. (Yr. 1)   JRD, p. 20
    3rd Sun. (A)   ENH, p. 47; SWB, p. 29; JRD, p. 25
    3rd Sun. (B)   PYW, p. 84; TBJ, p. 61
    3rd Sun. (C)   LSJ, p. 59; PYW, p. 90
    4th Sun. (A)   LSJ, p. 65; GOC, p. 79
    4th Sun. (C)   ENH, p. 53
    4th Mon. (Yr. 1)   TBJ, p. 67
    5th Sun. (A)   JRD, p. 30
    5th Sun. (B)   LSJ, p. 70; TCL, p. 55
    5th Sun. (C)   SWB, p. 34; TTP, p. 43
    5th Mon. (Yr. 1)   TTP, p. 48
    5th Fri. (C)   SWB, p. 40
    6th Sun. (A)   SWB, p. 42

6th Sun. (B)   GOC, p. 85; TCL, p. 55; TTP, p.53; TBJ, p. 72
6th Sun. (C)   LSJ, p. 75
6th Mon. (Yr. 2)   TTP, p. 57; TBJ, p. 79
6th Thurs. (Yr. 1)   TBJ, p. 75
7th Sun. (B)   CMC, p. 42
7th Sun. (C)   PYW, p. 97, LJE, p. 29
7th Mon. (Yr. 2)   JRD, p. 35
7th Tues. (Yr.1)   TBJ, p. 83
Pentecost Sunday   ENH, p. 59; TBJ, p. 87

Ordinary Time:

1st Mon. (Yr. 1)   TTP, p. 63
1st Tues. (Yr. 2)   TTP, p. 67
2nd Sun. (A)   LSJ, p. 83; ENH, p. 67; DBC, p. 59; SWB, p. 51
2nd Sun. (B)   PYW, p. 105
2nd Sun. (C)   LSJ, p. 88; ENH, p. 73
2nd Mon. (Yr. 1)   LJE, p. 35
2nd Mon. (Yr. 2)   TTP, p. 71
2nd Fri. (Yr. 1)   SWB, p. 57
3rd Sun. (A)   GOC, p. 93; JRD, p. 41
3rd Sun. (B)   GOC, p. 100; TCL, p. 63
3rd Sun. (C)   ENH, p. 80; DBC, p. 65; TTP, p. 75
3rd Mon. (Yr. 1)   JRD, p. 46; TTP, p. 80
3rd Fri. (Yr. 1)   SWB, p. 61
4th Mon. (Yr. 1)   TTP, p. 84
4th Mon. (Yr. 2)   LFL, p. 47
5th Sun. (A)   ENH, p. 86
5th Sun. (B)   TNG, p. 39; LFL, p. 51
5th Sun. (C)   TTP, p. 88
6th Sun. (A)   DBC, p. 71; SWB, p. 65; JRD, p. 51
6th Sun. (B)   GOC, p. 106; TBJ, p. 99
6th Sun. (C)   LSJ, p. 93; PYW, p. 111; SWB, p. 71
6th Mon. (Yr. 2)   TTP, p. 93
7th Sun. (A)   SWB, p. 76
7th Sun. (C)   LJE, p. 39
8th Sun. (A)   GOC, p. 111
8th Sun. (B)   LJE, p. 19
8th Mon. (Yr. 1)   JRD, p. 55
8th Mon. (Yr. 2)   LJE, p. 45
8th Thurs. (Yr.1)   TBJ, p. 104
9th Mon. (Yr. 1)   JRD, p. 59; TTP, p. 98
9th Tues. (Yr. 2)   TTP, p. 102
10th Mon. (Yr. 2)   JRD, p. 63, LJE, p. 50
10th Tues. (Yr. 2)   TTP, p. 107
11th Mon. (Yr. 1)   TTP, p. 112
11th Sun. (C)   PYW, p. 117
12th Sun. (A)   JRD, p. 68
12th Mon. (Yr. 1)   JRD, p. 74
13th Sun. (B)   LSJ, p. 99
13th Mon. (Yr. 1)   JRD, p. 79

13th Wed. (C)   SWB, p. 100
13th Thurs. (Yr. 1)   LFL, p. 57
15th Sun. (C)   LSJ, p. 105
16th Sun. (C)   SWB, p. 104
16th Mon. (Yr. 1)   JRD, p. 83
17th Sun. (B)   CMC, p. 51
18th Mon. (Yr. 2)   LFL, p. 61; TBJ, p. 113
18th Thurs. (Yr. 1)   TBJ, p. 108
22nd Thurs. (Yr. 2)   CMC, p. 64
23rd Sun. (A)   CMC, p. 67
23rd Sun. (B)   TTP, p. 116
23rd Sun. (C)   DBC, p. 83
24th Sun. (A)   LSJ, p. 110; GOC, p. 118; TCL, p. 69; LFL, p. 66
24th Sun. (B)   TCL, p. 74; CMC, p. 72
24th Mon. (Yr. 2)   LFL, p. 72
25th Sun. (A)   GOC, p. 124; TCL, p. 80
25th Sun. (B)   LSJ, p. 115; PYW, p. 123; TCL, p. 86
25th Sun. (C)   ENH, p. 92
25th Mon. (Yr. 1)   LFL, p. 76
25th Thurs. (Yr. 2)   TTP, p. 122
26th Sun. (A)   GOC, p. 130
26th Sun. (B)   ENH, p. 98; LFL, p. 80
26th Sun. (C)   PYW, p. 128; DBC, p. 89; SWB, p. 107
26th Mon. (Yr. 1)   JRD, p. 89
27th Sun. (A)   TBJ, p. 118
27th Sun. (B)   ENH, p. 104
27th Sun. (C)   ENH, p. 110; SWB, p. 112
27th Mon. (Yr. 2)   LFL, p. 85, LJE, p. 56
27th Tues. (Yr. 2)   TTP, p. 127
27th Fri. (Yr. 1)   TBJ, p. 123
28th Sun. (A)   LSJ, p. 121; GOC, p. 135; TCL, p. 90
28th Sun. (B)   PYW, p. 134; ENH, p. 116
28th Sun. (C)   LSJ, p. 126; SWB, p. 118; TTP, p. 132
28th Mon. (Yr. 1)   LFL, p. 89
29th Sun. (A)   JRD, p. 99; TBJ, p. 128, LJE, p. 61
29th Sun. (B)   TCL, p. 96; LFL, p. 93
29th Sun. (C)   ENH, p. 122; JRD, p. 94, LJE, p. 66
29th Mon. (Yr. 1)   LJE, p. 71
29th Mon. (Yr. 2)   JRD, p. 104
30th Sun. (A)   GOC, p. 140
30th Sun. (B)   LSJ, p. 132
30th Sun. (C)   PYW, p. 139
30th Mon. (Yr. 1)   LFL, p. 98
31st Sun. (A)   JRD, p. 108
31st Sun. (B)   ENH, p. 128; TCL, p. 102
31st Mon. (Yr. 1)   LJE, p. 77
31st Mon. (Yr. 2)   JRD, p. 113
32nd Sun. (B)   PYW, p. 144
32nd Sun. (C)   DBC, p. 93
32nd Mon. (Yr. 1)   LFL, p. 102; TTP, p. 138

32nd Mon. (Yr. 2)	JRD, p. 117
33rd Sun. (A)	LSJ, p. 137; GOC, p. 146; TCL, p. 107
33rd Sun. (B)	LSJ, p. 143; PYW, p. 149; TCL, p. 113
33rd Sun. (C)	PYW, p. 155; ENH, p. 134; SWB, p. 123
34th Mon. (Yr. 1)	JRD, p. 121
Christ the King:	TNG, p. 63; PYW, p. 174

FEASTS:

Baptism of the Lord	JRD, p. 127
Body and Blood of Christ (B)	LSJ, p. 157; JRD, p. 136
Body and Blood of Christ (C)	PYW, p. 168; TCL, p. 121
Epiphany	CMC, p. 27
Epiphany, Mon.	LFL, p. 10
Sacred Heart	TBJ, p. 139
Solemnity of BVM, Mother of God:	TBJ, p. 12
Immaculate Conception	LJE, p. 93
Trinity Sunday (A)	LSJ, p. 151
Trinity Sunday (B)	TTP, p. 145
Trinity Sunday (C)	DBC, p. 77; SWB, p. 82
Trinity Mon. (C)	SWB, p. 88
Trinity Tues. (C)	SWB, p. 92
Trinity Wed. (C)	SWB, p. 96
Triumph of the Cross	LSJ, p. 168
Arrupe, Pedro, SJ	CMC, p. 179
John Paul I	TNG, p. 216
Murray, John Courtney	TNG, p. 211
Sadat, Mohammed el	LSJ, p. 196
Birth of John the Baptist	CMC, p. 57; LFL, p. 131
Conversion of St. Paul	PYW, p. 163; SWB, p. 174
North Amer. Martyrs	TTP, p. 175
Our Lady of Sorrows	TTP, p. 149
St. Alphonsus Rodriquez	LFL, p. 140
St. Aloysius Gonzaga	JRD, p. 149, LJE, p. 88
Sts. Andrew Kim, Paul Chong, & Companions	TBJ, p. 144
St. Barnabas	ENH, p. 201
St. Boniface	TBJ, p. 153
St. Charles Borromeo	TBJ, p. 158
St. Charles Lwanga/ Companions	JRD, p. 145
St. Claude de La Colombière	TBJ, p. 139
Bl. Diego de San Vitores	ENH, p. 188
St. Frances Xavier Cabrini	JRD, p. 167
St. Francis de Sales	ENH, p. 194
St. Ignatius of Antioch	SWB, p. 170; JRD, p. 162
St. Ignatius Loyola	LSJ, p. 163; SWB, p. 165

St. Jerome	JRD, p. 158
St. John Don Bosco	TBJ, p. 135
St. John Lateran	LSJ, p. 173; TTP, p. 154
St. John Neumann	TTP, p. 159
St. Joseph the Worker	JRD, p. 141
Bl. Kateri Tekakwitha	TTP, p. 171
St. Luke	DBC, p. 185
St. Philippine Duchesne	TCL, p. 149
St. Robert Bellarmine	JRD, p. 154
Sts. Simon & Jude, Apostles	TBJ, p. 148
St. Teresa of Avila	GOC, p. 197
St. Thérèse of Lisieux	LJE, p. 83
St. Thomas More	TTP, p. 165
St. Vincent de Paul	LFL, p. 135

THEMES:

45th Assembly, Greater Dallas Community of Churches	JRD, p. 203
Baccalaureate	TNG, p. 116; GOC, pp. 179, 185, 191; PYW, p. 195; ENH, pp. 143, 149; DBC, p. 179; CMC, pp. 208, 213, 219; SWB, p. 186
Baptism	TNG, pp. 71, 75; TCL, p. 135; CMC, pp. 185, 188; JRD, p. 215, LJE, p. 129
Blessing of Pipe Organ	DBC, p. 190
Broadcasting	TNG, p. 194
Cathedral Centennial	DBC, p. 167
Catholic/Jewish Relations	TNG, p. 156
Catholic Social Thought	CMC, p. 198
Child Advocacy themes	JRD, p. 94, 99; TTP, p. 230; TBJ, p. 128
Children's Defense Fund	LJE, pp. 61, 66, 144
Christmas Chorale	LFL, p. 160
Christian Living	TNG, p. 129
Christian Unity	TNG, p. 148
Church Renewal	TNG, p. 134
College/Univ./H.S. Anniv.	TCL, pp. 142, 155; JRD, p. 230
Loyola College (MD)	LJE, p. 137
Conference on Authority	DBC, p. 163
Death/Funeral	TNG, pp. 205, 211, 216; LSJ, p. 192; ENH, p. 184; TCL, p. 139; JRD, p. 235, LJE, p. 163
Dominican Preachers	SWB, p. 179
Eucharist	LJE, p. 19
Evangelization	LSJ, p. 181
Forgiveness	TBJ, p. 17
Freedom	TNG, p. 175
Gonzaga H.S. bldg. dedication	TBJ, p. 214
Graduation, College	TNG, p. 109
Graduation, Med. School	SWB, p. 191; LFL, pp. 149, 155; JRD, p. 219; TTP, p. 224

Graduation, Prison   TNG, p. 163
Holy Childhood Assoc.   SWB, p. 203
Holy Spirit themes   PYW, pp. 183, 189; TTP, p. 211; TBJ, p. 87
Ignatian Year   CMC, pp. 158, 164
Labor Day   TCL, p. 161; TBJ, p. 204
Jewish Holocaust   GOC, p. 202
Marian themes   TNG, p. 197; TCL, p. 127; CMC, p. 170; JRD, p. 211;
                               TTP, p. 7; TBJ, p. 12, LJE, p. 93

Rev. Martin Luther King, Jr.   LJE, p. 119
Medical Profession   TNG, p. 25
Mission Congress   PYW, p. 219
Missions   TNG, p. 140
Mother's Day   DBC, p. 196
Ordination Anniversary   TNG, pp. 100, 104; CMC, p. 141; TBJ, p. 199
Parish Anniversary   DBC, p. 173, SWB, p. 196; LFL, p. 144
Peace and Justice   CMC, p. 203; TTP, pp. 93, 138, 218; LJE, p. 150
Priests' Jubilee/Retreat   CMC, p. 148, LJE, p. 160
Radio Mass (Baltimore)   LJE, p. 125
Red Mass   TNG, p. 121; TCL, p. 167; CMC, p. 192; TTP, p. 218
Reformation Sunday   PYW, p. 226; TBJ, p. 220
Religious Profession   TNG, p. 85
Religious Anniversary   LSJ, p. 203; CMC, pp. 135, 141; JRD, p. 211
          Jesuit, 50th Anniv. TBJ, p. 209
          Jesuit, 70th Anniv. LJE, p. 133
Retreat House Anniv.   PYW, p. 211
Search for God   TNG, p. 19
Seniors Clubs   SWB, p. 208
Social Justice   TNG, p. 167
Stewardship   TNG, p. 186
Teaching Anniversary   TNG, p. 93
Terror/Fear   LJE, p. 150
University Opening Mass   PYW, pp. 183, 189; ENH, p. 157; JRD, p. 225
War/Peace   TNG, p. 181
Wedding   TNG, p. 83; LSJ, pp. 186, 189; GOC, pp. 155, 160,
                               165, 170, 175; PYW, pp. 201, 206; ENH, pp. 163, 168,
                               173, 177, 182; TCL, pp. 174, 180, 186, 191, 196, 201;
                               DBC, pp. 101, 106, 112, 117, 123, 129, 135, 141, 146,
                               152, 157; CMC, pp. 81, 87, 93, 98, 103, 109, 115, 121,
                               127; SWB, pp. 131, 141, 146, 151, 157; LFL, pp. 109,
                               114, 120, 125; JRD, pp. 175, 180, 186, 191, 196; TTP,
                               pp. 183, 188, 193, 198, 204; TBJ, pp. 165, 170, 175,
                               181, 186, 191, LJE, pp. 99, 105, 111
Wedding: 50th Anniv.   CMC, p. 153

SCRIPTURE READINGS:

Genesis 1:11–12   TBJ, p. 108
Genesis 1:24–31   LJE, p. 99
Genesis 1:26–28, 31   TBJ, p. 181

Genesis 1:26–2:3	PYW, p. 206; TCL, p. 186; DBC, p. 152; CMC, p. 98; SWB, pp. 131, 151; LFL, pp. 120, 125; JRD, pp. 141, 180; TBJ, p. 204
Genesis 2:4–9, 15	TCL, p. 161
Genesis 2:18–24	PYW, p. 201; GOC, p. 160; ENH, pp. 173, 177; TCL, p. 196; DBC, pp. 101, 106; CMC, pp. 81, 93; SWB, p. 141; JRD, pp. 175, 191; TTP, p. 193
Genesis 3:9–15, 20	LJE, p. 93
Genesis 6:5–8; 7:1-5, 10	LJE, p. 133
Genesis 9:8–15	TBJ, p. 17
Genesis 12:1–4a	LSJ, p. 41; DBC, p. 16; SWB, p. 19; JRD, p. 15
Genesis 12:1–9	JRD, p. 74
Genesis 14:18–20	DBC, p. 179; LSJ, p. 157; JRD, p. 136
Genesis 18:16–33	JRD, p. 79
Genesis 22:1–19	LFL, p. 57
Exodus 12:1–8, 11–14	TNG, p. 58; PYW, pp. 61, 67; JRD, p. 132
Exodus 14:5–18	JRD, p. 83
Exodus 17:3–7	GOC, p. 31; ENH, p. 26; TTP, p. 17
Exodus 17:8–13	ENH, p. 122; JRD, p. 94, LJE, p. 66
Exodus 23:20–24	JRD, p. 89
Leviticus 13:1–2, 44–46	TBJ, p. 99
Leviticus 19:1–2, 11–18	JRD, p. 10
Leviticus 25:8–12, 17–19	TBJ, p. 87
Numbers 6:22–26	CMC, p. 153; TBJ, p. 12
Numbers 21:4–9	LSJ, p. 168
Numbers 24:2–7, 15–17	LJE, p. 3
Deut. 4:32–34, 39–40	CMC, p. 208; TTP, p. 145
Deut. 6:4–7	JRD, p. 219
Deut. 10:12–22	SWB, p. 136
Deut. 15:7–11	LJE, p. 144
Deut. 26:4–10	DBC, p. 173
Ruth 1:16–17	DBC, p. 129
1 Sam. 1:9–20	TTP, p. 67
1 Sam. 15:16–23	TTP, p. 71
1 Sam. 16:1, 6–7, 10–13	TTP, p. 28
1 Sam. 26:2, 7–9, 12–13, 22–23	LJE, p. 39
2 Sam. 15:13–14, 30; 16:5–13	LFL, p. 47
1 Kings 17:1–6	JRD, p. 63, LJE, p. 50
1 Kings 17:7–16	TTP, p. 107
1 Kings 19:4–8	TBJ, p. 209
1 Kings 19:9–15	LSJ, p. 163
1 Kings 21:1–16	SWB, p. 88
1 Kings 21:17–29	SWB, p. 92
2 Kings 1:1, 6–14	SWB, p. 96
2 Kings 5:1–15	TTP, p. 22
2 Kings 5:14–17	LSJ, p. 126; SWB, p. 118; TTP, p. 132
2 Kings 17:5–18	TTP, p. 165
1 Chron. 15:3, 16, 19–21, 25	LFL, p. 144
Ezra 1:1–6	LFL, p. 76
Nehemiah 8:2–10	ENH, p. 80; DBC, p. 65; TTP, p. 75

Tobit 1:3; 2:1-8   JRD, p. 59; TTP, p. 98
Tobit 8:4-9   GOC, pp. 155, 170; ENH, p. 182; DBC, pp. 112, 117,
                                   146; CMC, pp. 121, 127; LFL, p. 114; JRD, p. 186

Job 1:6-22   JRD, p. 158
Psalm 138   CMC, p. 219
Proverbs 8:22-31   ENH, p. 143
Ecclesiastes 1:2-11   TTP, p. 122
Ecclesiastes 3:1-8   GOC, p. 165
Songs 2:8-10, 14, 16; 8:6-7   TCL, pp. 174, 191, 201; DBC, p. 123; CMC, pp. 87,
                                   115; LFL, p. 109; TTP, pp. 183, 204; TBJ, pp. 175,
                                   186, 191, LJE, p. 111

Songs 2:10-12   DBC, p. 157; TBJ, p. 170
Songs 4:8-16   TCL, p. 180
Songs 8:6-7   TBJ, p. 165
Wisdom 1:17   LFL, p. 102; JRD, p. 167; TTP, p. 138
Wisdom 2:12, 17-20   TCL, p. 167; TBJ, p. 214
Wisdom 6:12-20; 7:7-12   PYW, p. 195; GOC, p. 185
Sirach 2:1-11   CMC, p. 148
Sirach 6:5-6, 14-17   DBC, p. 141
Sirach 15:15-20   DBC, p. 71; SWB, p. 65; JRD, p. 51
Sirach 17:19-24   JRD, p. 55
Sirach 42:15-25   TBJ, p. 104
Isaiah 5:1-7   TBJ, p. 118
Isaiah 6:1-8   TTP, p. 88
Isaiah 7:1-9   TTP, p. 171
Isaiah 8:23-9:3   GOC, p. 93; JRD, p. 41
Isaiah 11:1-10   TBJ, p. 5
Isaiah 32:14-20   TTP, p. 93
Isaiah 35:4-7   ENH, p. 157; TTP, p. 116
Isaiah 40:25-31   DBC, p. 135; CMC, p. 219; JRD, pp. 196, 230
Isaiah 42:1-4, 6-7   JRD, pp. 127, 225; TBJ, p. 36; TBJ, p. 41
Isaiah 43:1-4   SWB, p. 186
Isaiah 45:1, 4-6   JRD, p. 99; TBJ, p. 128, LJE, p. 61
Isaiah 49:1-6   LFL, p. 131
Isaiah 52:7-10   LSJ, p. 181; ENH, p. 194; TCL, p. 149, LJE, p. 6
Isaiah 52:13-53:12   TBJ, p. 47
Isaiah 58:9-14   DBC, p. 13
Isaiah 61:1-3   ENH, p. 188; LFL, p. 149
Isaiah 65:17-21   CMC, p. 38; TTP, p. 34, LJE, p. 15
Isaiah 66:10-14   LSJ, p. 203, LJE, p. 83
Jeremiah 1:4-10   PYW, p. 219
Jeremiah 9:23-24   ENH, p. 149; TCL, p. 155; CMC, p. 213
Jeremiah 18:18-20   CMC, p. 198
Jeremiah 20:7-13   JRD, p. 68
Jeremiah 22:1-4   TTP, p. 224
Jeremiah 28:1-17   LFL, p. 61; TBJ, p. 113
Jeremiah 31:31-34   TBJ, pp. 30, 220
Lamentations 3:17-26   LSJ, p. 196
Ezekiel 11:17-21   JRD, p. 203
Ezekiel 18:25-28   CMC, p. 158

Ezekiel 34:11–12, 15–17	TCL, pp. 135, 142
Ezekiel 37:1–14	LJE, p. 137
Ezekiel 37:12–14	TBJ, p. 23
Ezekiel 47:1–12	TTP, p. 154
Daniel 1:1–6, 8–20	JRD, p. 121
Daniel 9:4b–10	TTP, p. 12
Daniel 12:1–3	ENH, p. 184
Hosea 2:16b, 17b, 21–22	LJE, p. 19
Joel 1:13–15; 2:1–2	TBJ, p. 123
Amos 5:14–15, 21–24	SWB, p. 100
Micah 5:1–4	CMC, p. 141; TTP, p. 7
Micah 5:6–8	CMC, p. 103
Micah 6:6–8	CMC, p. 192, 203; TTP, p. 218, LJE, p. 35
Habakkuk 1:2-3; 2:2–4	LJE, p. 125
Zechariah 8:1–8	LFL, p. 135
Malachi 1:14b–2:2b, 8–10	JRD, p. 108
Matt. 1:18–23	CMC, pp. 141, 170; SWB, p. 8
Matt. 2:1–12	CMC, p. 27; LFL, p. 160
Matt. 3:1–12	PYW, p. 19; ENH, p. 5; SWB, p. 3; TBJ, p. 5
Matt. 3:13–17	JRD, p. 127
Matt. 4:1–11	ENH, p. 19
Matt. 4:12–23	GOC, p. 93; JRD, p. 41
Matt. 4:12–17, 23–25	LFL, p. 10; TTP, p. 159, LJE, p. 10
Matt. 5:1–9	LSJ, p. 196; GOC, p. 175
Matt. 5:1–12	TCL, p. 201; DBC, p. 106; DBC, p. 157; JRD, p. 63; TBJ, pp. 108, 165, 191, LJE, p. 35, LJE, p. 50, LJE, p. 119
Matt. 5:1–16	SWB, p. 146, LJE, p. 111
Matt. 5:13–16	GOC, p. 155; ENH, p. 86; TCL, p. 155; DBC, pp. 117, 123; LFL, pp. 109, 149; JRD, pp. 196, 219; TTP, p. 107; TBJ, p. 181
Matt. 5:17–37	DBC, p. 71; SWB, p. 65; JRD, p. 51
Matt. 5:23–24	LSJ, p. 173
Matt. 5:38–48	SWB, pp. 76, 88, 92; TTP, p. 112
Matt. 6:1–6, 16–18	GOC, p. 27; SWB, p. 96; JRD, p. 149
Matt. 6:24–34	LSJ, p. 189; GOC, p. 111;
Matt. 6:31–34	TCL, p. 161; TBJ, p. 204
Matt. 7:1–5	JRD, p. 74; TTP, p. 165
Matt. 7:21, 24–29	GOC, p. 170; TCL, pp. 191, 196; SWB, p. 141; JRD, p. 175
Matt. 8:18–22	JRD, p. 79
Matt. 8:28–34	SWB, p. 100
Matt. 9:1–8	LFL, p. 57
Matt. 10:7–13	ENH, p. 201
Matt. 10:16–33	JRD, p. 68
Matt. 11:2–11	LSJ, p. 29, LJE, p. 3
Matt. 11:20–24	TTP, p. 171
Matt. 12:38–42	JRD, p. 83
Matt. 13:54–58	JRD, p. 141
Matt. 14:13–21	LFL, p. 61; TBJ, p. 113

Matt. 17:1-9   LSJ, p. 41; DBC, p. 16; SWB, p. 19; JRD, p. 15
Matt. 17:14-20   DBC, p. 135
Matt. 18:1-4   LJE, p. 83
Matt. 18:1-5, 10   JRD, p. 89
Matt. 18:15-20   CMC, p. 67
Matt. 18:21-35   LSJ, p. 110; GOC, p. 118; TCL, p. 69; LFL, p. 66
Matt. 19:13-15   JRD, p. 215; TTP, p. 230
Matt. 20:1-16   GOC, p. 124; TCL, p. 80
Matt. 20:17-28   CMC, pp. 192, 198; JRD, p. 230
Matt. 21:28-32   GOC, p. 130; CMC, p. 158
Matt. 21:33-43   TBJ, p. 118
Matt. 22:1-14   LSJ, p. 121; GOC, p. 135; TCL, p. 90
Matt. 22:15-21   JRD, p. 99; TBJ, p. 128, LJE, p. 61
Matt. 22:34-40   GOC, p. 140; TCL, p. 180; DBC, p. 146; CMC, p. 127;
                      LFL, p. 120; JRD, p. 186, LJE, p. 88
Matt. 23:1-12   JRD, p. 108
Matt. 24:37-44   LSJ, p. 17; DBC, p. 5
Matt. 25:14-30   LSJ, p. 137; GOC, p. 146; TCL, p. 107; CMC, p. 213
Matt. 25:31-40   LJE, p. 105
Matt. 25:31-46   TCL, p. 135; JRD, p. 10
Matt. 26:14—27:66   GOC, p. 49; DBC, p. 35
Matt. 27:46   LFL, p. 30
Matt. 28:16-20   CMC, p. 208; TTP, pp. 145, 175
Mark 1:1-8   LSJ, p. 23; TCL, p. 21
Mark 1:12-15   PYW, p. 33; TCL, p. 35; TBJ, p. 17
Mark 1:14-20   GOC, p. 100; TCL, p. 63; TTP, p. 63
Mark 1:21b-28   TTP, p. 67
Mark 1:40-45   GOC, p. 106; TBJ, p. 99
Mark 2:18-22   TTP, p. 71, LJE, p. 19
Mark 3:13-19   SWB, p. 57
Mark 3:22-30   JRD, p. 46
Mark 4:26-34   SWB, p. 61
Mark 5:1-20   LFL, p. 47; TTP, p. 84
Mark 5:21-43   LSJ, p. 99
Mark 7:31-37   ENH, p. 157; TTP, p. 116
Mark 8:14-21   LJE, p. 133
Mark 8:27-35   TCL, p. 74; CMC, p. 72
Mark 9:30-38   LSJ, p. 115; PYW, p. 123; TCL, p. 86; TCL, p. 167;
                     CMC, pp. 148, 188; TBJ, p. 214
Mark 9:35-37; 10:13-15   LJE, p. 144
Mark 9:38-48   ENH, p. 98; LFL, p. 80
Mark 10:2-9   PYW, p. 201; CMC, p. 87; LFL, p. 114; JRD, p. 191
Mark 10:2-16   ENH, p. 104
Mark 10:13-16   LJE, p. 129
Mark 10:17-30   PYW, p. 134; ENH, p. 116; JRD, p. 55, LJE, p. 45
Mark 10:35-45   TCL, p. 96; LFL, p. 93
Mark 10:46-52   LSJ, p. 132; TBJ, p. 104
Mark 12:1-12   JRD, pp. 59, 145; TTP, p. 98
Mark 12:13-17   TTP, p. 102
Mark 12:28-34   ENH, p. 128; TCL, p. 102

Mark 12:38-44	PYW, p. 144
Mark 13:12	LJE, p. 150
Mark 13:24-32	LSJ, p. 143; PYW, p. 149; TCL, p. 113
Mark 13:33-37	GOC, p. 19; CMC, p. 15
Mark 14:1–15:47	GOC, p. 54; PYW, p. 51; TCL, p. 41
Mark 14:12-16, 22-26	PYW, p. 168; TCL, p. 121
Mark 15:34	LFL, p. 30
Mark 16:15-18	PYW, p. 163; SWB, p. 174
Luke 1:1-4; 4:14-21	ENH, p. 80; DBC, p. 65; TTP, p. 75
Luke 1:26-38	SWB, p. 208; JRD, p. 211, LJE, p. 93
Luke 1:26-38, 46-55	LSJ, p. 203; TCL, p. 127
Luke 1:39-45	TTP, p. 7
Luke 1:57-66, 80	CMC, p. 57; LFL, p. 131
Luke 2:1-20	LFL, p. 160
Luke 2:16-21	TBJ, p. 12
Luke 2:33-35	TTP, p. 149
Luke 3:1-6	PYW, p. 25; TCL, p. 27
Luke 3:10-18	LSJ, p. 33; ENH, p. 11
Luke 4:1-13	DBC, p. 173; SWB, p. 14
Luke 4:16-21	CMC, p. 203; SWB, p. 179; JRD, p. 225; TTP, p. 218; TBJ, p. 87
Luke 4:24-30	TTP, p. 22
Luke 5:1-11	CMC, p. 64; TTP, p. 88
Luke 5:27-32	DBC, p. 13
Luke 6:17, 20-26	LSJ, p. 93; PYW, p. 111; SWB, p. 71
Luke 6:27-38	LJE, p. 39
Luke 6:36-38	LFL, p. 155; TTP, p. 12
Luke 7:1-10	LFL, p. 72
Luke 7:11-17	JRD, p. 154
Luke 7:36-50	PYW, p. 117
Luke 8:16-18	LFL, p. 76
Luke 9:7-9	TTP, p. 122
Luke 9:11-17	LSJ, p. 157; DBC, p. 179; JRD, p. 136
Luke 9:18-26	SWB, p. 165
Luke 9:28-36	DBC, p. 22
Luke 9:46-50	LFL, p. 135; JRD, p. 158
Luke 10:1-9	DBC, p. 185
Luke 10:25-28	DBC, p. 141; LFL, p. 85
Luke 10:25-37	LSJ, p. 105; ENH, p. 184; SWB, p. 146; TTP, p. 224, LJE, p. 56
Luke 10:38-42	SWB, p. 104; TTP, p. 127
Luke 11:15-26	TBJ, p. 123
Luke 11:29-32	LFL, p. 89
Luke 11:37-41	JRD, p. 162
Luke 12:8-12	SWB, p. 170
Luke 12:13-21	JRD, p. 104, LJE, p. 71
Luke 12:22-34	LJE, p. 99
Luke 12:49-53	LSJ, p. 163
Luke 13:10-17	LFL, p. 98
Luke 14:1, 7-11	LFL, p. 140

Luke 14:12–14	JRD, p. 113, LJE, p. 77
Luke 14:25–33	DBC, p. 83
Luke 15:1–3, 11–32	LSJ, p. 46; DBC, p. 29
Luke 16:1–13	ENH, p. 92
Luke 16:19–31	PYW, p. 128; DBC, p. 89; SWB, p. 107
Luke 17:1–6	LFL, p. 102; JRD, p. 117; JRD, p. 167; TTP, p. 138
Luke 17:5–10	ENH, p. 110; SWB, p. 112, LJE, p. 125
Luke 17:11–19	LSJ, p. 126; SWB, p. 118; TTP, p. 132
Luke 18:1–8	GOC, p. 202; ENH, p. 122; JRD, p. 94, LJE, p. 66
Luke 18:9–14	PYW, p. 139
Luke 18:15–17	SWB, p. 203
Luke 20:27–38	DBC, p. 93
Luke 21:1–4	JRD, p. 121
Luke 21:5–19	PYW, p. 155; ENH, p. 134; SWB, p. 123
Luke 21:25–28, 34–36	CMC, p. 20
Luke 22:14–23:56	PYW, p. 55
Luke 22:19	JRD, p. 203
Luke 22:24–27	DBC, p. 163
Luke 23:34	LFL, p. 17
Luke 23:43	LFL, p. 22
Luke 23:46	LFL, p. 41
Luke 24:1–12	ENH, p. 41
Luke 24:13–35	ENH, p. 47; SWB, p. 29; JRD, p. 25, LJE, p. 163
Luke 24:35–48	PYW, p. 84; TBJ, p. 61
Luke 24:46–53	LSJ, p. 181
John 1:1–18	LJE, p. 6
John 1:1–11	DBC, p. 101,
John 1:6–8, 19–28	LFL, p. 5
John 1:29–34	LSJ, p. 83; ENH, p. 67; DBC, p. 59; SWB, p. 51
John 1:35–42	PYW, pp. 105, 211
John 2:1–14	LSJ, p. 88; PYW, p. 90; ENH, p. 73; SWB, p. 131; TTP, p. 188
John 2:13–22	TTP, p. 154
John 3:1–8	SWB, p. 25; JRD, p. 20
John 3:13–17	LSJ, p. 168
John 3:14–21	CMC, p. 33
John 3:16–18	LSJ, p. 151
John 4:5–42	GOC, p. 31; ENH, p. 26; TTP, p. 17; TBJ, p. 87
John 4:43–54	CMC, p. 38; TTP, p. 34, LJE, p. 15
John 6:1–15	CMC, p. 51
John 6:41–51	LSJ, p. 186; SWB, p. 136; TBJ, p. 209
John 7:37–39	GOC, p. 191
John 8:1–11	PYW, p. 45
John 8:31–36	TBJ, p. 220
John 9:1–41	TTP, p. 28
John 10:1–10	LSJ, p. 65; GOC, p. 79
John 10:11–18	CMC, p. 164; TBJ, p. 67
John 10:27–30	ENH, p. 53; SWB, p. 186
John 11:1–45	GOC, p. 37; ENH, p. 32
John 11:17–27	TCL, p. 139; JRD, p. 235

John 11:20–27	LSJ, p. 192; TCL, p. 149; CMC, p. 170
John 11:1–45	TBJ, p. 23
John 12:1–11	TBJ, p. 36; TBJ, p. 41
John 12:20–33	GOC, p. 43; PYW, p. 39; TBJ, p. 30
John 12:24–26	ENH, p. 188
John 13:1–15	TNG, p. 58; PYW, pp. 61, 67; JRD, p. 132
John 13:3–5, 12–15	DBC, p. 129
John 13:31–35	SWB, p. 34; TTP, p. 43
John 14:1–12	GOC, p. 179; DBC, p. 196; JRD, p. 30
John 14:15–17, 25–29	LJE, p. 137
John 14:15–17, 26	PYW, pp. 183, 189; TTP, p. 211
John 14:15–21	SWB, p. 42
John 14:21–29	LSJ, p. 75; TTP, p. 93; TTP, p. 48
John 15:1–8	LSJ, p. 70; GOC, p. 197; TCL, p. 55; SWB, p. 191
John 15:1–17	ENH, p. 168
John 15:9–12	GOC, p. 165; PYW, p. 206; TCL, p. 186; CMC, pp. 98, 115, 135; SWB, p. 157; LFL, p. 125; TTP, p. 198; TBJ, pp. 175, 186
John 15:9–17	GOC, p. 85; ENH, pp. 173, 177, 182; ENH, p. 194; TCL, p. 55; TCL, p. 142; TCL, p. 174; DBC, p. 152; CMC, pp. 93, 121, 153; JRD, p. 180; TTP, pp. 53, 183, 193; TBJ, p. 72
John 15:12–17	GOC, p. 185; ENH, p. 163; CMC, p. 81; SWB, pp. 40, 151; TTP, p. 204
John 15:26–16:4a	TTP, p. 57; TBJ, p. 79
John 16:12–15	PYW, p. 195; ENH, p. 143; DBC, p. 77; SWB, p. 82
John 16:16–20	TBJ, p. 75
John 16:29–33	JRD, p. 35
John 17:1–11	TBJ, p. 83
John 17:11–19	CMC, p. 42
John 17:20–23	PYW, p. 226
John 17:20–26	GOC, p. 160; PYW, p. 97; DBC, p. 167; CMC, p. 103, LJE, p. 29
John 18:1–19:42	LSJ, p. 52; GOC, pp. 59, 65; TBJ, p. 47
John 18:33–37	PYW, p. 174
John 19:26–27	LFL, p. 26
John 19:28	LFL, p. 34
John 19:30	LFL, p. 37
John 20:1–9	LJE, p. 25
John 20:10–23	PYW, p. 219
John 20:19–23	ENH, p. 59; CMC, p. 109; PYW, p. 219; TBJ, p. 55; TBJ, p. 199, LJE, p. 160
John 20:19–31	GOC, p. 73; PYW, p. 77; DBC, pp. 45, 51; SWB, p. 196; TTP, p. 38
John 21:1–9	LSJ, p. 59
Acts 1:12–14	JRD, p. 211
Acts 2:1–8, 11b	PYW, p. 183; CMC, p. 109
Acts 2:1–11	TBJ, p. 87; TBJ, p. 199
Acts 2:1–17	TTP, p. 211
Acts 2:14, 22–33	ENH, p. 47; SWB, p. 29; JRD, p. 25, LJE, p. 163

Acts 2:41	LJE, p. 160
Acts 2:42–47	SWB, p. 196
Acts 3:13–15, 17–19	TBJ, p. 61
Acts 4:8–12	CMC, p. 164
Acts 4:23–31	SWB, p. 25; JRD, p. 20
Acts 4:32–35	TBJ, p. 55
Acts 5:12–16	TTP, p. 38
Acts 6:1–7	GOC, p. 179; DBC, p. 196; JRD, p. 30
Acts 7:55–60	DBC, p. 167, LJE, p. 29
Acts 10:25–26, 44–48	GOC, p. 85; TCL, p. 55; TTP, p. 53; TBJ, p. 72
Acts 10:34–38	JRD, p. 127
Acts 10:34a, 37–43	LJE, p. 25
Acts 11:1–8	TBJ, p. 67
Acts 11:21–26; 13:1-3	ENH, p. 201
Acts 13:22–26	LFL, p. 131
Acts 14:5–18	TTP, p. 48
Acts 14:21b–27	SWB, p. 34; TTP, p. 43
Acts 15:22–29	SWB, p. 40
Acts 16:11–15	TTP, p. 57; TBJ, p. 79
Acts 18:1–8	TBJ, p. 75
Acts 19:1–8	JRD, p. 35
Acts 20:17–27	TBJ, p. 83
Acts 22:3–16	PYW, p. 163; SWB, p. 174
Romans 1:1–7	LFL, p. 89
Romans 1:16–25	JRD, p. 162
Romans 3:19–28	TBJ, p. 220
Romans 4:20–25	LJE, p. 71
Romans 5:1–5	ENH, p. 143
Romans 5:1–2, 5–8	GOC, p. 31; ENH, p. 26; TTP, p. 17
Romans 5:15b–19	JRD, p. 68
Romans 8:8–11	TBJ, p. 23
Romans 8:12–17	CMC, p. 208; LFL, p. 98; TTP, p. 145
Romans 8:28–30	CMC, p. 141
Romans 8:31–35, 37–39	PYW, p. 206; GOC, p. 170; DBC, p. 152; CMC, p. 103
Romans 10:8–13	DBC, p. 173
Romans 10:13–17	SWB, p. 179
Romans 11:29–36	LJE, p. 77
Romans 12:1–2, 9–18	TCL, p. 191; CMC, p. 127; SWB, pp. 131, 151, 157; LFL, p. 109; TBJ, p. 181
Romans 12:4–12	ENH, p. 168
Romans 12:9–13	LJE, p. 105
Romans 12:9–21	CMC, p. 121; LFL, p. 149; TTP, p. 198
Romans 15:4–9	TBJ, p. 5
1 Cor. 1:4–9	LFL, p. 144
1 Cor. 1:10–13, 17	GOC, p. 93; JRD, p. 41
1 Cor. 1:26–31	LJE, p. 150
1 Cor. 2:6–10	DBC, p. 71; SWB, p. 65; JRD, p. 51
1 Cor. 2:9–13	PYW, p. 189
1 Cor. 3:9–11, 16–17	TTP, p. 154; TBJ, p. 214
1 Cor. 3:18–23	CMC, p. 64

1 Cor. 9:16–19, 22–23 — LFL, p. 51

1 Cor. 10:31–11:1 — TBJ, p. 99

1 Cor. 11:17–26, 33 — LFL, p. 72

1 Cor. 11:23–26 — TNG, p. 58; LSJ, p. 157; PYW, pp. 61, 67; DBC, p. 179; JRD, p. 132; JRD, p. 136

1 Cor. 12:3–7, 12–13 — GOC, p. 191; CMC, p. 109; JRD, p. 225; TBJ, p. 199

1 Cor. 12:4–13 — SWB, p. 191

1 Cor. 12:12–27 — ENH, p. 80; DBC, p. 65; TTP, p. 75

1 Cor. 12:12–14, 27–31a — JRD, p. 154

1 Cor. 12:27–13:13 — PYW, p. 201; GOC, p. 175; ENH, pp. 177, 182; TCL, pp. 174, 180, 201; DBC, pp. 101, 106, 157; CMC, pp. 81, 93, 98, 115; SWB, p. 146; LFL, pp. 120, 125; TTP, p. 198

1 Cor. 12:31–13:8 — TBJ, pp. 165, 170, 191

1 Cor. 12:31–13-13 — LJE, p. 105

1 Cor. 13:1–13 — LSJ, p. 189; DBC, p. 135; TTP, p. 204, LJE, p. 99

1 Cor. 14:1, 6–12 — TTP, p. 188

1 Cor. 15:1–11 — TTP, p. 88

1 Cor. 15:12–20 — TCL, p. 139; JRD, p. 235

1 Cor. 15:20–26, 28 — TCL, p. 135

1 Cor. 15:45–49 — LJE, p. 39

2 Cor. 3:1b–6 — LJE, p. 19

2 Cor. 4:7–15 — TTP, p. 175

2 Cor. 5:14–17 — TCL, p. 149

2 Cor. 6:1–10 — TTP, p. 112

2 Cor. 9:6–11 — JRD, p. 149

Gal. 1:1–6 — LFL, p. 85

Gal. 1:6–12 — LJE, p. 56

Gal. 1:13–24 — TTP, p. 127

Gal. 3:27–28 — CMC, p. 185

Gal. 4:4–7 — CMC, p. 170; TBJ, p. 12

Gal. 4:22–24, 26–27, 31; 5:1 — GOC, p. 197

Gal. 5:1, 13–14 — TCL, p. 155; DBC, p. 163; CMC, p. 213

Gal. 5:16–25 — LSJ, p. 163

Ephesians 1:3–6, 11–12 — LJE, p. 93

Ephesians 1:15–23 — SWB, p. 170

Ephesians 2:1–10 — JRD, p. 104

Ephesians 3:2–12 — LSJ, p. 181

Ephesians 3:14–21 — PYW, p. 211; TCL, p. 142; SWB, pp. 136, 165, LJE, p. 137

Ephesians 4:1–7, 11–13 — ENH, p. 194; JRD, p. 203

Ephesians 4:30–5:2 — TBJ, p. 209

Ephesians 5:8–14 — TTP, p. 28

Ephesians 5:21–33 — CMC, p. 87; TTP, p. 188

Ephesians 6:10–18 — LFL, p. 140

Philippians 1:3–11 — LSJ, p. 168, 203; GOC, p. 185; CMC, p. 153

Philippians. 2:1–4 — ENH, p. 163; SWB, p. 141; JRD, p. 113

Philippians 2:1–11 — CMC, p. 158; JRD, p. 230

Philippians 2:5–8 — CMC, p. 179

Philippians 4:1–7 — JRD, p. 5

Philippians 4:4–9	LFL, p. 155
Philippians 4:6–9	TBJ, p. 118
Colossians 1:3–4, 9–14	JRD, p. 219
Colossians 3:1–4	LJE, p. 25
Colossians 3:12–15	LJE, p. 119
Colossians 3:12–17	GOC, pp. 160, 165; ENH, pp. 173, 184; TCL, p. 186; DBC, pp. 112, 117, 129, 146, 190; CMC, p. 135; SWB, pp. 157, 186; LFL, p. 114; JRD, pp. 175, 180, 186, 196; TTP, pp. 183, 193, 224, LJE, p. 111
1 Thess. 1:1–5b	JRD, p. 99; TBJ, p. 128, LJE, p. 61
1 Thess. 2:7b–9, 13	JRD, p. 108
2 Thess. 3:6–12, 16	TCL, p. 161; TBJ, p. 204
1 Tim. 2:1–8	TTP, p. 149
2 Tim. 1:6–8, 13–14	LJE, p. 125
2 Tim. 1:8b–10	LSJ, p. 41; DBC, p. 16; SWB, p. 19; JRD, p. 15
2 Tim. 2:8–17	LSJ, p. 126; SWB, p. 118; TTP, p. 132
2 Tim. 3:14–4:2	ENH, p. 122; JRD, p. 94, LJE, p. 66
2 Tim. 4:9–17	DBC, p. 185
Titus 1:1–9	JRD, p. 117
Hebrews 1:1–6	TTP, p. 63, LJE, p. 6
Hebrews 5:7–9	TBJ, p. 30
Hebrews 8:6–13	SWB, p. 57
Hebrews 9:15, 24–28	JRD, p. 46; TTP, p. 80
Hebrews 10:5–10	TTP, p. 7
Hebrews 10:32–39	SWB, p. 61
Hebrews 11:32–40	TTP, p. 84
James 2:1–5	ENH, p. 157; TTP, p. 116
James 2:14–17	TTP, p. 218
James 3:16–4:3	TCL, p. 167
1 Peter 1:3–9	SWB, p. 196, LJE, p. 45
1 Peter 1:17–21	ENH, p. 47; SWB, p. 29; JRD, p. 25, LJE, p. 163
1 Peter 2:4–9	GOC, p. 179; DBC, p. 196; JRD, p. 30
1 Peter 3:18–22	TBJ, p. 17
2 Peter 1:2–7	JRD, p. 145
2 Peter 3:12–18	TTP, p. 102
1 John 2:1–5	TBJ, p. 61
1 John 3:1–2	CMC, p. 164
1 John 3:18–24	GOC, p. 155; DBC, p. 123
1 John 3:22–4:6	LFL, p. 10; TTP, p. 159, LJE, p. 10
1 John 4:7–13	GOC, p. 85; TCL, p. 55; SWB, p. 191; JRD, p. 191; TTP, p. 53; TBJ, pp. 72, 175, 186
1 John 4:11–17	DBC, p. 141
1 John 5:1–6	TBJ, p. 55, LJE, p. 88
2 John 4–6	SWB, p. 203
Rev. 1:9–13, 17–19	PYW, p. 77; DBC, p. 51; TTP, p. 38
Rev. 3:14, 20–21	ENH, p. 188
Rev. 12:1–12	SWB, p. 208
Rev. 21:1–5a	SWB, p. 34; TTP, p. 43
Rev. 22:12–14, 16–17, 20	DBC, p. 167, LJE, p. 29